SECOND EDITION

THE FARM BUSINESS

L. Norman
R. A. E. Turner
K. R. S. Wilson

Hampshire College of Agriculture,
Sparsholt, Winchester, Hampshire

LONGMAN
LONDON AND NEW YORK

LONGMAN GROUP LIMITED
Longman House, Burnt Mill, Harlow
Essex CM20 2JE, England
Associated companies throughout the world
Published in the United States of America
by Longman Inc., New York

First published 1971
Second edition 1985

British Library Cataloguing in Publication Data
Norman, Leonard
  The farm business. – 2nd ed
  1. Farm management
  I. Title   II. Turner, R.A.E.
  III. Wilson, K.R.S.
  630'.68   S561

ISBN 0-582-44255-9

Library of Congress Cataloging in Publication Data
Norman, L. (Leonard), 1938–
  The farm business.

  Bibliography: p.
  Includes index.
  1. Farm management.   2. Farm management–Great Britain.
  I. Turner, R. A. E. 1939–   . II. Wilson, K. R. S., 1943–   . III. Title.
  S561.N72 1985   338.1   83–22220
  ISBN 0–582–44255–9

Set in 10/12pt Bembo Roman
Printed in Great Britain at
The Bath Press, Avon

CONTENTS

ACKNOWLEDGEMENTS

We are indebted to the following for permission to reproduce copyright material:

The Farming Press & the Authors, P. Needham & R. F. Ridgeon for fig 4.2 & Table 7.22 (R. F. Ridgeon 1980); Granada Publishing Ltd for fig 7.3; the Controller of Her Majesty's Stationery Office for Table 3.14; Imperial Chemical Industries plc for fig 6.3, Tables 3.4, 3.5, 8.2–8.5; Longman Group Ltd for Tables 3.6, 7.25; Meat & Livestock Commission for Tables 7.1–7.10, 7.13–7.18; Milk Marketing Board for fig 6.2, Tables 6.4, 6.5, 6.10, 6.12; Potato Marketing Board for Tables 8.13, 8.14 from the Board's Statistical Records; the Editor, Power Farming for Table 3.1; UKF Fertilisers for figs 8.6–8.8; University of Cambridge, Department of Land Economy & the Author, R. F. Ridgeon for fig 7.12, Table 7.20; Wye College (University of London) For Tables 3.2 (Farm Business Unit 1980), 5.11, 6.7, 6.11, 6.16, 7.12, 8.7–8.11, 8.15, 8.16.

FOREWORD

It is a tribute to the first version of *The farm business* – written some 15 years ago by Len Norman and Roger Coote – that it can now be rewritten and published in a general format which remains so close to the original.

This time Len Norman has collaborated with his Sparsholt colleagues Dick Turner and Ken Wilson, and their combined feel for, and practical experience of, farm management – not to mention their eye for detail – is impressive.

Few books on farm management have been so well illustrated with examples and it has been a major task, alone, to update all of these. The updating, however, does not stop there. It extends to the detailed content of the book and keeps it in line with the way in which farm business management has developed as a subject over the past decade. In particular, it keeps as its main target clientele those who are following the City and Guilds of London Institute course in farm business management and again provides some worked answers to a sample of recent examination questions.

But it is not only 'City and Guilds' students who will be grateful for a revised edition of this book. Farmers, farm managers, teachers and students at all levels will find help from it – not least from the fact that, as in the first edition, so much of the book is devoted to the management of individual enterprises. This, again, is rare among farm management texts. I have personally always found the diagrams of factors affecting the profitability of individual enterprises an especially valuable framework for examining and thinking about those enterprises.

The authors should be thanked and congratulated, and I wish their book the success in its second decade that it so clearly enjoyed in its first.

Professor Tony Giles
Director of the Farm Management Unit
University of Reading
National Examiner in Farm Business
    Management for
The City and Guilds of London
    Institute 1971–81

AUTHORS' NOTE

The agricultural industry is continually changing and farm business management is essentially concerned with costs and prices. Inevitably, the agricultural industry will experience changes in both levels of prices and government policy which, together with other influencing factors, make it essential for those involved in farm business management work to keep themselves well informed and up to date on such information.

The costs and outputs used as illustrations throughout this book were those currently obtaining at the time of writing, but it must be appreciated that these will not remain appropriate for very long. Such figures are, however, used with the prime objective of illustrating principles to be applied in assessing the productivity of enterprises and, therefore, readers are exhorted to keep these constantly under review.

L.N.
R.A.E.T.
K.R.S.W.

PREFACE

It is now over 20 years since the City and Guilds of London Institute launched their first syllabus and examination course in farm organization and management. That course and examination were primarily designed for adult students of sound practical background. The demand for such a course grew rapidly as the general interest in farm business management as a subject also developed.

During the 1960s, other developments in farm business management were taking place. The Ministry of Agriculture developed specialized advice in farm business management. The Farm Management Association was formed and branches developed in many counties: private management consultants, recording and secretarial agencies were also formed. This rapid spread of interest in farm business management meant that many farmers, farm managers, teachers and students sought some source of business management information that was presented in a logical, systematic way that could be applied to farm case studies and practical management in the field.

In response to that demand, the textbook *The farm business* by L. Norman and R. B. Coote was first published in 1971. While that text may have served to meet various needs during the 1970s, clearly a lot of the data presented in that book has become outdated although the basic principles and techniques of farm business management remain the same. Recently, a new examination syllabus in farm business management has been developed by the City and Guilds of London Institute (the Phase IV – 028 Scheme launched in 1980). Consequently, it was felt that *The farm business* textbook needed to be updated and rewritten so that readers have access to reasonably up-to-date information which can be applied to the various farm business management techniques outlined in the text.

The task of completely rewriting this book has been undertaken by Mr R. A. E. Turner and Mr K. R. S. Wilson – two heads of department at the Hampshire College of Agriculture, in conjunction with Mr L. Norman one of the original authors of the first edition. The authors have tried to draw together their practical farming knowledge as well as farm business management expertise. The whole text has been completely revised, and with the development of computer application to farm business management in recent years, considerable references are made to the application of computer techniques in this field.

This revision does not include the field of taxation, since the purpose of this book is to enable the farmer to appreciate and apply farm business management techniques. No doubt tax planning will become an essential aspect of the successful business. In this case, the full knowledge and experience of the accountant and solicitor should be sought and brought to bear upon the unique combination of circumstances posed by each business.

In presenting this new edition of *The farm business*, we would like to express our thanks to Professor A. K. Giles of Reading University who has again written the Foreword to this edition, and who has encouraged us with this work. We would also like to thank Professor J. Nix of the Farm Business Unit, School of Rural Economics, Wye College, University of London, for permission to quote from his *Farm management pocketbook* (13th and 14th editions). Our gratitude is also expressed to the City and Guilds of London Institute for permission to include past examination questions in the text.

Finally, we would like to thank colleagues on the staff of the Hampshire College of Agriculture, and in particular Mr I. D. Hamilton, Vice-Principal/Farms Director, for checking the text, Mr I. J. Rennie, Farm Management Consultant, for advice and help with the computerized data, Mr A. Bishop, Barclays Bank, for invaluable financial advice and Mr M. D. Ridout Tutor/Librarian at Hampshire College of Agriculture. Any errors, must remain our own responsibility.

L. Norman   Hampshire College of Agriculture,
R. A. E. Turner   Sparsholt, Winchester, Hampshire
K. R. S. Wilson

1 | ANALYSIS OF THE FARM BUSINESS

COMPARATIVE ACCOUNT ANALYSIS

The physical and financial records of the farm business will, if properly analysed and interpreted, provide essential information upon which to make effective management decisions. Analysis will pinpoint weaknesses in the business which can be corrected and will also highlight satisfactory levels of performance which may be exploited more fully. This is a simple diagnostic technique which involves the calculation of a number of 'efficiency factors', which can be compared with similar measures calculated for comparable farms.

When beginning to analyse a farm business the various physical and financial records of the farm should be examined. Some farmers may keep a very comprehensive set of records, while others may keep very few. Whatever the case, all farmers will have a farm trading account relating to each year's trading, since this is necessary for taxation purposes. Inevitably, there is always some delay between the end of the trading year and the actual completion of the trading account. Because of this, it can be argued that the information it contains is out of date. While this cannot be denied, the trading account, if properly presented, does contain useful information which can be analysed to produce a number of meaningful efficiency measures which can be of value to the farmer. In the short term these measures may assist him in the management and running of his farm; in the longer term they will be of value in the planning and organization of his business.

A farm trading account normally covers a 12 months' period which may be the calendar year from 1 January to 31 December, the financial year from 5 April to 4 April of the following year, or the farming year from 1 October through to 30 September. In fact, any period can be covered and the trading year can begin at any time. In reality though, the starting date is often influenced by the major enterprises on the farm or simply the month of the year the farmer started farming.

Layout of a farm trading account

The basic layout of the farm trading account covers four sections:
1. Opening valuation of livestock, crops and cultivations, and stores on the farm at the beginning of the trading year.
2. The items of actual expenditure in the farm business during the year.
3. The sums of revenue (receipts) received by the farm business during the trading year.
4. The closing valuation at the end of the year of the same items as in the opening valuation.

FARM TRADING ACCOUNT

1. *Opening valuation*	£	2. *Receipts*	£
e.g. Dairy cows		e.g. Sales of milk	
Sheep		Sales of cull cows	
Wheat		Sales of wheat	
Feedingstuffs (in store)			
Fuel and oil etc.			
3. *Expenditure*		4. *Closing valuation*	
e.g. Feedingstuffs		e.g. Dairy cows	
Replacement heifers		Sheep	
Wages		Wheat	
Fuel and oil, etc.		Feedingstuffs (in store)	
		Fuel and oil, etc.	
Profit		Loss	
£ Balancing total		£ Balancing total	

Compiling a farm trading account

The information set out in a farm trading account comes from financial records and an annual valuation. The trading account must reflect a true picture of trading by the farm during the year and, therefore, it may be necessary to adjust items of expenditure and receipts to allow for any debtors and creditors which were outstanding both at the beginning and at the end of the trading year.

When the trading account is made up the items comprising the opening valuation and expenditure (shown on the left-hand side of the account) are totalled, and those items comprising receipts and closing valuation (shown on the right-hand side of the account) are also totalled. The figure at the bottom of each side of the account is made to balance and the balancing figure is called 'profit' if it falls on the left and 'loss' if it falls on the right.

Standardizing the farm trading account

The final profit figure shown in a farm trading account will be influenced by a number of factors besides the success or otherwise of the farm itself. Some farms are saddled with certain charges, e.g. interest on overdrafts or mortgages on capital borrowed to purchase land. Some farms will carry a rent charge while others may be owned with no rent paid. Some farms may be 'staffed' by family labour for which no allowance may be made in the trading account. It can be seen, therefore, that considerable variations in the final 'profit' figure between similar farms may result, depending on the number of these items included in the trading account. This being the case, it is necessary to standardize the farm trading account before valid interfarm comparisons can be made. The following adjustments should be made when standardizing a farm trading account:

1. Remove from the trading account the following items:
   (a) interest charges (e.g. interest on bank overdraft);
   (b) mortgage payments;
   (c) capital repayments (e.g. to private lenders);
   (d) expenditure on owner/occupier's repairs.
2. If the farm is owned then impute a rent to the farm – a figure representative of rents actually being paid by similar farms in the area should be used.
3. A sum should be included in the account for any family labour used on the farm, i.e. actual manual effort as opposed to managerial effort. This should be done to ensure that family manual labour, for which no actual payment is made, is set against the 'profit' of the farm business.

The 'profit' figure which now results from the standardized trading account can be compared with the figure in the standardized accounts of similar farms; also any efficiency measures calculated from the standardized accounts can be similarly compared.

Information in the standardized trading account
The standardized trading account itself reveals the following information:

1. The 'profit' or 'loss' during the trading year which can, genuinely, be compared with that of other similar farms.
2. The amount of tenant's capital invested in the farm at the beginning and end of the year (excluding that in farm machinery, car and tenant's fixtures).
3. The details, and totals, of actual expenditure and receipts of the farm over the trading year.

The need for analysis of the standardized trading account
The information shown by the farm trading account, even after standardization, is very limited and reveals little that can be used either by a farmer to correct faults which are present in his farm business or to plan future changes for his farm. The information does not indicate which enterprises are doing well and which ones are not 'pulling their own weight'. In fact, the good enterprises may be 'masking' the poor ones quite unbeknown to the farmer.

The expenditure and receipts sections indicate purchases and sales, respectively, but do not indicate actual inputs and outputs of the farm.

It is obvious, therefore, that some further detailed investigation of the standardized trading account will be necessary and efficiency measures must be calculated which can be compared with the standards of achievement of similar farms in the same area.

ANALYSIS OF A FARM BUSINESS

When beginning the analysis of a farm business it is most important to visit the farm and meet the farmer or manager so as to be familiar

Table 1.1   *Littledown Farm: hectares of crops – Years 1, 2 and 3*

	1	2	3
Winter wheat	48	50	50
Winter barley	24	30	35
Spring barley	32	24	24
Maincrop potatoes	8	8	8
Leys	130	130	125
Permanent pasture	20	20	20
Total	262	262	262

Conservation of grass in Year 2: Hay   10 ha
                                   Silage   58 ha of ley
                                   Reseeding 33 ha of ley

Table 1.2   *Livestock numbers*

Enterprise   Year 2

Cattle

	Opening no.	Purchased	Transferred in	Died	Sold	Closing no.	Avg. no. Year 2
Dairy cows	125	2	27	1	18	135	130
0–1 year	35	—	—	—	—	35	35
1–2 year	30	—	—	—	—	30	30
2–2½ year	26	—	—	—	—	26	26

Sheep

Ewes	540	135	—	8	207	460	500
Rams	12	3	—	—	3	12	12

Pigs

Sows	112	20	—	2	42	88	100
Boars	6	2	—	—	2	6	6
Sucklers	200	—	—	—	—	230	—

with background details of the business. In this case details of a 264 ha farm have been constructed and a detailed analysis of this farm business will be followed through. The background information is as follows.

Littledown Farm is situated in the south-east of England and has some medium loam soil with some clay and some chalk land. The farm grows cereals and potatoes and carries a herd of Friesian dairy cows and followers and a flock of Kerry Hill ewes crossed with a Suffolk ram, which graze leys and permanent pasture. There is also a Large White × Landrace pig enterprise producing weaners for sale. The farm employs eight men full time, plus the farmer with occasional help from his wife. Details of the cropping and stocking of the farm are given in Tables 1.1 and 1.2.

Trading account for Littledown Farm

A trading account for this farm for Year 2 from 1 January to 31 December is presented in Table 1.3. From the trading account it will be seen that no family labour is included in the expenses section of the account; a rent is included since the farm is a tenant farm and some bank interest charges are also included.

Table 1.3   Littledown Farm: farm trading account – Year 2. 1 January–31 December

Opening valuation	£	£	Receipts	£	£
Dairy cows	47 500		Dairy cows	6 300	
Dairy young stock	14 450		Calves	7 200	
Sheep	17 112		Milk	104 000	
Breeding pigs	11 020		Sheep	6 300	
Other pigs	2 400		Lambs	27 500	
Wheat	38 765		Sows	4 092	
Spring barley	14 586		Other pigs	48 000	
Straw	1 500		Wool	1 625	
Potatoes	10 500		Wheat	40 274	
Forage	12 000		Spring barley	13 676	
Tillages	19 650		Winter barley	20 670	
FYM	650		Potatoes	11 200	
Fertilizer	14 000		Milk to house	350	
Seeds	1 055		Private use of car	450	
Fuel and oil	550		Private use of elec.	300	
Concentrate feed	4 200		Rental value of farmhouse	800	
Sprays	1 200		Sundries	800	293 537
Livestock sundries	320				
Miscellaneous sundries	480	211 938			

Expenditure			Closing valuation		
Heifers	920		Dairy cows	53 000	
Sheep	9 375		Dairy young stock	20 350	
Pigs	3 150		Sheep	16 520	
Concentrate feed	81 150		Breeding pigs	9 750	
Hay	500		Other pigs	3 450	
Seed	10 182		Wheat	45 000	
Fertilizer	35 670		Spring barley	10 925	
Sprays	7 452		Straw	1 750	
Wages and NI	62 000		Potatoes	12 000	
Casual labour	1 720		Forage	12 500	
Machinery dep.	19 500		Tillages	20 580	
Fuel, oil and elec.	6 723		FYM	650	
Repairs, tax and ins.	8 444		Fertilizer	16 000	
Contract	1 620		Seed	2 050	
Dep. tenant's fixtures	1 878		Fuel and oil	625	
Vet., med., AI	11 970		Concentrate feed	4 515	
Haulage	600		Sprays	800	
Water	1 399		Livestock sundries	400	
Rent	21 578		Miscellaneous sundries	320	231 185
Rates	665				

Table 1.3   (continued)

Expenditure (contd.)			Closing valuation (contd.)
Office and Gen. ins.	3 907		
PMB levy	1 200		
Bank interest	6 000	297 603	231 185
Profit	15 181		
		£524 722	£524 722

Standardization of the trading account for Littledown Farm – Year 2

The trading account must be standardized before efficiency measures can be calculated from it and compared with those for other farms. The adjustments that are necessary are shown in Table 1.4.

Table 1.4   *Adjustments necessary to standardize the trading account*

	£
Trading account 'Profit' (see Table 1.3)	15 181
Adjustments	
Add back – bank interest	6 000
∴ Net farm income	21 181
Subtract – value of family labour: farmer	4 000
wife	450
∴ Management and investment income	16 731

Net farm income is the income to the farm as a result of the year's trading. Management and investment income is the reward to the farmer for the management of his farm business and the return on the tenant's capital employed in the farm business, since an allowance has been made for the manual labour put into the farm during the year by the farmer and his family.

Systematic analysis of the standardized farm trading account

In analysing the standardized trading account for Littledown Farm a logical sequence should be followed which can be applied to any farm trading account. A set of analysis worksheets had been drawn up and these will be followed through sheet by sheet.

If a number of farm accounts are to be analysed it is suggested that the seven worksheets (Tables 1.5–1.7, 1.9–1.12), which are presented in the following pages, be stencilled and used in each case, since the design of the worksheets is such that they can be used in the analysis of any farm trading account.

Worksheet 1

Description of the farm
On Worksheet 1 (Table 1.5) details of the farm can be set out for reference purposes. The information under 'classification of

Table 1.5   Worksheet 1
Farm account analysis Work Sheet

Farm	Farm reference	Littledown Farm
Hectares 264	Year ending	31 Dec. Year 2
Tenant/owner-occupier	Full-time workers	
	(inc. farmer)	9
	Part-time workers	
	Date visited	

System of farming	Dairy cows and followers; sheep; breeding sows; cereals and potatoes
Soil types	Medium loam, clay and chalkland
Buildings	Yard and parlour
	Farrowing house and sow yard
	On-floor grain storage for 950 tonnes
Livestock	Friesian cows
	Kerry Hill ewes × Suffolk ram
	Large White sows × Landrace boar

Cropping			*Hectares*	%
		Winter wheat	50	19.0
	Cereals	Winter barley	30	11.4
		Spring barley	24	9.0
	Permanent pasture		20	7.6
	Leys		130	49.2
	Other crops: maincrop potatoes		8	3.0
	Roads and buildings		2	0.8
	Total		264	100.0

Table 1.5   (continued)

Classification of farm	
Farm type	Milk, sheep, cattle and arable
Hectare size group	Over 200 ha
Comparative data reference	Farm Business Unit (1983)
Comparative data Year	1981/82

Published by Wye College (University of London) Farm Business Unit, School of Rural Economics & Related Studies

farm'cannot be filled in at this stage, but must be left until enough information had been revealed about the farm to enable it to be classified for comparative purposes with similar farms.

Worksheet 2

Calculation of gross output

The standardized farm trading account can now be taken and various efficiency measures calculated from it. These will be defined as the analysis progresses:

Gross output.   The gross output of an enterprise is the receipts of that enterprise (including value of products consumed) adjusted for valuation changes less purchase of livestock replacements. The total gross output of the farm is the total of the enterprise gross outputs, plus sundry receipts.

When calculating gross output it is not sufficient to take just the sales of a particular enterprise – obviously consideration must also be given to products in store (valuations), products consumed and livestock purchases.

A simple formula for calculating gross output is:

$$\text{Gross output} = \left(\begin{array}{c}\text{receipts +} \\ \text{closing valuation}\end{array}\right) - \left(\begin{array}{c}\text{opening valuation} \\ \text{+ expenditure}\end{array}\right)$$

For example the pig enterprise in Year 2 as shown in the trading account:

$$\begin{array}{lll}
\text{Gross output} \\
\text{of pigs}
\end{array} = \left\{\begin{array}{l}\text{£4 092 culls} \\ \text{(receipts)} \\ \text{£48 000 progeny} \\ \text{sales}\end{array}\right. + \left\{\begin{array}{l}\text{£9 750 closing valua-} \\ \text{tion sows} \\ \text{£3 450 closing valua-} \\ \text{tion suckling pigs}\end{array}\right.$$

$$Minus \quad \left\{\begin{array}{l}\text{£3 150 gilts} \\ \text{purchased} \\ \text{(livestock} \\ \text{replacements)}\end{array}\right. + \left\{\begin{array}{l}\text{£11 020 opening} \\ \text{valuation sows} \\ \text{£2 400 opening valua-} \\ \text{tion pigs}\end{array}\right.$$

$$= \text{£48 722}$$

Worksheet 2 (Table 1.6) clearly shows how each enterprise in the farm trading account is taken and its gross output calculated.

The total gross output of the farm is obtained by totalling the gross output of each enterprise including sundry receipts. The total gross output of this farm in Year 2 was £294 384

What does gross output measure? The gross output of an enterprise reflects the total output of that enterprise irrespective of the costs of producing that output. The total gross output of the whole farm similarly reflects total output and will be influenced by:

1. Yield of the various enterprises;
2. Price per unit received for products;
3. Scale of the enterprises;
4. Valuation changes.

Worksheet 3

'Inputs' or cost items

When calculating levels of 'inputs' or costs for the farm business during the trading year, opening and closing valuations of those items which can be stored must not be ignored. It must be remembered that the expenditure section of the trading account indicates actual expenditure during the year; in this analysis the actual amount used in the farm business must be calculated. For instance, a farmer may actually purchase £15 000 worth of fertilizer in a trading year, but only use £11 000 worth of it in that trading year, leaving £4 000 of fertilizer in the closing valuation. Clearly, it follows that only £11 000 worth of fertilizer 'input' went into the farm business in that particular trading year and not the whole £15 000 worth which was purchased.

In calculating levels of inputs from the information in the trading account the expenditure on an item is taken and adjusted in the following ways:

(a) for valuation changes;
(b) the rental value of the farmhouse should be deducted from the total farm rent because the function of the analysis is to indicate the performance of the farm itself;
(c) a rental value should be imputed to the farm if the farmer is an owner-occupier;
(d) manual labour of the farmer and his family should be evaluated and included;
(e) private use of car, fuel and electricity is deducted from the relevant cost items;

Table 1.6   Worksheet 2
Analysis of financial information for year 2

	1	2	3	4	5	6	7
Livestock replacement purchases* OUTPUT	*Opening valuation* (£)	*Expenditure** (£)	*Sub total* 1 + 2 (£)	*Receipts* (£)	*Closing valuation* (£)	*Sub total* 4 + 5 (£)	*Gross output* 6 − 3 (£)
1a Dairy cattle	47 500	920	48 420	6 300 7 200	53 000	66 500	18 080
1b Other cattle	14 450		14 450		20 350	20 350	5 900
2 Milk (plus milk used in house)					104 000 350		104 350
3 Sheep and wool	17 112	9 375	26 487	6 300 27 500 1 625	16 520	51 945	25 458
4 Pigs Sow and sucklers	2 400 11 020	3 150	16 570	4 092 48 000	3 450 9 750	65 292	48 722
5 Poultry and eggs (plus home consumed)							
6							
7							
Total livestock 1–7 (A)							202 510
8 Cereals Wheat Spring barley Winter barley	38 765 14 586		53 351	40 274 13 676 20 670	45 000 10 925	130 545	77 194
9 Straw	1 500		1 500		1 750	1 750	250
10 Potatoes	10 500		10 500	11 200	12 000	23 200	12 700
11 Forage Tillage FYM	12 000 19 650 650	500	32 800		12 500 20 580 650	33 730	930
Total crops 8–11 (B)							91 074
12							
13							
14							
15							
16							
17 Sundry receipts				800		800	800
18							
Total miscellaneous 12–18							800
Gross output (C)							294 384

(f) sales of resources of purchased commodities, e.g. feedingstuffs, should be credited back to the appropriate item.

A simple formula for calculating levels of inputs is:

$$\text{Input} = \left\{ \begin{array}{l} \text{opening} \\ \text{valuation} \end{array} + \text{expenditure} \right\} - \left\{ \begin{array}{l} \text{closing} \\ \text{valuation} \end{array} + \text{receipts} \right\}$$

For the input of fertilizer on the farm in Year 2 the calculation would be as follows:

$$\begin{array}{l} \text{Input of} \\ \text{fertilizer} \end{array} = (\pounds 14\ 000 \text{ opening valuation} + \pounds 35\ 670 \text{ expenditure})$$

Minus (£16 000 closing valuation) = £33 670

Worksheet 3 clearly shows how each input item is calculated from information in the trading account.

Variable costs

Input (cost) items on Worksheet 3 (Table 1.7) have been grouped: those numbered 20 to 28 inclusive are called variable costs. These are the cost items which alter with any change in scale of enterprise and can be easily allocated to particular enterprises, e.g. feed, seed, fertilizers, casual labour, contract work, sprays, veterinary and medicines. These costs are also referred to as allocatable or direct costs.

Table 1.7   Worksheet 3

		1	2	3	4	5	6	7
		Opening valuation	Expenditure	Sub total 1 + 2	Receipts	Closing valuation	Sub total 4 + 5	Total input 3 − 6
INPUTS		(£)	(£)	(£)	(£)	(£)	(£)	(£)
20	Bought feed	4 200	81 150	85 350		4 515	4 515	80 835
21	Bought seed	1 055	10 182	11 237		2 050	2 050	9 187
22	Fertilizers	14 000	35 670	49 670		16 000	16 000	33 670
23	Casual labour		1 720	1 720				1 720
24	Contract work		1 620	1 620				1 620
25	Crop protection	1 200	7 452	8 652		800	800	7 852
26	Other crop VCs PMB levy		1 200	1 200				1 200
27	Vet. med. and other L/S VCs	320	11 970	12 290		400	400	11 890
28	Other miscellaneous variable costs Haulage		600	600				600

Table 1.7   (continued)

	1	2	3	4	5	6	7
	Opening valuation	Expenditure	Sub total 1 + 2	Receipts	Closing valuation	Sub total 4 + 5	Total input 3 − 6
INPUTS	(£)	(£)	(£)	(£)	(£)	(£)	(£)
29 Total variable costs							148 574
30 Regular labour paid		62 000	62 000				62 000
31 Regular labour unpaid		4 450	4 450				4 450
32 Machinery depreciation★		19 500	19 500	200		200	19 300
33 Fuel and oil★ and electricity	550	6 723	7 273	50 300	625	975	6 298
34 Machinery repairs Tax and insurance★		8 444	8 444	200		200	8 244
35 Electricity and coal							
36 Rent (less rental value of farmhouse)		21 578	21 578	800		800	20 778
37 Rates (less rates on farmhouse)		665	665				665
38 Water		1 399	1 399				1 399
39 Office expenses and general insurance		3 907	3 907				3 907
40 Deprecn. on tenant's fixtures		1 878	1 878				1 878
41 Other misc. overheads	480		480		320	320	160
42							
43 Total fixed costs							129 079
Total costs (variable and fixed)							277 653

★ Less private use, e.g. car, electricity, etc.

Management & investment income	£16 731
Family manual labour	£ 4 450
Net farm income	£21 181

Fixed costs

Those cost items numbered 29 to 41 are referred to as fixed costs. These are the cost items which do not alter very much with small changes in scale of an enterprise and are items which are not easily allocated to particular enterprises, e.g. machinery costs, labour and general overhead costs.

It is most important to note that with large changes in scale then fixed costs will alter substantially – for example, if a farmer decreases his dairy herd by three cows the relevant variable costs will automatically decrease, i.e. feed, veterinary and medicines and forage variable costs, but the fixed cost items of labour, machinery, etc. will not alter. If, however, the farmer decreases his dairy herd substantially then the fixed costs' will change as well as the relevant variable costs.

Management and investment income and net farm income

When the total input for the farm has been calculated (the sum of the variable and fixed costs' items) and is subtracted from the total gross output of the farm (as calculated on Worksheet 2 (Table 1.6)), the resulting margin is called Management and Investment Income (MII). This represents the reward to the farmer for the management of his farm and the income on the tenant's capital invested in the farm business – whether or not borrowed capital is involved. In summary the calculation is:

MII   = gross output – total inputs (variable and fixed costs)
£15 676 = £294 384 – £278 708

In calculating management and investment income the manual work of family labour was evaluated and included in the fixed costs. Sometimes it is difficult to calculate the value of family labour (called unpaid labour), and therefore a useful measure which eliminates this problem is called Net Farm Income (NFI). This is simply the income to the farm for the year's trading, and completely ignores any family labour. NFI can be calculated as follows:

NFI   = gross output – total inputs (excluding unpaid
                                                    manual labour)

or

NFI   = MII *plus* unpaid manual labour.

Points to observe when calculating gross output and inputs

The following suggestions may prove useful when analysing a trading account to produce gross output and inputs:
1. Sundry cost items often appear in a trading account. These should be classified as variable or fixed costs if possible: otherwise regard them as fixed costs.
2. When working through the trading account and extracting data

to be entered on the worksheets, tick off each item on the trading account when it has been extracted on to the analysis worksheet. This will help when checking later, especially if an error has been made.
3. If the total inputs (Worksheet 3 (Table 1.7)), when subtracted from the gross output (Worksheet 2), do not give the right answer for the farm's management and investment income, then each column on Worksheets 2 and 3 (Tables 1.6, 1.7) can be totalled down the worksheet, thus giving a built-in check – a quick way to spot arithmetical errors.

Worksheet 4

Forage hectares
In order to measure and compare the efficiency of stocking density of this farm with that of similar farms it is necessary to calculate the total amount of forage used in the farm business during the trading year in terms of both hectares and 'hectares equivalent' of grass and forage. Obviously, it would be inadequate to take only hectares of grass in any calculation which was to measure efficiency of forage used on the farm. Three basic terms are commonly used:

Farm forage hectares.   These are the total hectares of crops grown for feeding to livestock (excluding cereals).

Forage hectares.   These are the farm forage hectares after allowing the equivalents for hay sales, forage valuation changes and let and rented keep.

Adjusted forage hectares.   These are forage hectares plus a hectare allowance for bought hay and other bulk feeds. The average output per hectare of forage is taken as £155 and can be assessed as follows: Average yield per hectare of hay – say, 3.8 tonne at £40 tonne = £155
   In the calculation of adjusted forage hectares for the 264 ha farm on Worksheet 4 the hectares of grass (leys 130, permanent pasture 20) are taken and the 'hectare equivalents' of purchased forage as well as those of the opening and closing valuation of forage are calculated taking £155 as equal to 1 ha.
   The resulting adjusted forage hectares for the farm in Year 2 is 149.99 ha.

Tenant's capital

This is the amount of capital invested in the farm by the farmer as a tenant and embraces his investments in livestock, crops, cultivations, stores, machinery, car and tenant's fixtures. By definition, items of landlord's capital – land, buildings, etc. – are not included, even if the farmer is an owner-occupier.

In analysis of the farm business and the subsequent calculation of efficiency measures relating to the business, the average level of investment in tenant's capital during the trading year must be

Table 1.8   Littledown Farm: details of tenant's capital items

Tenant's capital items	Opening valuation (£)	Closing valuation (£)
Livestock		
Dairy cows	47 500	53 000
Dairy young stock	14 450	20 350
Sheep	17 112	16 520
Breeding pigs	11 020	9 750
Other pigs	2 400	3 450
Total	£92 482	£103 070
Crops and cultivations		
Winter wheat	38 765	45 000
Winter barley	—	—
Spring barley	14 586	10 925
Straw	1 500	1 750
Potatoes	10 500	12 000
Forage	12 000	12 500
Tillage	19 650	20 580
FYM	650	650
Total	£97 651	£103 405
Stores		
Fertilizers	14 000	16 000
Seeds	1 055	2 050
Fuel and oil	550	625
Concentrate feed	4 200	4 515
Sundry stores	2 000	1 520
Total	21 805	24 710
Machinery and equipment	129 703	110 203
Total	129 703	110 203
Total – Tenant's capital	£341 641	£341 388

known. To obtain this the average of the opening and closing valuations of tenant's capital items is taken as shown in Table 1.8. The livestock, crops and cultivations and stores items are taken from the opening and closing valuations of the trading account. The level of investment in machinery, car and tenant's fixtures are extracted from the farmer's capital account.

In Worksheet 4 (Table 1.9) the average level of investment in tenant's capital per hectare for each item is given and this can be

Table 1.9 Worksheet 4
Adjusted forage hectares

	Hectares	
	Sub-total	Total
Grass		
Leys	130	
Permanent pasture	20	150
Kale		
Rape		
Feed roots		
Rented keep		
Purchased forage $\dfrac{£}{155}$*	$\dfrac{500}{155}$	3.22
Opening valuation of forage, i.e. hay, silage, etc. $\dfrac{£}{155}$	$\dfrac{12\ 000}{155}$	77.42
Total available		230.64
Less		
Let keep		
Closing valuation of forage, i.e. hay, silage, etc. $\dfrac{£}{155}$	$\dfrac{12\ 500}{155}$	80.65
Forage sold $\dfrac{£}{155}$		
Adjusted Forage hectares		149.99

*£155 = 3.8 tonnes of hay per hectare at £40 tonne approx.

Tenant's capital

	Opening valuation	Closing valuation	Average of O/V and C/V	£/ha* Avg. valuation	Comparative data £/ha	
				264	Avg.	premium
Livestock	92 482	103 070	97 776	370.3	357.2	344.1
Crops and cultivations	97 651	103 405	100 528	380.78	134.1	125.7
Stores, etc.	21 805	24 710	23 257.5	88.09	75.5	85.5
Machinery and equipment	129 703	110 203	119 953	453.36	351.7	349.5
Total	341 641	341 388	341 514.5	1 293.53	918.5	904.8

* Use farm hectares.

compared with the levels of investment on similar farms. The information for the comparative farm groups cannot be entered on Worksheet 4 until this farm has been classified for comparative purposes, and this will be done on Worksheet 5 (Table 1.10).

Worksheet 5

Calculations of comparative data
Worksheet 5 (Table 1.10) is designed for the calculation of certain standards for the hectares of crops and head of livestock on the farm; these standards will be compared later with similar ones for comparable farms. The number of hectares for each crop enterprise and the average number of head of livestock for the year is taken. If a weighted monthly average of livestock numbers is available then this should be used.

Calculation of standard output
Standard output is in fact the gross output that the farm would have obtained during the trading year if average levels of yields and prices had been realized. Data is available from university departments of agricultural economics indicating levels of standard output for farm enterprises in their respective areas. In calculating standard output only sale crops are included; the output of feed crops is accounted for in the value of livestock products derived from them.

   When standard outputs have been calculated for each enterprise, these can be totalled to give the total farm standard output and this will be used as a basis for calculating certain efficiency factors which will be discussed later.

Grazing livestock units
Most farms will carry various types of grazing livestock which need to be reduced to a common denominator for comparison purposes with other farms, since head of cows, ewes and dairy young stock, as such, cannot be added together. The measure used is the grazing livestock unit which permits a comparison of like with like. In the calculation of grazing livestock units all types of grazing animals are equated to the cow which is equal to 1.0 grazing livestock unit. (g.l.u.), e.g. 1 cow = 1.0 g.l.u., 1 ewe = 0.2 g.l.u. (i.e. 5 ewes = 1 cow). Grazing livestock units will be used to calculate certain efficiency measures later in the analysis.

Standard man-days

A standard man-day represents 8 hours of work by an adult male worker. Standards are available indicating the 'average' amount of labour required for particular farm enterprises, e.g. one cow requires 5.0 standard man-days per year.

Using these standard man-day figures it is possible to calculate the total theoretical labour requirement of a farm in standard man-days. Normally 15 per cent is added to this total to cover general farm work which is not allocated to particular enterprises, e.g. hedging, ditching, general farm maintenance and holidays.

When the total theoretical labour requirement for the farm has been calculated this can be compared with the number of man-days actually available on the farm and can also be used to calculate other efficiency measures relating to the utilization of labour.

Tractor units

A tractor unit represents one hour of tractor work (note no additional 15 per cent is added). As in the case of standard man-days, standards are available indicating the average number of tractor hours required per year by each farm enterprise – see Worksheet 5 (Table 1.10).

Table 1.10 Worksheet 5
Calculations of standard output, livestock units, standard man-days and tractor hours

	OV no.	CV no.	Avg. no.	Standard output		Grazing livestock units		Standard man-days		Tractor units	
Stock bulls				—		1		4		7	
Dairy cows	125	135	130	700	91 000	1	130	5	650	7	910
Dairy heifers (2+ years)	26	26	26	130	3 380	0.8	20.8	2.5	65	4.5	117
Breeding stock (1–2 years)	30	30	30	130	3 900	0.6	18.0	2	60	2.5	75
Breeding stock (under 1 year)	35	35	35			0.4	14.0	1	35	3	105
Beef cows				—		0.8		2.0		4.5	
Beef heifers (2+ years)				130		0.8		2.5		4.5	
Fattening cattle (2+ years)				130		0.8		2.5		4.5	
Fattening cattle (1–2 years)				120		0.6		2		2.5	
Fattening cattle (under 1 year)				160		0.4		1		2.5	

Table 1.10   (continued)

	OV no.	CV no.	Avg. no.	Standard output		Grazing livestock units		Standard man days		Tractor units	
Rams	12	12	12	—	—	0.2	2.4	0.5	6	1	12
Ewes	540	460	500	42	21 000	0.2	100	0.5	250	1.3	650
Other sheep (over 1 year)				17		0.2		0.3		1	
Other sheep (under 1 year)				17		0.2		0.3		1	
Boars	6	6	6	—		—	—	2	12	0.5	3
Sows and gilts	112	88	100	460	46 000	—	—	4	400	2.0	200
Fattening pigs				120		—		0.6		1.0	
Others (weaners, young store pigs)				120		—		0.6		1.0	
Piglets				120		—		0.6		1.0	
Chicks and pullets	4.5			4.5		—		0.08		0.01	
Hens and cocks				8.5		—		0.05		0.01	
Table chickens				2.7		—		0.01		0.01	
Other poultry				20		—		0.2		0.01	
Standard L/S output					165 280		285.2		1 478		2 072
	Hectare										
Wheat			50	650	32 500			2.5	125	11	550
Barley Winter			30	530	15 900						
Barley Spring			24	460	11 040			2.5	135	11	594
Oats and mixed corn				500				2.5		11	
Beans – threshed				425				1.75		13	
Peas – threshed				500				1.75		13	
Vining peas				600				4.9		27.2	
Potatoes			8	1 850	14 800			22	176	48	384
Herbage seeds				650				1.8		10	
Oilseed rape				675				1.8		17.3	
Feed roots – cut				—				10		40	
Feed roots – folded								5		15	
Kale – cut								10		40	
Kale – folded								2		9	
Hay and Silage 1 cut			68					2.5	170	14	952
2 cuts								4		23	
Arable silage								4		15	
Grazing			150					1	150	2.5	375
								—		—	

Table 1.10 (continued)

	Avg. no.	Standard output	Grazing livestock units	Standard man days	Tractor units
Keep let		170		1.0	
Bare fallow		—		1.5	14
Standard crop output		74 240			
Total standard output		239 520		Total 2 234	
Total grazing L/S units			285.2	+15% 335	
Total standard man-days				2 569	
Total tractor work units					4 927

Standard output:	£	%		
Milk	91 000	37.99		
Sheep and cattle	28 280	11.80		
Pigs and poultry	46 000	19.20		Cattle,
Arable	74 240	30.99	Farm type	milk,
Total SO	239 520	100	classification	sheep,
				and arable

When the total farm requirement of tractor units has been calculated this figure is later used as a basis upon which certain efficiency measures relating to machinery are calculated.

Classification of Littledown Farm for comparison purposes

The basis of classification of farms for comparative purposes is the percentage standard output from the main enterprises. Now that the standard output has been calculated for each enterprise on Littledown Farm it is a simple exercise to calculate the percentage from the main enterprises.

The comparative data that will be used in this exercise is that published by Wye College University of London for farms in the south-east of England in 1983.

Using percentage standard output for classification does not mean that all farms when analysed will automatically 'fit' neatly into a classification group. In the case of Littledown Farm, 80 per cent of its standard output comes from three categories when combined and is best compared with those grouped as 'Milk, sheep/cattle and arable'.

Now that the farm has been classified, a reference for this group can be completed at the bottom of Worksheet 1 (Table 1.5). (This was left unexplained when Worksheet 1 was referred to since it is only at this stage of the analysis that the section can be completed.) Obviously, this is useful when checking through various case studies where a set of worksheets similar to these are being used.

It is now possible to enter the levels of investment of tenant's capital items for 'average' and 'premium' farms in the table of tenant's capital in Worksheet 4.

Worksheet 6

Comparative analysis of financial information

Now that the farm trading account has been standardized and the farm classified on a basis of standard output, it is possible to compare the farm's achievements (both physical and financial) with the group of comparative farms from the Wye College data. Worksheet 6 (Table 1.11) brings together, in summary form, the financial efficiency measures for this farm and the comparative data for 'average' and 'premium' farms is also presented. The grouping of farms as 'average' and 'premium' refers to their profitability as measured by their return on tenant's capital.

Table 1.11   Worksheet 6

	Total	£ per hectare		
Summary of financial information	This	This	Group	
Enterprise outputs	farm	farm	Average	Premium
Dairy cattle and milk	122 430	463.8	259.7	246.1
Other cattle	5 900	22.3	138.8	156.1
Sheep and wool	25 458	96.4	48.1	61.4
Pigs	48 722	184.6	—	—
Poultry and eggs				
Total livestock	202 510	767.1	446.9	463.7
Cereals (inc. straw)	77 444	293.3	164.9	187.3
Fruit and hops				
Other crops — potatoes	12 700	48.1	57.4	96.3
Total crops	90 144	341.5	227.1	291.1
Miscellaneous receipts	800	3.0	9.2	9.0
Forage and tillage valuation changes	930	3.5	2.8	7.6
Gross output	294 384	1 115.1	688.5	776.3
Inputs				
Bought feed	80 835	306.2	123.7	113.2
Bought seed (inc. home grown)	9 187	34.8	20.3	23.8
Other livestock VCs	11 890	45.0	25.4	26.5
Haulage	600	2.3		
Fertilizers	33 670	127.5	52.2	51.9
Crop protection	7 852	29.7	14.8	17.4
Other crop VCs	1 200	4.5	7.3	9.7

Table 1.11 (continued)

Summary of financial information	Total This farm	£ per hectare This farm	Group Average	Group Premium
Casual labour	1 720	6.5	14.3	14.0
Contract work	1 620	6.1	8.5	10.4
Total variable costs	148 574	562.8	288.4	296.2
Total gross margin	145 810	552.3	400.2	480.1
Regular labour (paid)	62 000	234.8	121.6	138.8
Regular labour (unpaid)	4 450	16.8	33.9	21.0
Machinery depreciation	19 300	73.1	51.9	51.0
Fuel and oil (electricity and coal)	6 298	23.8	34.7	38.8
Mach. repairs, tax and insurance	8 244	31.2	37.6	43.7
Rent and rates	21 443	81.2	83.9	86.3
General overhead costs	7 344	27.8	36.5	40.2
Total fixed costs	129 079	488.9	400.1	419.8
Total inputs (fixed + variable costs)	278 708	1 055.7	688.5	716.0
Management & investment income	16 731	63.4	0.0	60.3
Net farm income	21 181	80.2	22.8	65.5

In Worksheet 6 one new measure appears:

Total gross margin. Total gross margin is simply the total gross output of the farm less the total variable costs. Gross margins will be covered thoroughly later when gross margins will be calculated for each of the farm enterprises.

Worksheet 7

Further measures of efficiency for the farm business
As a result of the calculations made earlier in the analysis further measures of efficiency can now be calculated for the farm business relating to intensity of the business and yields, livestock performance and forage productivity, efficiency of labour and machinery and finally level of investment and return on that investment.

A. Measures of yield and intensity

1. Standard output (SO) per hectare This efficiency measure indicates the expected level of gross output (GO) for the farm at average levels of yields and prices.

2. System index   This index provides a guide to the general level of intensity of the farm compared with similar farms. It is calculated by expressing the standard output per hectare over the group average standard output (SO) per hectare as an index:

$$\text{System index} = \frac{\text{Farm SO per hectare}}{\text{Group SO per hectare}} \times 100$$

In effect, it is what this farm would produce per hectare at standard yields and prices compared with the comparative group farms' output per hectare at standard yields and prices. If the farm standard output per hectare is greater than the group standard output per hectare then the system index will be greater than 100 (and vice versa).

3. Yield index   This index gives a guide to the actual farm's yields and prices compared with average 'standard' levels of yields and prices for the area.

$$\text{Yield index} = \frac{\text{GO}}{\text{SO}} \times 100$$

The index can be split into a crop and livestock yield index:

$$\text{Crop index} = \frac{\text{Gross Output (crops)}}{\text{Standard Output (crops)}} \times 100$$

$$= \frac{90\ 144}{74\ 240} \times 100$$

$$= 121$$

$$\text{Livestock yield index} = \frac{\text{Gross Output (livestock)}}{\text{Standard Output (livestock)}} \times 100.$$

$$= \frac{202\ 510}{165\ 280} \times 100$$

$$= 123$$

B. Measures of livestock performance and forage production

1. Grazing livestock output per adjusted forage hectare   This measure indicates the actual gross output from livestock utilizing forage and, therefore, indicates the production from adjusted forage hectares.

2. Adjusted forage hectares per grazing livestock unit   This measure shows the stocking rate on the adjusted forage hectares of the farm.

3 and 4. Milk yield per cow and milk sales per cow   The total milk yield in Year 2 was 695 666 litres and, therefore, the average yield and average value of milk sold per cow over the year can be calculated as shown.

5. Margins of milk sales over concentrates   This measure is easily calculated and is a quick guide to the efficiency of concentrate usage in milk production.

Note: When interpreting these results all the measures relating to livestock performance should be considered together, since checking one measure in isolation can be very misleading.

C. Measures of labour and machinery efficiency

Labour and machinery costs per hectare (see Worksheet 6, Table 1.11)   When assessing labour and machinery efficiency in a farm business, the levels of labour and machinery costs per hectare can be examined and compared with those/ for similar farms. Any such comparisons must be interpreted with great care since labour costs are affected by intensity of enterprises.

1. Labour cost per 100 standard man-days

2. Machinery cost per 1000 tractor hours   These measures of labour and machinery efficiency, based on the theoretical requirement of the farm for each resource, overcome the weakness of the per hectare measures. The theoretical requirements for labour and machinery were calculated in Worksheet 5 as standard man-days for labour, and tractor units for machinery. Although it may be argued that the 'standard' figures used in these calculations do not suit all farms, the calculation does provide, nevertheless, a useful comparison between similar farms.

3. Gross margin per £100 labour

4. Gross margin per £100 machinery

5. Gross margin per £100 labour and machinery   So far labour and machinery have been assessed only on a physical basis in relation to costs. The most important consideration will be their financial productivity in terms of gross margin per unit cost. Although these measures, based on gross margin, are easy to calculate it must be remembered that many factors combine together to influence the gross margin of a farm. If gross margin is high enough, poor physical use of labour and machinery may be justified. If, however, there is a poor level of gross margin, these measures will be low when compared with similar farms, yet the physical efficiency of the labour and machinery on the farm may be satisfactory. The reason for calculating gross margin per £100 labour and machinery together is that these resources can, to some extent, replace one another, i.e. machines can replace men and costs of one may be high if costs of the other are low.

From the above measures of labour and machinery efficiency it is apparent that each measure has its limitations and deals with separate aspects of labour and machinery efficiency within the business. It is essential, therefore, that any conclusions made on the labour and machinery efficiency on a farm should not be drawn until all the measures have been considered together. Any conclusions drawn from just one or two measures in isolation may give a false impression of the facts.

Table 1.12   Worksheet 7

| | | | Group reference | |
		This farm per ha 264	Average per ha	Premium per ha
A. Measures of yield and intensity				
1. Standard output/ha				
$\dfrac{\text{Total SO}}{\text{Hectares}}$	$\dfrac{239\ 520}{264}$	907	686	715
2. System index				
$\dfrac{\text{SO} \times 100}{\text{Group avg. SO}}$	$\dfrac{907 \times 100}{686}$	132	100	104
3. Yield index				
$\dfrac{\text{GO} \times 100}{\text{SO}}$	$\dfrac{294\ 384 \times 100}{239\ 520}$	123	100	108
B. Measures of livestock performance and forage performance and forage production				
1. Grazing livestock output (less conc.) per adjusted forage hectare	Cattle 23 980 Milk 104 350 Sheep 25 458			
	153 788 −51 185			
$\dfrac{\text{GO from milk+cattle+sheep−conc.}}{\text{Adjusted forage hectares}}$	$\dfrac{102\ 603}{149.99}$	684	475	564
2. G.L.U. per adjusted forage hectare	$\dfrac{285.2}{149.99}$	1.9	2.1	2.2

Table 1.12 (continued)

	This farm per ha 264	Group reference Average per ha	Premium per ha
3. Milk yield per cow	$\dfrac{695\ 666}{130}$ 5 351	5 250	6 250
4. Milk sales per cow	$\dfrac{104\ 350}{130}$ 803	840	1 000
5. Margin of milk sales over concentrates			
$\dfrac{\text{Total milk sales} - \text{value of concs. to cows}}{\text{Average number of cows}}$	$\dfrac{104\ 350 - 40\ 210}{130}$ 493	563	632

C. Measures of labour and machinery efficiency

1. Labour cost per 100 standard man-days (including unpaid)

$\dfrac{\text{Labour cost} \times 100}{\text{Total SMD}}$	$\dfrac{68\ 170 \times 100}{2\ 569}$ 2 653	2 113	1 947

2. Machinery costs per 1 000 tractor hours

	Total	Per 1 000 tractor hours	Per 1 000 tractor hours	Per 1 000 tractor hours
$\dfrac{\text{Machinery costs} \times 1\ 000}{\text{Total tractor hours}}$				
Licences, insurance and repairs	8 244	1 673	2 303	2 598
Fuel and electricity (power)	6 298	1 278	2 095	2 229
Contract	1 620	329	550	698
Depreciation	19 300	3 917	3 095	2 862
Total machinery costs	35 462	7 197	8 043	8 387

3. GM/£100 labour

$\dfrac{\text{GM} \times 100}{\text{Labour cost (inc. unpaid)}}$	$\dfrac{145\ 810}{68\ 170}$ 214	246	292

4. GM/£100 machinery costs

$\dfrac{\text{GM} \times 100}{\text{Machinery cost}}$	$\dfrac{145\ 810}{35\ 462}$ 411	319	333

5. GM/£100 Labour and Machinery costs

$\dfrac{\text{GM} \times 100}{\text{L and M costs}}$	$\dfrac{145\ 810}{103\ 632}$ 141	136	154

D. Measures of investment and return

1. Tenant's capital per ha

	$\dfrac{341\ 514}{264}$ 1 294	919	905

2. Return on tenant's capital

$\dfrac{\text{MII} \times 100}{\text{Tenant's capital}}$	$\dfrac{16\ 731}{341\ 514}$ 4.9%	0%	6.8%

D. Measures of level of investment and return on capital

1. Tenant's capital per hectare (see also Worksheet 4 (Table 1.9))   This is the measure of the tenant's level of investment in the farm business. The details of the average levels of investment in 'productive' items, e.g. livestock, and 'non-productive' items, e.g. machinery, were calculated in Worksheet 4, where the average of the opening and closing valuations were taken from the trading account and the details of machinery, car and tenant's equipment were extracted from the farm's capital account.

2. Return on tenant's capital   This is calculated by expressing the management and investment income as a percentage of the tenant's capital. The percentage return on tenant's capital is the yield obtained from the tenant's capital invested in the farm business. Since an allowance was made for family manual labour, this is a measure which can be fairly compared with likely returns from investments in any form of business, whether in farming or otherwise.

Trading account analysis: Conclusions
Now that the farm trading account has been systematically analysed, it is very apparent that all the efficiency measures that have been calculated relate to the farm business as a whole and not to individual enterprises. It is necessary, therefore, to examine each enterprise on the farm individually since the good ones may be 'masking' the poor ones – a fact that would not have been identified in the trading account analysis. The analytical technique that will be used for the examination of individual enterprises is that of gross margin analysis, and when the gross margins for each of the farm enterprises have been calculated, then the results of both the trading account analysis and the gross margins' analysis will be interpreted, giving a complete picture of the strengths and weaknesses of the farm business.

GROSS MARGIN ANALYSIS

The gross output for each individual enterprise is calculated and its variable costs deducted, leaving a margin which is called the 'gross margin'. Fixed costs items are completely ignored in this form of analysis and do not enter into it.

For each individual enterprise on Littledown Farm gross margins are to be calculated. For the livestock enterprises gross margins are usually calculated for the same 12 months' period as is covered by the trading account. The information required to calculate gross margins for the livestock enterprises will, therefore, be found in a particular year's trading account, and by examining the physical and financial records relating to that year's trading.

The crops enterprise gross margins will need to be calculated for a particular *crop year* so that the gross margin of each particular crop is found. The information that will be required for crop gross margins may well bridge 2, or even 3 years' trading accounts. Figure 1.1 for the winter wheat crop on Littledown Farm illustrates this point.

Figure 1.1 clearly shows how some variable costs items fall into Year 1 as well as Year 2, and the receipts items for grain fall into Year 3. It will be necessary, then, to have information from different years' trading accounts before the final gross margin figures can be calculated for the winter wheat, winter barley and spring barley

Trading account year	Technical operations for winter wheat	Variable costs incurred	Receipts received
Year 1 October October	Winter wheat sown Wheat sprayed, pre-emergent; broad-leaved weeds/blackgrass	Seed Seedbed fertilizer Pre-emergent spray chemical	
Year 2 February/March	First top dressing of fertilizer	Nitrogen fertilizer	
March	Spray with eyespot fungicide/straw strengthener	Spray chemical	
March	Second top dressing of fertilizer	Nitrogen fertilizer	
March/April	Third top dressing of fertilizer	Nitrogen fertilizer	
April/May	Spray with Septoria fungicide	Spray chemical	
June/July	Spray with aphicide	Spray chemical	
August/September	Harvest, clean, dry and store		
November/December			Grain sales
Year 3 January/April			Grain sales

Figure 1.1   Information needed to calculate gross margin for winter wheat crop harvested in Year 2

Table 1.13 Littledown Farm: allocation of all variable cost items for the Year 2 trading account, and other relevant variable costs for crops enterprises harvested in Year 2

Harvest year	Year 2 harvest						Year 3 harvest		Total
Crop Enterprise	Winter wheat (£)	Winter barley (£)	Spring barley (£)	Maincrop potatoes (£)	Forage (£)	Unallocated variable costs	Winter wheat (£)	Winter barley (£)	Variable costs from trading acc. Year 2 (£)
Seed	—	—	1 032	2 960	16 501	—	2 250	1 295	9 187
Fertilizer (seedbed)	—	—	840	1 600	2 720	—	2 000	1 410	8 560
Spray (pre-emergent)							1 600	1 120	2 720
Fertilizer (top dressing)	2 850	1 500	480	—	20 280	—	—	—	25 110
Sprays	2 000	900	672	960	600	—			5 132
Casual labour	—	—	—	1 720	—	—			1 720
Contract	—	—	—	420		1 200			1 620
PMB levy and sundries	—	—	—	1 200	—	—			1 200
Haulage	—	—	—	—		600			600
Relevant variable costs from Year 1 trading account:									
Seed	2 100	1 050	—	—	—	—			—
Fertilizer (seedbed)	1 400	780	—	—	—	—			—
Spray (pre-emergent)	1 500	690							

crops harvested in Year 2. The same is true of the potatoes which were not sold until Year 3.

It follows, then, that information will probably be needed from two or even three years' trading accounts when calculating crop gross margins. If gross margin calculations are being done for a crop at a time when the product is still in store, then the valuation of the crop in store should be taken.

Crops enterprise gross margins

A breakdown of the variable costs for crops and forage on Littledown Farm is given in Table 1.13. The winter wheat and winter barley are crops where information on variable costs has had to be extracted from Year 1 trading account. Some of the variable costs in the Year 2 trading account do, however, relate to the winter wheat crop which will be harvested in Year 3 – see Table 1.13. This crop will, of course, have been sown in the autumn of Year 2.

The fact that variable costs items have been extracted from the previous year's trading account for gross margin analysis does not alter the final profit figure for the Year 2 trading account. This is so, because these items will have been included in the tenant right (forage and tillage) valuation made at the end of Year 1, and appear, therefore, in the opening valuation of the Year 2 trading account.

It should be noted that the totals column in Table 1.13 provides a check against the total inputs of each of these variable costs items which were calculated in Worksheet 3.

In calculating the gross margins for the crop enterprises on Littledown Farm it is assumed that the calculations are being done fairly soon after the end of Year 2 (which ended on 31 December).

Table 1.14 Littledown Farm: the spring barley, winter barley and winter wheat crop harvested in Year 2

Spring barley	
Hectares grown	24 ha
Yield/hectare	5 tonnes
Total yield	120 tonnes
Amount fed by 31 December – end of Year 2	25 tonnes at £110/tonne = £2 750
Remainder in closing valuation Year 2	95 tonnes at £115/tonne = £10 925
Total	120 tonnes = £13 675
Amount to be fed Year 3	35 tonnes
Amount to be sold Year 3	60 tonnes
Total (= amount in closing valuation)	95 tonnes

Table 1.14   (continued)

Winter barley	
Hectares grown	24 ha
Yield/hectare	6.8 tonnes
Total yield	163 tonnes
All sold by 31 December – end of Year 2	£20 670 (195 tonnes at £127/tonne) – malting sample.

Winter wheat	
Hectares grown	48 ha
Yield/hectare	7.5 tonnes
Total yield	360 tonnes
All in closing valuation of Year 2 trading account	£45 000 (375 tonnes at £125/tonne)

At the end of Year 2 all of the wheat harvested in Year 2 was still in store (valued in the closing valuation, see Table 1.14); some of the spring barley harvested in Year 2 had already been fed by 31 December of Year 2, but the remainder was in store valued in the closing valuation, see Table 1.14. Of this amount of barley in store

Table 1.15   Littledown Farm: gross margins for crops harvested in Year 2

Crop Enterprise Hectares grown Year 2	Winter wheat 48 (£)	Winter barley 24 (£)	Spring barley 24 (£)	Maincrop potatoes 8 (£)
Gross output				
Sales	—	20 670	—	
Fed on the farm	—	—	2 750	
Closing valuation		—		
(Year 2 trading account)	45 000		10 925	12 000
Total	45 000	20 670	13 675	12 000
Variable costs:★				
Seed	21 000	1 050	1 032	2 960
Fertilizers	4 250	2 280	1 320	1 600
Sprays	3 500	1 590	672	960
Casual labour	—	—	—	1 720
Contractor	—	—	—	420
PMB levy and sundries	—	—	—	1 200
Total	9 850	4 920	3 024	8 860
Gross margin	35 150	15 750	10 651	3 140
Gross margin per ha	£732	£656	£444	£393

★ See Table 1.13.

at the end of Year 2, some will be fed and the rest sold in Year 3. All the potatoes lifted in Year 2 were in store at the end of Year 2 and appear in the closing valuation; all of the winter barley has been sold.

The details of the calculations of the crop enterprise gross margins for crops harvested in Year 2 are shown in Table 1.15.

Livestock enterprise gross margins

Firstly, the forage variable costs should be allocated between the various grazing livestock enterprises. Unless very detailed records are kept so that forage seed, fertilizer and spray costs can be allocated to each grazing enterprise, the allocation should be done on a basis of livestock units (details of which were given on Worksheet 5, Table 1.10) The details of the forage costs for Littledown Farm were given in Table 1.13 – seed £1 650, fertilizers £23 000, spray £600 = £25 250. To allocate this on basis of grazing livestock units the number of grazing livestock units in each enterprise should be calculated (these were calculated in Worksheet 5, Table 1.10).

Dairy cows – average no.	130×1.0	$= 130$ g.l.u.
Dairy young stock – average no.		
0–1 year	35×0.4	$= 14$
1–2 years	30×0.6	$= 18$ 52.8
2–2½ years	26×0.8	$= 20.8$
Sheep	512×0.2	$= 102.4$
		285.2

The forage variable costs of £25 250 can now be allocated using the following formula:

$$\frac{\text{Total forage cost}}{\text{Total no. of g.l.u. on farm}} \times \text{No. of g.l.u. in enterprise}$$

1. Dairy cows $\quad \dfrac{£25\ 250 \times 130}{285.2} = £11\ 509$

2. Dairy young stock $\quad \dfrac{£25\ 250 \times 52.8}{285.2} = £4\ 675$

3. Sheep $\quad \dfrac{£25\ 250 \times 102.4}{285.2} = £9\ 066$

$$£25\ 250$$

In addition to the allocation of forage variable costs to the various grazing livestock enterprises the following information – see Tables 1.16 and 1.17 – is also required, in addition to that in the trading account for Year 2 (Table 1.13)

Table 1.16   Littledown Farm: details of transfers between enterprises

1. *Livestock*
   (a) 35 heifer calves transferred from the dairy herd to the dairy young stock enterprise valued at £70 each = £2 450.
   (b) 27 down-calving heifers transferred from the dairy young stock enterprise back to the dairy herd, valued at £420 = £11 340.
2. *Barley fed to livestock*
   The following amounts were fed to livestock:

	Dairy cows		Sheep		Total	
	tonne	£	tonne	£	tonne	£
Barley (harvested Year 2) (valued at £95/tonne)	20	2 200	5	550	25	2 750
Barley (harvested Year 1) (valued at £85/tonne)	20	2 000	6	600	26	2 600
	40	4 200	11	1 150	51	5 350

Table 1.17   Littledown Farm: allocation of variable costs to livestock enterprises

Enterprise	Dairy cows (£)	Dairy young stock (£)	Sheep (£)	Pigs (£)	Total (£)
Purchased feed	36 010	6 125	3 700	35 000	80 835
Vet., medicine	1 950	485	1 150	1 200	4 785
Sundries	2 080	225	600	2 200	5 105
AI, recording fees	2 000				2 000

The gross margin calculations for the livestock enterprises on Littledown Farm are presented in Table 1.18.

For comparison with the crops enterprises the gross margin per forage hectare should be calculated for the grazing livestock enterprises. Details of these calculations for each of the grazing livestock enterprises on Littledown Farm are given in Table 1.19.

Notes on calculating livestock gross margins
The opening and closing valuations of all livestock enterprises should be included as shown in the calculations in Table 1.18 since changes in these valuations will influence gross output and consequently gross margin.

Table 1.18   Littledown Farm: livestock enterprise gross margin

	Dairy cows (£)	Dairy young stock (£)	Sheep (£)	Pigs (£)
Gross output				
Closing valuation at end of Year 2	53 000	20 350	16 520	13 200
Sales				
Culls	6 300	—	6 300	4 092
Progeny	7 200	—	27 500	48 000
Products	104 350	—	1 625	—
Transfers out	2 450	11 430	—	—
Subtotal	173 300	31 780	51 945	65 292
Less opening valuation at beginning of Year 2	47 500	14 450	17 112	13 420
Livestock purchases	920	—	9 375	3 150
Transfers in	11 430	2 450	—	—
Subtotal	59 850	16 900	26 487	16 570
Gross output	113 450	14 880	25 458	48 722
Variable costs				
Purchased feed	36 010	6 125	3 700	35 000
Home-grown grain	4 200	—	1 150	—
Vet. and medicine	1 950	485	1 150	1 200
AI and recording fees	2 000	—	—	—
Other livestock variable costs	2 080	225	600	2 200
Total	46 240	6 835	6 600	38 400
Gross margin (exc. forage costs)	67 210	8 045	18 858	10 322
Less forage costs	11 509	4 675	9 066	—
Gross margin after forage	55 701	3 370	9 792	10 322
Avg. stock number per enterprise	130 cows	52.8 livestock units	500 ewes	100 sows
Gross margin per head (excluding forage costs)	£517 per cow	£152 per livestock unit	£38 per ewe	£103 per sow
Final gross margin per head (after deducting forage costs)	£429 per cow	64 per livestock unit	£19.6 per ewe	£103 per sow

Table 1.19   Littledown Farm: gross margin calculations per adjusted forage hectare for grazing livestock

Gross margin per adjusted forage hectare		$\dfrac{\left(\begin{array}{c}\text{Enterprise} \\ \text{gross margin}\end{array} - \begin{array}{c}\text{Allocated} \\ \text{forage costs}\end{array}\right) \times \begin{array}{c}\text{Total number of} \\ \text{g.l.u.s on farm}\end{array}}{\begin{array}{c}\text{No. of g.l.u.s} \\ \text{in enterprise}\end{array} \times \begin{array}{c}\text{Total adjusted forage} \\ \text{hectares on farm}\end{array}}$
Dairy cows	=	$\dfrac{(67\,210 - 11\,509) \times 285.2}{130 \times 149.99} = \text{£}814.7/\text{adjusted forage hectare}$
Dairy young stock		$\dfrac{(8\,045 - 4\,675) \times 285.2}{52.8 \times 149.99} = \text{£}121/\text{adjusted forage hectare}$
Sheep	=	$\dfrac{(18\,858 - 9\,066) \times 285.2}{102.4 \times 149.99} = \text{£}181.8/\text{adjusted forage hectare}$

Reconciliation of the enterprise gross margins with the total farm gross margin

The total of the individual enterprise gross margins will not necessarily balance with the total farm gross margin shown on Worksheet 6 (Table 1.11), which comprises total gross output less total variable costs.

Enterprise gross margins must, however, be reconciled with the total farm gross margin and a balance drawn up to prove that the enterprise gross margins have been correctly calculated, and that nothing has been overlooked.

A table should be drawn up – see Table 1.20 – to show that all items included in calculating farm gross output can be accounted for, and a further table – see Table 1.21 – can be used to balance the variable costs items between the enterprises.

$$\begin{array}{lll}\text{Total farm} & = \text{total farm} & \\ \text{gross margin} & \text{gross output} & -\text{total variable costs} \\ \text{£}145\,810 & = \text{£}294\,384 & -\text{£}148\,574\end{array}$$

The next stage in reconciling the gross margins is to total the individual gross margins for all the enterprises costed. This will give the total enterprise gross margin which must now be adjusted in order to balance with the total farm gross margin.

The necessary adjustments have been made in Table 1.22 and are enumerated as follows:
1. Sundry receipts must be added since they do not occur in the enterprise gross margins.
2. Any crops' costs which have occurred in the previous year's trading account and have been used in calculating enterprise gross margins must be added back.
3. Crops from the previous year which were in store at the begin-

Table 1.20 Littledown Farm: allocation between enterprises of farm gross output from Year 2 trading account

	Year 1 crops	Year 2 crops Spring barley	Winter barley	Winter wheat	Potatoes	Dairy cows	Dairy young stock	Sheep	Pigs	Unallocated	Transfers	Total
1. Cattle						18 080	5 900					23 980
2. Milk						104 350						104 350
3. Sheep — wool								25 458				25 458
4. Pigs									48 722			48 722
5.												
6.												
7.												
Total livestock						113 450	14 880	25 458	48 722			202 510
8. Cereals Wheat*	1 509			45 000								
S. Barley*	1 690	13 675										
Winter barley			20 670								−2 600† −2 750‡	77 194
9. Straw										250		250
10. Potatoes	700*				12 000							12 700
11. Forage and tillage										930		930
Total crops	3 899	13 675	20 670	45 000	12 000					1 180	−5 350	91 074
Sundry receipts										800		800
Total misc.										800		800
Gross output	3 899	13 675	20 670	45 000	12 000	113 450		25 458	48 722	1 980	−5 350	294 384

*Gains upon realization of OV. † Barley from Year 1. ‡ Barley from Year 2.

Table 1.21 Littledown Farm: allocation of variable costs from Year 2 trading account

	Year 2 crops				Year 3 Crops		Dairy cows (£)	Dairy young stock (£)	Sheep (£)	Pigs (£)	Forage (£)	Unallocated (£)	Total (£)
	Winter wheat (£)	Winter barley (£)	Spring barley (£)	Potatoes (£)	Winter wheat (£)	Winter barley (£)							
Purchased feeds							36 010	6 125	3 700	35 000			80 835
Purchased seeds			1 032	2 960	2 250	1 295					1 650		9 187
Fertilizer	2 850	1 500	1 320 (840 + 480)	1 600	2 000	1 400					23 000		33 670
Casual labour				1 720									1 720
Contract				420								1 200	1 620
Sprays	2 000	900	672	960	1 600	1 120					600		7 852
Livestock sundries							2 080	225	600	2 200			5 105
Vet. and med.							1 950	485	1 150	1 200			4 785
AI and recording fees							2 000						2 000
Misc. PMB levy, sundries				1 200									1 200
Haulage												600	600
Total variable costs	4 850	2 400	3 024	8 860	5 850	3 815	42 040	6 835	5 450	38 400	25 250	1 800	148 574

Table 1.22 *Littledown Farm: reconciliation of enterprise gross margins with total farm gross margin*

			Total farm gross margin from Worksheet 6 (Table 1.11)
			£
Wheat		35 150	145 810
Winter barley		15 750	
Spring barley		10 651	
Maincrop potatoes		3 140	
Dairy cows		55 701	
Dairy young stock		3 370	
Sheep		9 792	
Pigs		10 322	
Total enterprise gross margin		143 876	
Plus:			
1. Sundry receipts		800	
2. Crop costs occurring in Year 1 account			
Seed	3 150		
Fertilizer	2 180		
Spray	2 190	7 520	
3. Gains on OV relating to Year 1 crops			
Wheat	1 509		
Barley	1 690		
Potatoes	700	3 899	
4. Forage and tillage valuation change		9 030	13 149
Valuation change Straw		250	157 275
Less:			
5. Unallocated v. cost			
Contract	1 200		
Haulage	600	1 800	
6. Crop costs relating to Year 3			
Seed	3 545		
Fertilizer	3 400		
Spray	2 720	9 665	
		11 465	
		145 810	145 810

Gains upon realization of Year 1 crops in store at 1 January:

	Wheat		Spring barley		Potatoes	
	£	£	£	£	£	£
Opening valuation	38 675		14 586		10 500	
Value fed				2 600		
Sales		40 274	13 676			11 200
Gain	1 509		1 690		700	
	40 274	40 274	16 276	16 276	11 200	11 200

ning of the trading year may have been sold. Any gains above the opening valuation figure should be added back, and any losses subtracted.

4. Forage and tillage valuation changes must be added if positive, or deducted if negative.
5. Not all the variable costs shown on the trading account can be directly allocated among the enterprises. Any unallocated variable costs should, therefore, be deducted.
6. Deduct any payments or bonuses which have been estimated for the purpose of calculating enterprise gross margins, but which have not actually occurred in the trading account.
7. Any crop costs which have occurred in the trading account, but which relate to crops sown for the following harvest year, should be deducted.
8. Valuation changes occurring in stores or produce, e.g. straw, which are not included in the enterprise gross margins should be added if positive and deducted if negative.

Table 1.22 clearly shows how the reconciliation of enterprise gross margins should be presented and made to balance mathematically with the total farm gross margin figure. In the analysis of other farm businesses, other items might appear which must not be ignored in striking this balance, e.g. receipts for keeper sheep (agistment receipt); it follows, therefore, that each farm business must be examined carefully to ensure that all items are considered, otherwise reconciliation will be impossible.

Interpretation of the trading account analysis, comparative data and gross margin analysis

Now that the trading account for Year 2 has been analysed and efficiency measures are available, together with comparative data from similar farms and gross margins for each of the enterprises on the farm, an interpretation of all these measures should be made. The analytical work so far has really been routine – a job which a competent clerk can easily do, but now the more interesting aspects of farm business analysis come to light in the interpretation of these results.

It is recommended that a logical sequence be followed when undertaking an interpretation of data from a farm business analysis. The sequence shown in Fig. 1.2 has been drawn up for this purpose.

Interpretation of the results of the analysis of Littledown Farm business

Following the suggested scheme of interpretation of the analysis results (see Fig. 1.2), the first measure to examine is the return on tenant's capital.

Standardize account and compare results with those achieved by

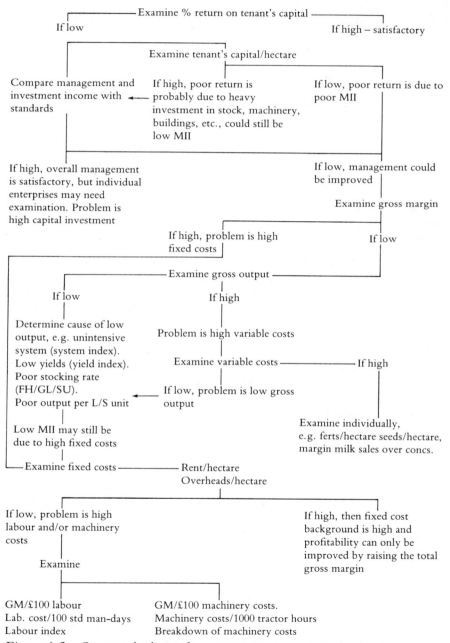

Figure 1.2   Suggested scheme for systematic interpretation of efficiency measures

similar farms, i.e. group comparison.

Return on tenant's capital.   At 4.9 per cent this is above average levels of return and below the premium for the group; comparison figures being 0 per cent and 6.8 per cent respectively. The return on tenant's capital as achieved is a function of the management and investment income and the tenant's capital invested.

Management and investment income.   At £63/ha this is well above average levels of performance at £18/ha and £3.0/ha above premium.

Tenant's capital.   A high level of tenant's capital at £1293/ha compared with average and premium investments of £918 and £904 combines with the MII achieved to produce a 4.9 per cent return on tenant's capital investment. In comparative group terms the return is satisfactory, but still leaves ample room for improvement.

Total gross margin.   The total gross margin per hectare is £552, which is well above the average and premium group figures of £400 and £480. This gross margin is the result of a very high gross output which can more than adequately cope with the high level of variable costs.

Fixed costs.   Total fixed costs for the farm at £488/ha are well above the average and premium figures. The high management and investment income figure is primarily due to the high gross output which is able to carry the high fixed and variable costs. Fixed costs should be examined more carefully.

Levels of fixed costs.   The machinery costs per hectare in total are above the average and below the premium for the group. With the total farm gross margin well above the comparison figures, the relatively low machinery costs combine to produce a very good gross margin per £100 spent on machinery. The most significant item contributing to this is a spares and repairs figure being kept creditably low. Machinery costs per 1 000 tractor hours, as might be expected, providing the use is sound, are also below both average and premium.

General overheads are well within reason, while rent and rates are below both average and premium although it is unlikely that these are controllable by management.

Labour cost £/ha is well above both average and premium comparisons. Labour costs in relation to theoretical labour requirements expressed as standard man-days are very high and the picture presented is further endorsed when gross margin per £100 labour is examined. The high gross margin is completely counteracted by the high labour costs.

When labour and machinery are examined together the gross margin per £100 labour and machinery is only just above average, the effect of high labour costs being sufficient to counteract low machinery costs and a high gross margin.

The level of fixed costs and in particular labour, are the main reason for the return produced. The high total farm gross margin per hectare would suggest that the efficiency with which variable costs have been used in relation to output is generally good. Examination of enterprise gross margins will help in deciding this.

Crop enterprise gross margins.   Gross margins for the cereal crops confirm that these enterprises are making a satisfactory contribution to the farm business – see Table 1.23.

The gross margin per hectare for winter wheat and both winter and spring barley are above average. Maincrop potatoes show a poor gross margin, with output well below average and variable costs above average.

Livestock enterprise gross margins.   The gross margins for livestock enterprises were calculated in Table 1.18. In Table 1.24 they are presented on a per unit basis in summary form.

From the information given it is clear that the breeding sow herd is producing below average performance. A premium result would show an extra £100 per sow in gross margin. With a breeding herd of 100 sows, £100 extra gross margin could be used to offset some of the fixed costs being incurred.

The grazing livestock enterprises require close examination. Dairy cow output at £873 per cow is above average and the use of variable costs excluding forage gives rise to a gross margin per cow of £517, the average being £525 and the high £559. The grazing implications look even less soundly based, resulting in a gross margin per forage hectare of below average performance. Stocking rate, as measured by grazing livestock units per adjusted forage hectare, compares well with comparison farms (Table 1.12, Worksheet 7). Forage costs are, however, much higher.

The dairy young stock show a similar trend, but are an unreliable enterprise to draw many useful comparative conclusions.

Sheep show a similar trend to the other grass using livestock. Output per ewe being just above average. The gross margin before and after, deducting forage costs reflects a very low level of performance.

Table 1.23 *Littledown Farm: gross margins of crop enterprises for Year 2 with comparative figures*

Enterprise	Winter wheat			Winter barley			Spring barley			Maincrop potatoes		
	This farm (£)	Average (£)	Premium (£)	This farm (£)	Average* (£)	Premium* (£)	This farm (£)	Average† (£)	Premium† (£)	This farm (£)	Average (£)	Premium (£)
Gross output per hectare	900	765	935	689	625	725	569	500	585	1 500	2 080	2 755
Variable costs per hectare	197	195	195	164	170	170	126	130	130	1 107	1 115	1 150
Gross margin per hectare	732	570	740	656	455	555	444	370	455	393	965	1 605

* Malting barley.
† Feed barley.

Table 1.24 *Littledown Farm: gross margins for Livestock enterprises for Year 2 with comparative figures*

Enterprise	Sows				Dairy cows						Dairy young stock				Sheep		
	This farm	Average	Premium		This farm	Low	Average	High	Very high		This farm	Average	Premium		This farm	Average	Premium
	(£)	(£)	(£)		(£)	(£)	(£)	(£)	(£)		(£)	(£)	(£)		(£)	(£)	(£)
Gross output	Per sow	487	485	592	Per cow	873	735	855	935	1 015	Per livestock unit	281.8	585*	585*	Per ewe	51.0	50.2	59.5
Variable costs (exc. forage)	Per sow	384	375	389	Per cow	356	274	330	376	425	Per livestock unit	129	207	182	Per ewe	13.2	11.1	11.1
Gross margin (exc. forage)	Per sow	103	110	203	Per cow	517	461	565	559	590	Per livestock unit	152	378	403	Per ewe	37.7	39.1	48.4
Gross margin after deducting forage costs					Per forage hectare	815	725	844	906	964	Per forage hectare	121.4	360	460	Per forage hectare	181.8	288	467

★ Per heifer reared

Conclusion
The return on investment, while above the average comparative figure, could well be improved. The high output achieved is not culminating in a sufficiently high total farm gross margin to cover the high fixed cost and leave an adequate management and investment income.

On close examination two areas stand out which should be examined much more closely:
1. The fixed costs and, in particular, the labour element;
2. The use of forage in relation to the costs involved, quality and productivity of the pastures being worthy of an initial examination. Costs in relation to stocking rate must also be closely looked at.

Cash crops on the farm, potatoes excepted, contribute well. For the long term, planning should begin to ensure that the structure of the business, labour/machinery, enterprise combination, etc are soundly based. Expanding existing enterprise combinations does not always lead to an improvement in business performance.

COSTING SYSTEMS

Comparative farm account analysis

In the analysis of the Littledown Farm business the technique of comparative farm account analysis was thoroughly covered. Unfortunately, like all analysis techniques, this has its limitations and shortcomings.

Limitations of comparative farm account analysis
Comparative farm account analysis only shows the levels of outputs and inputs per hectare over the whole farm. There is no attempt to divide costs and outputs between enterprises and, therefore, the relative profitability between different enterprises is not shown. It follows, therefore, that one very profitable enterprise may be 'covering up' for an unprofitable one.

Cost accounting or enterprise costing

There is, however, an analysis technique which is used in farm business analysis, which does allocate both outputs and inputs to particular enterprises. This technique is called 'cost accounting' or 'enterprise costing.' This particular analysis technique was not applied to the enterprises on Littledown Farm, but if it had been, a profit figure for each enterprise on the farm could have been calculated as well as for each item of output, e.g. profit per tonne of potatoes, profit per hectare of wheat and profit per cow or per litre of milk.

Limitations of cost accounting

First impressions suggest that cost accounting is a useful technique for analysing farm enterprises, since all cost and output items are allocated to particular enterprises overcoming the 'weakness' of comparative farm account analysis. Unfortunately, this apparent advantage of costs allocation involves the problem of allocating fixed costs, and since this cannot be done accurately the final profit figure is not reliable.

It would be easy to allocate wages if time sheets were kept of time spent on each enterprise, but there would still remain the problem of allocating holidays, national insurance, and time spent on maintenance and non-productive work. At first sight it would seem that rent and rates would present no problems since they could be allocated on a per hectare basis, unfortunately this system would not be acceptable to pig and poultry 'concrete' enterprises which use a very limited area. Similar problems arise when trying to allocate other fixed cost items. Some machinery costs can be allocated by keeping hourly records, but the problem arises of unproductive work and its allocation to particular enterprises. It may be argued that electricity and water can be easily allocated by installing meters, but a very real problem will be encountered when trying to allocate general overhead costs viz.:

(a) all miscellaneous costs, fees, subscriptions, office expenses;
(b) telephone and other sundry items.

What basis of allocation should be adopted? A number could be used:

1. Percentage gross output of each enterprise;
2. Percentage standard output of each enterprise;
3. Percentage of allocated costs to each enterprise;
4. Percentage hectares of each enterprise;
5. Percentage labour requirements of each enterprise.

All of these are acceptable by accounting standards, but none are reliable.

The outcome of cost accounting is, therefore, a profit figure for each enterprise which is very largely affected by the proportion of the farm's fixed costs that it carries, depending upon the method of allocation or apportionment of fixed costs that was employed.

Gross margin analysis

Since the early 1960s the gross margin has become recognized as a useful comparative measure between enterprises. Originally the gross margin was intended as a measure of productivity for cash crops, but it has since been extended to almost every agricultural (and horticultural) enterprise.

It is possible, therefore, to calculate gross margins for individual enterprises and total these to give the total farm gross margin. The difference between this and the fixed costs gives the farm's management and investment income. The level of fixed costs which exist on a farm will, to a large extent, dictate the type of enterprise which will be carried since a high level of fixed costs will necessitate a high gross margin if a margin is to be left as a trading profit. Conversely, where the overall level of fixed costs is low, a margin will still be achieved from enterprises producing a relatively low gross margin.

Limitations of gross margin analysis
There are a number of restraints which must be considered when applying gross margin analysis to a farm business. These are:
1. The gross margin is confined to strictly defined cost areas. It does not take into account any changes that may occur in fixed cost structure of the business and therefore must be used with care in farm planning. This caution is necessary since fixed costs are, of course, not fully fixed. Some fixed cost items do not change except over a period of time, e.g. rent, while others do alter, e.g. labour and machinery costs. It is dangerous in farm planning to assume that all fixed costs will remain constant, since some of these will undoubtedly alter, particularly when major changes of policy are being considered.
2. The gross margin of an enterprise is not necessarily an indication of its profitability. This is only one aspect of an enterprise; many other items and factors are involved before the ultimate profitability is known.
3. Confusion and misinterpretation can easily occur unless the full gross margin calculation can be examined, i.e. an insight into exactly how the figures were calculated:

    Example: *Potato enterprise*
             Contract harvesting   = variable cost
             Using own harvester   = fixed cost
             Casual labour   = variable cost
             Regular labour   = fixed cost

     If gross margins were calculated for two farmers A and B,

both of whom had the same hectares of potatoes, same yield, same sale price, same percentage ware, same seed, fertilizer and spray costs, but;

> Farmer A harvests by contract and uses casual labour, while Farmer B uses his own harvester and uses his regular labour force

Then Farmer B's gross margin for his potato enterprise will be much higher than that of Farmer A.

Similarly with cereal enterprises; crops harvested by contractor will, other factors being equal, show a lower gross margin than crops harvested with farm-owned machinery. The profitability may be in reverse.

4. Increasing the intensity of enterprises on a farm may well increase the total farm gross margin, but it will not necessarily increase the total farm profit, since the fixed costs may also rise in greater proportion, i.e. profit is not proportional to gross margin. In fact, a higher gross margin may be achieved on a farm, but this could easily lead to a lower farm profit if the resultant increase in fixed costs was greater than the increase in gross margin.

5. Gross margin makes no allowance for the complementary interrelationships which often exist between enterprises, for example:

> stock and arable crops;
> dairy cows and sugar beet;
> sheep and grass seed production.

6. Outputs and costs alter with scale of enterprises. It follows, therefore, that if an enterprise is increased it may not necessarily maintain its gross margin per hectare or per animal unit.

7. Outputs and costs alter with seasons; to allow for this gross margins ought to be normalized over at least a 3 year period, if using them as a basis for farm planning.

8. Gross margins should always be interpreted in relation to the total farm business rather than in terms of allocated gross margin per hectare: (see Fig. 1.3).

The gross margins per hectare and the average level of fixed costs per hectare figures in Fig. 1.3 are those for enterprises on Littledown Farm in Year 2. When this information is presented in such a way it might be assumed that neither the sheep not the dairy young stock were profitable and, therefore, they should be discontinued. This would be a completely incorrect interpretation of the situation and a disastrous action to effect since the sheep contribute to the total farm gross margin and also help to maintain fertility and yield levels of other crops. Furthermore, the proportion of fixed

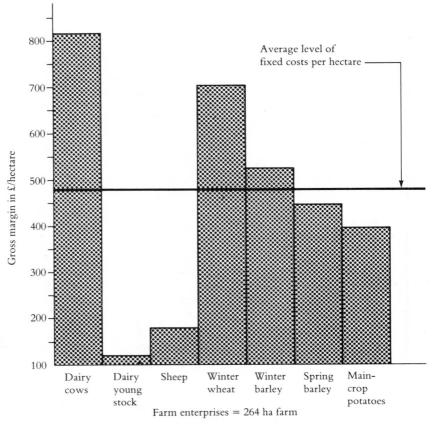

Figure 1.3   Littledown Farm: gross margins and average levels of fixed costs per hectare for Year 2

costs incurred by the sheep enterprise is unfairly represented in the average level of fixed cost per hectare figure.

This form of misinterpretation of gross margin calculation is frequently applied to sheep and break-crop enterprises since neither of these generate a very high gross margin in themselves, but they do help to maintain the level of gross margin achieved by other enterprises. The overall objective, therefore, should be to maximize total farm gross margin.

MONITORING THE FARM BUSINESS

The way in which the business at Littledown Farm is monitored is shown in Fig. 1.4.

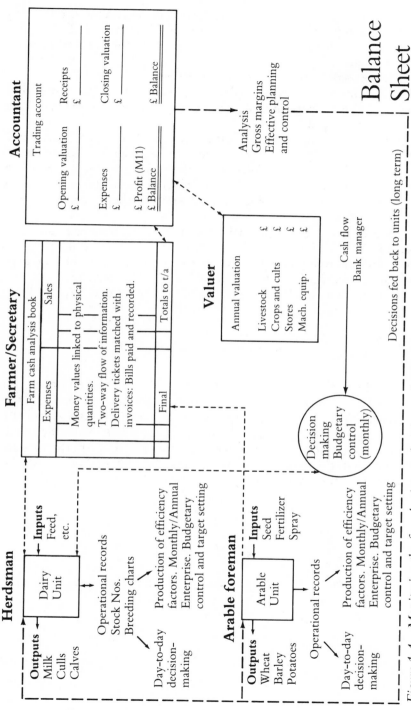

Figure 1.4   Monitoring the farm business: planning and control

Each section of the farm keeps a recording system monitoring the physical inputs to the unit (see examples, Fig. 1.4, Dairy unit and arable cropping). The operational records for each section on the farm enable:
1. Informed daily decisions to be made; and
2. The production of meaningful efficiency factors on a monthly basis where appropriate. This is a computerized system provided by a commercial company.

The farm office in common with many, still retains a cash analysis book system albeit computerized. Money values, via invoices, for goods and services received are linked either to the appropriate delivery tickets or service sheets received on the farm and then recorded, e.g. dairy concentrates, or service sheet repairs to the combine.

At the end of each financial year a farm trading account and balance sheet are drawn up and an analysis is carried out.

Forward planning and control is carried out with the aid of a Supercalc programme. The plans, cash flow, balance sheet, etc. for Year 3 on Littledown Farm can be found in Appendix A (p. 283)

GENERAL CONCLUSION

None of the analysis techniques or costing systems which have been described are perfect. Each system has its strong points and each one has its limitations. Nevertheless, each system is useful and the results of more than one analysis technique are very valuable when drawing conclusions about a farm business and its performance, provided that the interpreter of the results remains aware of the limitations of the analysis systems employed.

2 BUDGETING FOR THE FUTURE OF THE BUSINESS

The successful farm business is rarely the result of chance alone and although unpredictable biotic factors have considerable influence, the contributions made by sound planning, good decision-making, business control and sheer hard work cannot be dismissed easily.

These management activities employ many farm business techniques, but in all cases they are based upon the basic information revealed by the analysis and interpretation of past results.

Accounts and records show what has occurred in the past and where and why the business has succeeded or failed, but unless this information is used constructively in planning the future policy, there is little point in going to the trouble involved in its collection and analysis.

In this chapter, techniques are discussed which will enable a farmer to consider the possible future consequences of current decisions – decisions which will ultimately affect the whole future of the farm business and the future livelihood of those involved in it.

Although decisions in farming often involve imponderables there is no logic in disregarding the quantifiable element which, with its financial implications, has considerable importance for the well-being of the farm business. Generalizations such as 'beef don't pay', 'there's money in sheep' or 'rearing dairy replacements doesn't pay' may have their place in a conversational context but have little to offer to the farmer concerned with survival, the expansion of his business or the reduction of his bank overdraft. Such serious matters require careful thought and logical financial planning based upon the evidence of relevant data rather than conjecture.

Generalizations may have some foundation, but the truth of the matter is, of course, that no two sets of circumstances are quite the same and that what is sauce for the goose is not necessarily sauce for the gander. Just because Farmer A finds that it does not pay him to rear his replacement dairy heifers, there is no reason for Farmer

B to assume that the same conclusions can automatically be drawn about his own business.

In short, every case has to be judged on its own merits.

The right decision about any particular farm business can only be made after a careful examination of all the facts and by studying the likely implications of future policy upon the farm profitability, cash flow and funding.

This technique of estimating future income and expenditure is called 'budgeting' and is an essential aspect of farm planning. The technique of budgeting can be broadly considered in two forms:
1. Complete budgeting;
2. Partial budgeting.

In the complete budget the whole farm business is considered. This is a technique by which estimates are made of future income and expenditure in order to ascertain the future position of the total farm business with regard to capital requirements and expected profitability.

The partial budget, on the other hand, considers the likely effects of future policies or changes in future policy upon a given section or *part* of the farm business. This can be used as a logical approach towards deciding which will be the most profitable of possible alternative enterprises or alternative methods of using resources.

The two forms of budget are now considered in more detail.

THE COMPLETE BUDGET

The complete budget, involving the whole farm business can be used in the following ways:

1. *To obtain, as accurately as possible, an estimate of the future profit level of the business.* This involves making up an estimated trading account for some period in the future.

All cash income and expenditure will be included and provision must also be made for the 'paper' changes, i.e. changes in valuations of stock and crops and the depreciation incurred by machinery and fixed assets.

If the estimates of income and expenditure (Example I (Tables 2.1, 2.2)) are accurate the farmer can expect to make a net farm income of £3 189 in the next trading year.

2. *To obtain an estimate of future capital requirements of the business.* This type of budget is termed the 'capital budget' or 'cash flow budget', and examines future receipts and expenses in the light of the actual transactions which will be made either in cash or through the bank account.

EXAMPLE 1

Table 2.1 *Estimated profit and loss account for the next year's trading on a 33 ha dairy farm*

	£	£		£	£
Opening valuation			*Estimated sales and receipts*		
60 dairy cows at £410	24 600		277 550 litres of milk	30 530	
Stores	1 500		14 cull cows	3 900	
		26 100	58 calves	4 060	
					38 490
Estimated expenses					
19 replacement heifers	8 740		*Closing valuation*		
Feedingstuffs:			62 dairy cows at £410	25 420	
81 tonnes cake at £130 tonne	10 530		Sundry stores	1 500	
Seeds:					26 920
11 ha at £12/ha	132				
Fertilizers	1 683				
Vet., medicines and dairy sundries	1 403				
Wages and Nat. Insurance	1 710				
Fuel and oil	850				
Repairs and machinery insurance	1 500				
Rent and rates	2 442				
Sundry overheads	1 831				
		30 821			
Provision for depreciation on machinery and tenant's fixtures		5 300			
Estimated net farm income		3 189			
		65 410			65 410

Table 2.2 *Machinery account to show depreciation on machinery and tenant's fixtures (using historic cost accounting)*

	Written-down value*	Purchases	Sales	Written-down value†	Depreciation	Profit
	£	£	£	£	£	£
Tractor A	1 500	–	2 500	–	–	1 000
Tractor B	–	8 000	–	3 200	4 800‡	–
Sundry machinery	6 000	–	–	4 500	1 500	–
	7 500	8 000	2 500	7 700	6 300	1 000
Less Profit					1 000	
					5 300	

* At the start of the financial period.   † At the end of the financial period.   ‡ Taking 60% depreciation allowance in first year.

This is not the same as a future trading account and it is not intended to show a future measure of profit, since it makes no provision for either depreciation or valuation changes. The capital budget is designed to show the likely cash position in the future and will indicate the periods when capital must be borrowed and also when there is likely to be a surplus of available capital.

Such a budget can be calculated for any given period of time; it may be annual, quarterly, monthly or even weekly. The time interval chosen will vary according to specific needs, but the general rule is that the shorter the interval the more likely it is that the 'peaks' and 'troughs' will be exposed that might otherwise have been hidden where a longer interval was employed. The results of such budgets in terms of a surplus or a deficiency, can be plotted to show the 'capital profile' of the farm business.

Example II

Simple capital budget

A very simple illustration of a capital budget is as follows. It is assumed that a suitable building containing fattening space for twenty pigs is available, and that weaners are bought and fattened for pork. It takes three months to fatten a batch of pigs, and as soon as one lot is sold another is bought in. One pig is lost out of each batch, and the feed requirements increase as the pigs grow.

Purchase price per weaner £22
Price of feed   £390 per batch
Sale price per pig   £45 after levy and marketing expenses

The capital profile for this very simple business is calculated in Table 2.3 and illustrated in Fig 2.1.

The graph shows the capital position of this little business throughout the year. Starting with nothing, £440 has to be borrowed to buy in the first twenty weaners. By the end of the first month these pigs have eaten £78 worth of food. As they grow, they consume more food, the cost of which is added to the capital deficit so that by the end of the second month the business has an overdraft of £635. The fat pigs are sold by the end of the third month and the receipts from this sale more than balance the accumulated cost of the weaners and their feed, leaving a surplus of £25.

This surplus is immediately ploughed back and a further batch of pigs bought in. The same capital pattern follows in the next three-month periods so that by the end of the year a surplus or

Table 2.3 *Capital budget for a pig-fattening enterprise*

Month:	Jan. (£)	Feb. (£)	Mar. (£)	Apr. (£)	May (£)	June (£)	July (£)	Aug. (£)	Sept. (£)	Oct. (£)	Nov. (£)	Dec. (£)
Expenses												
Weaner pigs	440	—	—	440	—	—	440	—	—	440	—	—
Foodstuffs	78	117	195	78	117	195	78	117	195	78	117	195
Total expenses	518	117	195	518	117	195	518	117	195	518	117	195
Receipts												
Sales of porkers	—	—	855	—	—	855	—	—	855	—	—	855
Monthly balance	-518	-117	+660	-518	-117	+660	-518	-117	+660	-518	-117	+660
Cumulative balance	-518	-635	+25	-493	-610	+50	-468	-585	+75	-443	-560	+100

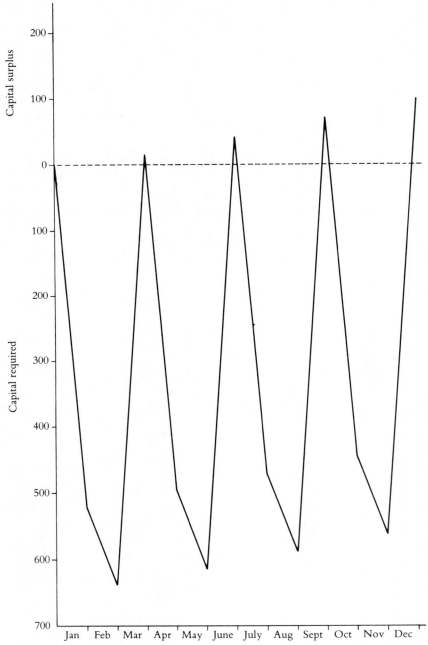

Figure 2.1   Capital profile for a pig-fattening enterprise (see Table 2.3)

margin of £100 has been built up, and the initial capital has been turned over approximately four times.

Additional items to be included in the capital budget

The cash flow sheet needs to go deeper than the farm account alone. Almost invariably the farmer's personal requirements need to be drawn from the same cash reservoir, so the cash flow sheet also needs to provide for:
1. Personal drawings;
2. Personal taxation (usually payable on the previous year's profits);
3. Repayment of borrowed capital;
4. Repayment of interest.
A complete budget for Littledown Farm is included in Appendix A (p. 283).

When to use the complete budget

The technique of complete budgeting can be of value to the farmer in the following circumstances:
(a) in estimating future profitability and capital requirements for the purpose of obtaining credit;
(b) when submitting a tender for a farm tenancy;
(c) in setting up and operating a system of budgetary control;
(d) in planning future tax commitments.

(a) Estimating capital requirements when arranging loans

It is particularly important to be able to estimate the likely movement of cash in and out of the bank account when arranging short-term loans. Most banks now require farmers applying for overdrafts to fill up a form designed to indicate the future cash flow of their businesses.

Such an estimate of cash flow is of value both to the borrower and to the lender (in this case, the bank manager) since it:
(a) sets a limit to the loan and serves as a prompt or warning should this be exceeded;
(b) shows the purpose for which the loan is required;
(c) indicates the length of time for which the loan is required;
(d) demonstrates the feasibility of the proposition.
This exercise also imposes a discipline upon the farmer by virtue of the need to think through the physical and financial implications fundamental to the construction of a cash flow.

(b) Submitting a tender for the tenancy of a farm

A prospective tenant will be well advised to carry out a careful examination of his likely expenditure and income in the first years of his tenancy, in order to determine whether he can raise sufficient capital to take on the farm and run it properly: How much rent he can afford to pay, and at the same time meet all his expenses, pay his interest charges, repay his loans and still have enough to live on and pay his income tax.

Many land agents now require both forms of the complete budget to be drawn up by prospective tenants when tendering for a farm.

(c) In setting up a system of budgetary control

Budgetary control is concerned with measuring physical and financial achievement against a budget. A very important aspect of business management, especially in farming, where, because of the interrelationships between enterprises the efficient enterprise may hide the inefficient one.

Future receipts and expenses are estimated on a monthly or quarterly basis, the time interval chosen being dependent upon the nature of the farm's enterprises. The actual result for each item is then recorded alongside the budgeted figure.

In this way any deviations from the expected levels of output and expenditure can be identified and investigated as and when they occur. The appropriate action may then be taken. See Appendix A (p. 283) for an example of whole farm budgetary control.

(d) In planning income tax commitments

This may be an area requiring serious consideration when carrying out farm business planning. Where profits fluctuate widely then the tax liability is likely to be greater than if the same total profit were to be evenly spread over the years, notwithstanding stock relief and the averaging of profits. The normal delay in the payment of tax relative to the profits taxed means that the payment of tax incurred by high profits may coincide subsequently with a poor trading year when cash may be less readily available.

The budgetary control system can thus be extended and used, not only as a yardstick with which to compare current performance, but also as an indicator of the level of anticipated profits before the end of the accounting year.

If the profit looks like being high, then there is still time before the end of the trading year to change a tractor or combine or start on repairs of buildings so that the maximum deductions can be claimed and the taxable income minimized. These courses of action, however, would not be prudent if the cash flow position were adverse, particularly if a period of high or rising interest rates prevailed.

Budgetary control has long been accepted as a necessary method of financial control in industry and is rapidly gaining recognition as a technique of farm management by progressive farmers, advisers and commercial firms offering management services.

THE PARTIAL BUDGET

This is a method for estimating the likely effects that changes in policy or prices in part of the business may have upon the future profitability of the farm business.

It is one method by which a farmer may test the financial implications of proposed improvements and alterations to the farm business.

If one looks at a farm business one is frequently faced with questions requiring decisions. Questions such as – whether or not to keep beef suckler cows or increase their stocking rate; whether or not to invest capital in machinery and thereby reduce labour costs; whether or not to use capital to intensify or enlarge a particular enterprise; which enterprise would best use a particular set of farm buildings.

These questions vary of course in complexity. Accordingly they vary in the basic question posed from 'Will it pay?' to 'Which will pay best?'. The technique of partial budgeting is one method which will help the farmer to make a good decision in circumstances in which it is possible to quantify the potential losses and gains from a proposed change, however small, in the farm business.

The technique of partial budgeting is very simple providing the basic rules are applied.

The rules of partial budgeting

Rule I
The budget should only include items which will actually appear or alter in the 'future trading account'.

For any proposed change in policy or for any pair of alternatives being considered, the changes can be examined under:

Potential loss   *Potential gain*
(a) extra costs   (c) extra revenue
(b) revenue foregone   (d) costs saved

Broadly speaking the partial budget will deal, under headings (a), (b), (c) and (d), with outputs and all relevant costs which will change. However, this technique does differ from the gross margin budget in that it recognizes changes in items usually defined as 'fixed costs', e.g. machinery, buildings, labour and interest on capital.

Gross margin figures can be used as a form of partial budget, but the user should take account of:

1. The element of valuations in the calculation;
2. Any changes in 'fixed costs';
3. That the gross margin may not necessarily expose a possible future variation in the output/cost structure of an enterprise(s).

With buildings, the basic capital cost is not permitted in the budget. Only the annual charges resulting from such an investment should be included. These are:

1. Depreciation on extra buildings;
2. Repairs on extra buildings;
3. Interest on capital invested in extra buildings.

These are the annual or running costs of the buildings and will occur in the trading account, whereas the initial investment in the buildings is a capital cost and will not.

Similarly with machinery, if a change in policy involves the purchase of a machine then the budget should include the annual costs of such a machine, i.e. depreciation, repairs and interest on the capital invested – not the original cost of the machine. Where a change in policy does not involve investing in extra buildings or machinery, the annual charges on existing machinery and buildings will not be included in the budget, since they remain unaltered by the change of policy, i.e. they do not come into any of the four categories mentioned.

Labour costs are also fairly easy to deal with in partial budgeting. The annual cost of the basic regular labour force is considered as a constant and will remain the same irrespective of small changes in policy. It is permissible, however, to include as extra costs or costs saved any changes in the requirements for casual labour or overtime labour since these are costs that will actually change in the annual trading account. The inclusion of regular labour charges is only permissible where a change in policy involves a change in the labour force, i.e. since men are indivisible, getting rid of one or more men or employing one or more extra men. It should not be assumed that a theoretical saving in man-hours will result in a saving in cash terms.

Where a budget involves breeding livestock then the same basic rules apply as is the case with buildings – the basic capital cost is not permitted in the budget. However, the budget should show the annual costs, i.e. replacement costs and the interest charges on the capital needed for the extra stock. Where the livestock can be defined as working capital, i.e. fattening stock such as weaners, or beef calves, then they will appear in the budget at cost price.

Rule 2

A budget should always be calculated on the basis of a common denominator to the alternatives being considered.

The common denominator used will always be one of the basic factors of production – namely land, labour or capital. The most important limiting factor which is common to both alternatives is always the basis upon which alternative policies are compared.

For example, if one were comparing the likely profitability of sheep or dairy cows one would be most likely to base the budget on the land requirement, e.g. 240 breeding ewes on 30 ha v. 50 dairy cows.

If one were budgeting the likely profitability of pigs or poultry one would base the budget on either the capital or labour requirements, since land is a minor consideration in such circumstances, for example:
(a) on the basis of labour:
    65 sows and their progeny fattened to pork
              v.
    8 000 laying-hens per man.
(b) on the basis of capital in the form of an existing building – say, 100 m²:

Pork pigs at 0.91 m²/pig	= 110 per batch
v.	
Poultry at 0.14 m²/bird	= 714

It will be possible to put 3–4 batchs of pork pigs through the house in a year, so the final comparison will be:
    385 porkers v. 714 laying-hens per year
If one were to budget the likely profitability of extending the business by increasing either the pigs or the dairy cows, the budget would have to be calculated on the basis of either their common capital or labour requirement, since land is only an important factor of production in the case of the cows.

Rule 3

Always be realistic in making estimates of future levels of production and conservative when putting a price on them. Guidance for the former can be obtained from past performances and trends, while in the case of the latter the guiding principle should be to avoid making unlikely increases.

Rule 4

Be impartial. Avoid prejudice and trying to weigh one alternative more favourably than the other. Obtain an answer in terms of 'hard cash' and then make the decision in the light of this and the non-financial considerations, i.e. reduction of drudgery, personal preference. Never let personal preferences interfere with the budget itself, although this may be more difficult than it would appear at first, since the subconscious weighting of the component parts of the budget may ultimately produce the result the 'author' desires.

Setting out a partial budget

The partial budget is a forward-looking 'trading account' for a section of the farm business and can be used to examine the effect of either:
(a) increasing the business by the expansion of one or more of its enterprises, or introducing new enterprises;
    or
(b) increasing the margin of the business by effecting a reduction in costs;
    or
(c) finding the most profitable of two or more alternative policies.
The basic layout of the budget is always as follows:
Heading, e.g.
385 porkers *v.* 714 laying hens

Extra costs Revenue foregone		Costs saved Extra revenue	
	A		B
Total		Total	

The two sides of this partial budget must balance. If the balancing figure comes on the left-hand side, i.e. at A, then the budget indicates that extra income is likely to be achieved. If, on the other hand, the budget balances on the right-hand side, i.e. at B, then the budget indicates a loss of income for the projected policy.

Always be careful, particularly when compiling a business report or when answering examination questions, to make a clear heading to the budget and to state clearly at the outset any assumptions that it is necessary to make.

Example of a partial budget

A farmer has a mixed livestock and arable farm comprising of winter and spring cereals, a dairy herd and a lowland sheep flock. Two main areas concern him at the moment. Firstly, the recent imposition of milk quotas and secondly, the wisdom, for a number of reasons, of continuing to grow winter barley. Let us deal with the dairy herd first.

The dairy herd currently numbers 96 cows and unless the production of this herd can be kept within the quota the farmer will be penalized. There are a number of alternative tactics that may be adopted but the farmer prefers the possibility of milking fewer cows. We will therefore explore the likely effect on his annual profit of reducing his dairy herd by 8 cows.

Certain assumptions have to be made but not, however, about his existing performances which are known. This reduction in the dairy herd will, at his current stocking rate of 2 cows per hectare, release 4 ha of land which could easily be absorbed by a marginal expansion in the area of winter wheat grown. Machinery and other fixed costs associated with growing the wheat crop will remain the same as the farmer already has his own production and grain-handling equipment. (The only possible cost likely to alter here will be the fuel, but it is unlikely that the fuel costs will differ sufficiently to have a significant effect upon the budget. For this practical reason their inclusion would not normally be considered worthwhile.) The fixed costs for the dairy herd will remain substantially the same with a very small reduction in the labour used which will be too small to be reflected in the wages bill. The fixed costs, on a per cow basis, will increase marginally but since they do not change overall they will not affect the partial budget. The layout of the partial budget would then appear as in Table 2.4.

The extra income, as shown in Table 2.4 is of course marginal but to this figure must be added the penalty costs of over production. This figure, which could run into several thousand of pounds, should when known be included in the partial budget under the

Table 2.4   Budget: additional 4 ha of winter wheat v. 8 dairy cows

Extra costs	£	Costs saved	£
Variable costs of 4 ha of winter wheat		2 replacement heifers/year	1 100
		Concentrates:	
Fertilizers at £86/ha	344	8 cows at 1.7 tonne/cow	
Seeds at £41/ha	164	£155/tonne	2 108
Sprays at £70/ha	280	Vet., medicines and sundries at	
Sundries at £7/ha	28	£53/cow	424
		Fertilizers to grassland at	
		£136 ha × 4 ha	544
		Annual share of seed costs	
		£12 ha/year × 4 ha	48
Revenue foregone		Extra revenue	
Milk:			
8 cows at 5 000 litres at		Output from 4 ha of winter wheat.	
14.7 p/litre	5 880	4 ha × 7.5 tonnes wheat at	
7 calves at £75 each	525	£130/tonne	3 900
2 cull cows/year at £350 each		4 ha × 2.5 tonnes straw at	
	700	£12/tonne	120
Extra Income	323		
	8 244		8 244

heading of costs saved. In this case making the intended change to additional wheat-growing well worthwhile.

An alternative to the expansion of the wheat crop at the expense of the dairy herd is a marginal increase in the existing lowland and flock which at the present levels of stocking would mean an additional 60 ewes utilizing the 4 ha released by the reduction in the dairy herd. In this case the stocking rates are comparable and therefore the forage costs for either enterprise will not be included in the budget. However, the extra 60 ewes and 2 rams will have to be purchased. Their cost of purchase will not be included in the partial budget since this cost will be represented in the budget by the difference between the cost of buying replacements and the value of cull ewes and rams. The interest charges associated with the initial purchases will be included. For the financial effects on the farm business of this change see Table 2.5, where it can be seen that, penalties apart, the effect is a lessening of the farm profit. A penalty of only £718 would produce a break-even position and any significant increase over this figure would result in the change being considered worthwhile.

Let us now turn our attention to the question of an alternative to the growing of the 25 ha of winter barley by the expansion of the existing ewe flock. The expansion of the ewe flock onto the barley ground will enable the flock to be uprated to a one-man unit and will increase the beneficial effects of the sheep flock on the arable rotation. The implications of such a change are that the handling

Table 2.5   *Budget: 60 extra ewes v. 8 dairy cows*

Extra costs	£	Costs saved	£
Concentrates:			
60 ewes at 50 kg/ewe at £144 tonne	432	2 replacement heifers per year Concentrates:	1 100
Vet., medicines at £2.3/ewe × 60	138	8 cows at 1.7 tonne/cow at £155 tonne	2 108
Sundries at £1.6/ewe × 60	96	Vet., medicine and sundries at £53 cow	424
Replacement ewes 13 at £65/head.	845		
Depreciation on 2 rams at £200 each *less* cull value £40 each $\frac{320}{4}$	80		
Interest on capital for 60 ewes 2 rams at 15% of $\frac{4\ 300}{2}$	323		
Revenue foregone		*Extra revenue*	
Milk:		Lamb sales:	
8 cows at 5 000 litres at 14.7 p/litre	5 880	60 ewes at 94% ewes lambing × 1.72 lambs/ewe at £41 lamb (overall lambing % 161.7)	3 977
7 calves at £75 each	525	Wool at £3.20/ewe × 60	192
2 cull cows/year at £350 each	700	Ewe premium at £3/ewe × 60	180
		Cull ewes 10 at £30 each	300
		Share of cull rams $\frac{80}{4}$	20
		Deficit	718
	9 019		9 019

facilities will have to be improved, labour costs at lambing and shearing time will increase and it would probably be prudent to budget on a slightly reduced lambing performance. There would be some saving of labour on the cereals which will be taken up by the extra sheep work over the year. Any reduction in fuel costs from the cereals will for practical purposes be absorbed by the grassland machinery work. The capital cost of the additional handling facilities will appear in the budget as:
1. Depreciation of the equipment
2. Interest on the capital involved
3. Repairs (if any)
The budget now reads as shown in Table 2.6.

Even with a lowered performance in respect of the ewe flock and the cost of additional handling facilities, the sheep look a better proposition than the winter barley. This does not take into account the less tangible benefits of the sheep break on the arable rotation. They do not, however look as good a proposition as they might had a gross margin budget been used as shown in Table 2.7.

Table 2.6   Budget: 375 extra ewes v. 25 ha of winter barley

Extra costs	£	*Costs saved*	£
Concentrates:		Variable costs on 25 ha of winter	
375 ewes at 50 kg/ewe		barley	
at £144 tonne	2 700	Fertilizer at £80/ha	2 000
Vet., medicines at £2.3/ewe × 375	863	Seed at £35/ha	875
		Sprays at £55/ha	1 375
Sundries at £1.6/ewe × 375	600	Sundries at £6/ha	150
Replacement ewes 83 × £65 each	5 395		
Replacement rams at 3 per year at			
£200 each	600		
Forage costs at £9.0/ewe × 375	3 375		
Annual share of seed costs at		*Extra revenue*	
£10 ha × 25	250	Lamb sales	
Extra labour at lambing	200	375 ewes at 94% ewes lambing	
Extra shearing costs at 70 p/ewe		× 1.7 lambs/ewe at £41 lamb	
× 375	263	(overall lambing % 159.8)	
Additional handling facilities			24 569
costing £2 400 (net)			
Depreciation $\frac{2\ 400}{10}$	240	Wool at £3.20/ewe × 375	1 200
Interest at 15% of $\frac{2\ 400}{2}$	180	Ewe premium at £3/ewe at 375	1 125
Interest at 15% of $\frac{26\ 175}{2}$		Cull ewes 75 at £30 each	2 250
(additional ewes and rams)	1 963		
Revenue foregone		Cull rams 2 at £40 each	80
Output from 25 ha of winter			
barley			
25 ha × 5.8 tonnes/ha at £106/tonne	15 370		
25 ha × 2 tonnes/ha at £12/tonne	600		
Extra income	1 025		
	33 624		**33 624**

The gross margin only deals with outputs and variable costs – no consideration is given to fixed costs at all. So unless the gross margin budget is adjusted for fixed-cost changes after the gross margin is established the full picture is not represented clearly enough for the right decisions to be made. In this case the extra income is considerably reduced but in other circumstances the result could have been reversed.

THE 'BREAK-EVEN' BUDGET

It is obvious, however, that if the yield of the winter barley was higher *or* if the lambing performance was lower, then it would be more profitable to continue with the winter barley enterprise.

Table 2.7 *Partial budget using gross margins only*

Sheep —	Sales:	£	£	£
	Lambs	24 569		
	Wool	1 200		
	Cull ewes	2 250		
	Cull rams	80	28 099	
	Add ewe premium		1 125	
			29 224	
	Less replacement ewes and tups	5 995	5 995	
	Gross output			23 229
	Less variable costs:			
	Concentrates	2 700		
	Vet. medicines	863		
	Forage costs	3 625		
	Casual labour	200		
	Shearing	263		
	Sundries	600	8 251	
	Gross margin			14 978
	i.e. £39.94/ewe or £599/ha at 15 ewes/ha			
Winter barley —	Sales			
	Winter barley	15 370		
	Straw	600		
	Gross output			15 970
	Less variable costs			
	Fertilizers	2 000		
	Seed	875		
	Sprays	1 375		
	Sundries	150	4 400	
	Gross margin			11 570

This is the basis of a calculation known as a 'break-even' budget, by which it is possible in any given set of circumstances to determine the necessary level of price or performance, which must be achieved by any given factors so that the profitability of the alternatives in question will be the same.

Let us firstly consider the factor of lambing performance in the last budget, Table 2.6.

Extra income £1 025

This represents $1\ 025 \times \frac{1}{41}$ lambs (at £41 lamb)

or $1\ 025 \times \frac{1}{41} \times \frac{100}{375}$ lambs sold per 100 ewes (lambing percentage).

i.e. 6.67%

Therefore the 'break-even' lambing percentage is 159.8 (see Table 2.6) less 6.67 = 153.13

Below this performance the winter barley is more profitable than sheep.

A similar calculation can be made to find the 'break-even' yield of barley.

Income lost of £1 025 for winter barley represents:

$$1\ 025 \times \frac{1}{106} \text{ tonnes of barley (at £106 tonne)}$$

$$\text{or } 1\ 025 \times \frac{1}{106} \times \frac{1}{25} \text{ tonne of barley/ha}$$

i.e. 0.387 tonnes barley/ha.

Therefore the 'break-even' yield is 5.8 tonnes plus 0.387 = 6.187 tonnes/ha. Below 6.187 tonnes/ha sheep are more profitable than barley. Above 6.187 tonnes/ha barley is more profitable than the sheep enterprise. This could be carried a stage further and for any given yield of winter barley per hectare, a corresponding lambing performance per ewe can be calculated so that the budget breaks even.

Example III

In the following example it is assumed, in the interests of simplicity, that the factors of lambing performance and barley yield are variable but that all other factors, e.g. concentrates use, fertilizer use, prices, stocking rates, etc. remain at the levels in the original budget (see Table 2.6).

Table 2.8 summarizes the budgetary margins for varying levels of lambing performance achieved for three possible levels of barley yield. By showing these results on a graph (see Fig. 2.2) it is possible to plot the corresponding 'break-even' point in lambing percentage for any given yield of barley and vice versa.

This technique of assessing the break-even point can be of immense value where it is not possible to quote a definite price or yield for a particular commodity. It is thus possible to plot the break-even price or yield in any given circumstances and to plot the likely profitability of a whole range of possible yields and prices.

These calculations would never claim to be precise arithmetical predictions but rather the probable outcomes of varying conditions and performances and, as such, should place one in a better position to make a sound decision.

Working capital within the partial budget. References to the treatment of such capital items as buildings, machinery and livestock in respect of interest charges have been made in the preceding pages. Working capital items, such as feed, seed, fertilizer, etc. have been

Table 2.8   *'Break-even' budget: 375 ewes v. 25 hectare of winter barley*

To find the budgetary margin in favour of lowland ewes at varying levels of barley yields and at different levels of lambing percentage

	Yield of winter barley (tonnes/ha)					
	4.8		5.8		6.8	
	£	£	£	£	£	£
1. *At 150 lambing %*						
Extra costs	16 629		16 629		16 629	
Revenue foregone						
Barley	12 720		15 370		18 020	
Straw	600		600		600	
	—	29 949	—	32 599	—	35 249
Costs saved	4 400		4 400		4 400	
Extra revenue						
Lamb sales	23 063		23 063		23 063	
Wool and culls	3 530		3 530		3 530	
Ewe premium	1 125		1 125		1 125	
	—	32 118	—	32 118	—	32 118
Margin		2 169		−481		−3 131
2. *At 159.8 lambing %*	16 629		16 629		16 629	
Extra costs						
Revenue foregone						
Barley	12 720		15 370		18 020	
Straw	600		600		600	
	—	29 949	—	32 599	—	35 249
Costs saved	4 400		4 400		4 400	
Extra revenue						
Lamb sales	24 569		24 569		24 569	
Wool and culls	3 530		3 530		3 530	
Ewe premium	1 125		1 125		1 125	
	—	33 624	—	33 624	—	33 624
Margin		3 675		1 025		−1 625
3. *At 170.0 lambing %*	16 629		16 629		16 629	
Extra costs						
Revenue foregone						
Barley	12 720		15 370		18 020	
Straw	600		600		600	
	—	29 949	—	32 599	—	35 249
Costs saved	4 400		4 400		4 400	
Extra revenue						
Lamb sales	26 138		26 138		26 138	
Wool and culls	3 530		3 530		3 530	
Ewe premium	1 125		1 125		1 125	
	—	35 193		35 193		35 193
Margin		5 244		2 594		−56

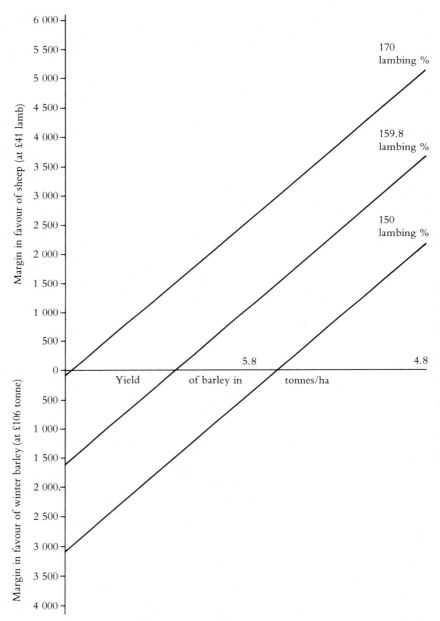

Figure 2.2   Graph to budgetary margins at varying levels of barley yields and at different lambing percentages

entered as incurred, but no mention has yet been made of the interest charges such costs may attract. If the farm account is already overdrawn, or does from time to time during the year, enter an overdraft position then it is likely that a partial budget requiring working capital is likely to attract additional interest charges at an appropriate level. The difficulty of identifying when in the year the working capital costs exceed the extra revenue, and thus incur interest charges, is not easily identified within the partial budget since it embraces a long period of time, normally a year, and does not, therefore, show the cash fluctuations at any given time. This difficulty could be overcome by drawing up a capital budget, as shown in Table 2.3, and charging the interest accordingly. The interest could then be entered under extra costs incurred in the partial budget. Such a consideration may be of some importance where the project under consideration requires the expenditure of working capital for a prolonged period before the return is expected, i.e. 18-month beef.

THE LIMITATIONS OF BUDGETING

All budgets suffer from one major shortcoming in that, at best, they are 'best estimates'. This is inevitable since the budget is concerned with the future outcome of present-day decisions and as such must involve the estimating of future income and expenditure. Implicit within such an exercise is the inclusion of risk and uncertainty. Many elements of the budget are possible to assess very accurately with the judicious use of information.

Other elements such as the expected prices for sale products and enterprise yield responses will be difficult to predict with any degree of certainty. One of the aims, therefore, when constructing a budget, must be to minimize the degree of uncertainty. This can be done by constructing a series of budgets to test the effects of a selected range of possible input and output variations in the critical parts of the budget. This technique, which lends itself to computerization, is known as sensitivity analysis. Even if aids are not available to reduce the arithmetical work there is a case for more than one budget: a 'best estimate' of what is expected to be the outcome of a proposition; a conservative budget illustrating the possible results of failure or only partial success; and a target budget towards which one might aim.

Less tangible, and yet none the less an important aspect in the construction of the budget, is the skill of the budgeter, who, if he is to be successful, must have considerable knowledge of the farm's performances and what may be achieved with the resources within his control. This then enables the budgeter to tailor the budget to suit the farm and the circumstances prevailing. The better this can be done, the more reliable the budget will be as a basis upon which to make a decision.

If personal knowledge of input–output responses for the particular farm is not available, then the planner has to resort to more general standards such as the level of yields achieved locally under similar conditions. If reliable information of this sort is not available from local farmers then the results achieved on research stations or government experimental husbandry farms under similar conditions may prove a useful guide.

On a broader field one can use country, regional or even national average figures or use standards, such as those published by university departments of agricultural economics.

A further limitation the budget has is that it cannot always allow adequately for the interdependence which often exists between enterprises on a farm. Enterprises must be considered as separate entities in the budget, whereas in practice they are often complementary to one another, e.g. a market garden enterprise may depend upon a pig enterprise for its muck; grass-seeds production may be dependent upon sheep at certain stages; cattle and sugar-beet may be interdependent, the one supplying the dung and the other beet tops and beet pulp fodder; in fact most arable rotations are at some stage dependent upon livestock to maintain fertility and to utilize grass breaks.

Budgeting, however, is not alone in this limitation, for no method of accounting has yet been devised which will accurately accommodate the financial effects of this interdependence. This is a limitation held in common with comparative farm analysis, gross margin analysis and planning and even full cost accounting.

A final point: never underestimate the importance of the human factor. Always make sure that the standards of performance that you have assumed in your budget can be achieved by the farmer or the person responsible for carrying out the plan. This is tremendously important, for individual ability may well be the most important limiting factor, and no matter how well a particular policy may be planned, it can never succeed unless it is within the capabilities of the staff involved and has their commitment.

3 FARM OVERHEADS OR FIXED COSTS

Fixed costs are defined as those farm cost items which are not easily allocated to particular farm enterprises and which do not vary very much with small changes in the scale (size) of an enterprise. These costs are also referred to as overhead costs, common costs and un-allocatable costs. Examples are: labour; machinery; buildings; rent and rates and miscellaneous overheads, e.g. office expenses.

It is much more difficult to allocate fixed costs to particular enterprises than it is to allocate variable costs, as has been explained. Allocation is only possible if detailed records are kept involving a large amount of time, effort and paper.

While small-scale changes may not affect the level of fixed costs, there will be a point at which an increase or decrease in the scale of an enterprise will begin to affect one or more of the fixed costs. If substantial alterations in the size of enterprises are being considered, then the consequent changes in fixed costs will occur.

The level of fixed costs on a farm varies with the average level of intensity of the farm enterprises. If there is an enterprise on the farm with high labour demands, or one which requires a special type of machine, then these items will tend to make the total level of fixed costs higher. Similarly, large areas of concrete, specialist farm buildings, tower silos and other items of high capital investment will lead to a high average level of fixed costs per hectare. On the other hand, on a hill farm with a very extensive system, e.g. hill sheep looked after by the farmer himself, then the level of fixed costs per hectare will be low, since he has no employees, little machinery and few buildings.

If savings can be made in a farm business by reducing fixed costs, this will improve profits – provided that levels of gross margin are maintained. A high level of fixed costs means that a high gross margin must be obtained to cover them, calling for a system which will produce such a gross margin. Therefore, in view of the importance of fixed cost items, an examination of each single one – machinery, labour, buildings and general farm overheads – will now be made.

FARM MACHINERY COSTS

There are a number of reasons why a farmer should carefully examine his machinery costs. These are summarized below.

Increase in the cost of purchasing farm machinery
The 1970s will be remembered as a period when the influence of oil prices affected almost all costs to the farmer, not least those of purchasing machinery and equipment. The early 1980s has seen inflation reduced and extremely keen competition between manufacturers and dealerships effectively peg or reduce some prices. This recent trend does not obviate the need to budget and plan carefully for machinery replacements. See Table 3.1 for price changes in tractors.

Machinery costs as a proportion of total farm costs
Machinery costs, made up of depreciation, fuel and oil, repairs and spares, vehicle tax and insurance, account for about 16–20 per cent of total farm costs on most farms. Considering machinery costs as a percentage of total fixed costs, then this input accounts for 33 per cent on most farms which is about £130–£135/ha in arable areas. Mixed farms, e.g. milk and arable under 200 ha, carry a figure of around £150/ha (see Table 3.2).

Table 3.1   Price changes of a typical 56 kW tractor

Year	Capital cost (£)	Price rise (£)	Percentage increase
1973	2 345		
1974	2 895	+550	+23
1975	4 061	+1 166	+40
1976	5 786	+1 725	+42
1977	6 552	+766	+13
1978	7 651	+999	+15
1979	8 700	+1 049	+14
1980	9 600	+900	+10
1981	10 250	+650	+7
1982	10 250	+0	+0
1983	10 750	+500	+5
1984	10 750	+500	+0

Source: 'Tractors and power systems: a problem of investment.' Stephen Howe. Paper 2, National Power Farming Conference 1981. (1973–1980 figures)1981–1984 calculated.

Table 3.2 Machinery and labour costs (£/ha) on size groups of farms in the south-east of England (average group figures for 1981–82)

Group	Predominantly milk farms		Milk and arable farms		Predominantly arable farms	
	Under 60 ha	Over 120 ha	Under 200 ha	Over 200 ha	Under 100 ha	Over 200 ha
Average hectares	39.3	232.1	153.9	306.2	62.7	363.8
No. of farms in group	9	11	6	11	14	17
Labour paid (£/ha)	82.1	176.8	130.9	131.7	43.5	101.0
Labour unpaid (£/ha)	195.9	26.5	53.8	22.9	85.1	9.5
Labour total (£/ha)	278.0 19.7%	203.3 19.5%	184.7 21.8%	154.6 19.9%	128.6 21.0%	110.5 17.7%
Machinery						
Depreciation (£/ha)	76.0	69.6	65.5	55.4	57.0	65.4
Fuel and oil (£/ha)	54.2	40.9	43.7	35.0	29.4	32.0
Repairs, tax and insurance (£/ha)	93.5	47.6	45.3	43.7	36.8	34.4
Machinery total (£/ha)	223.7 15.9%	158.1 15.2%	153.5 18.2%	133.1 17.2%	123.2 20.2%	131.8 21.1%
Total labour and machinery (£/ha)	501.7 35.5%	361.4 34.6%	338.2 40.0%	287.7 37.2%	251.8 41.3%	242.3 38.8%
Total inputs	1 410.3 100.0%	1 042.7 100.0%	843.6 100.0%	773.4 100.0%	609.4 100.0%	623.7 100.0%

Extracted from *Farm Business Statistics for South East England* (supplement for 1983) Wye College (University of London) Farm Business Unit School of Rural Economics and Related studies.

Table 3.3   Capital cost of 4.9 m cut combine harvester

Year	1971	1972	1975	1977	1979	1980	1981	1982	1983	1984
Capital cost (£)	6 350	7 160	14 400	21 565	27 340	28 721	28 000	28 000	30 000	36 000

The danger of over-mechanization

Over-mechanization is where too great a proportion of the total farm capital is invested in machinery.

Traditionally this is most likely to occur on smaller farms, big increases in the capital cost of specialist machines used for very short periods of the year has made this possible on almost any size of farm. (See Table 3.3).

The complementary effect of labour and machinery

Machinery costs should be examined critically from time to time, but not only in isolation, since the skilled labour required to operate farm machinery is an ever-increasing item of cost. Labour and machinery are complementary to each other and together comprise some 34–40 per cent of all farm costs on farms in the south-east of England – see Table 3.2.

Labour and machinery as a proportion of fixed costs

To achieve given levels of output variable costs will be incurred. If the relationship between output and variable costs is sound a good gross margin will result. Efficient, soundly run enterprises often leave little room for economy in the use of variable costs. The resulting total farm gross margin must therefore carry the fixed costs before a profit is made. Economies may be possible among the items comprising total fixed costs. Since labour and machinery together account for about 66–74 per cent of all fixed costs, a proportionately small saving on these items may significantly increase profits.

Benefits of mechanization

In addition to the above reasons for critically examining machinery costs, it must be remembered that a wise, planned investment in machinery can lead to many benefits.

Intangible benefits such as reduction in drudgery must never be ignored, while direct increases in returns to the farmer can also result from obtaining the correct machinery and equipment. Storage facilities for holding a product may mean a better market price. Cleaning and drying facilities may mean that the marketing of grain into intervention becomes possible. However, alternatives should be examined, e.g. buying storage space in a co-operative grain store rather than erecting on-farm storage.

The individual pressures of cash flow, borrowings, etc. will greatly influence this kind of machinery investment decision.

Timeliness has long been recognized as a prerequisite of profitable cropping. The importance is now understood to be of even greater significance. Taking maximum advantage of 'window time' when preparing ground, drilling, fertilizing and spraying can mean the difference between profit and loss.

Well-chosen, well-maintained and well-operated machinery combine together to give the most benefit from mechanization. The whole is the sum of the parts; get one wrong and the benefit from mechanization will not be realized to the full.

Obviously, a large number of factors must be considered before investment in extra machinery is made. In weighing these up, the financial effect of the machine upon the farm business must be foremost in the farmer's mind – what will be the increase in returns, what will be the extra annual cost in addition to the initial capital outlay? In attempting to answer these questions with accuracy, it is essential to know how annual machinery cost items are calculated. The terms fixed (or overhead) costs and running costs are commonly used as explained below.

Machinery fixed costs (overheads)

These are costs which apply to all items of farm machinery and are incurred whether the machine is used a lot or only a little. Machinery overheads consist of (1) depreciation; (2) interest charge on the capital invested when the machine was purchased; (3) tax and insurance for vehicles used on the road; (4) housing for the machine. If the machine is used a lot, then the cost of these items per working hour of the machine will be low; if the machine is used only a little, then their cost per working hour will be much higher.

Depreciation
Calculating machinery depreciation for farm business management purposes takes on a new dimension in times of high inflation.

The traditional concept of depreciation takes no account of the

Table 3.4   Replacement cost method of machinery depreciation compared with historic cost depreciation (present method)

Present method

			Previous crop year(s)			1979 crop year for a farm year ending 30 Sept.					
Original cost (£)	Year of purchase	Closing valuation 30 Sept. 1978	Opening valuation 1 Oct. 1978 Revaluation factor	£	Purchases	Sales	Total before revaluation	Revaluation Factor	£	Depreciation	Closing valuation 30 Sept. 1979
6 000 tractor	Oct. 1977	4 500 (1 year at 25%)★	—	4 500	—	—	4 500	—	4 500	1 125 (1 year at 25%)	3 375

Replacement cost method

			Previous crop year(s)			1979 crop year for a farm year ending 30 Sept.					
Original cost (£)	Year of purchase	Closing valuation 30 Sept. 1978	Opening valuation 1 Oct. 1978 Revaluation factor	£	Purchases	Sales	Total before revaluation	Revaluation Factor	£	Depreciation	Closing valuation 30 Sept. 1979
6 000 tractor	Oct. 1977	—	1.10† (Oc. 1977) / (Sept. 1978)	5 280 (−1 year depr. at 20%)★	—	—	5 280	1.11† (Sept. 1979) / (Oct. 1978)	5 861	1 172 (1 year at 20%)	4 689

★ The depreciation rates on most machines have been lowered, hence 25% depreciation using the present method, i.e. 20% for the replacement cost method.

† Revaluation factor based on the change in machinery prices indices provided by MAFF.

Source: ICI Record Farms 1979 crop year. Farm Advisory Service Report 13, Section 3, Appendix III, Table II, p. 25.

Table 3.5   Changes in depreciation rates (machinery)

Present method Historic cost depreciation			Replacement cost depreciation	
Depn. rate (%)	Group		Group	Depn. rate (%)
25	A	Tractors, vans, etc.	1	20
20	B	Combines, balers, forage harvesters, forage boxes hedge-cutters		15
30	C	Sprayers and fertilizer spreaders	2	15
30	D	Combined drills	3	10
25	E	Manure spreaders, slurry (tankers)	2	15
15	F	Sugar-beet and potato harvesters	2	15
15	G	Grain driers, milking equipment, etc.	4	10
15	H	All cultivation equipment except rotary	3	10
15	I	Rotary cultivators and direct drills	2	15
15	J	Fork lift trucks and lorries	4	10

Note: In most groups the depreciation rate has been lowered significantly affecting the written-down value rather than having a marked effect on the depreciation.
Source: ICI Recorded Farms 1979 crop year. *Farm Advisory Service Report 13*, Appendix II, p. 23.

trade-in value of a machine often being the same or very close to its original purchase price. In line with this apparent ability of a machine to retain a value close to its original price, inflation will accentuate the gap or difference between the trade-in value and the purchase price of a new machine, see Tables 3.4 and 3.5.

Funding this difference can produce a considerable machinery reinvestment problem.

Machinery depreciation methods useful for budgeting and machinery costings procedures are as follows in Table 3.6:

The diminishing balance method.   This is a method of calculating depreciation by taking a constant percentage each year over the 'life' of the machine. For example, if a tractor costing £15 000 new is depreciated at 16.5 per cent per annum, by this method the results given in Table 3.7 and Fig. 3.1 are obtained.

Straight-line method.   This is a simple method where the value of a machine is written off over a reasonable period of life. The calculation is

$$\frac{\text{Capital cost of machine} - \text{sale (scrap) value}}{\text{Life in years}}$$

Table 3.6   Rates of depreciation of farm machinery (percentage of new price)

Frequency of renewal (years)	Complex, high depreciation rate, e.g. potato harvesters, mobile pea viners, etc. (%)	Established machines with many moving parts, e.g. tractors, combines, balers, forage harvesters (%)	Simple equipment with few moving parts, e.g. ploughs, trailers (%)
1	34	26	19
2	24½	19½★	14½
3	20★	16½★	12½
4	17½†	14½	11½
5	15 ‡	13†	10½★
6	13½	12	9½
7	12	11	9
8	11	10 ‡	8½†
9	(10)	9½	8
10	(9½)	8½	7½ ‡

★ Typical frequency of renewal with heavy use.
† Typical frequency of renewal with average use.
‡ Typical frequency of renewal with light use.
Source: L. Norman and R. B. Coote. *The Farm Business*. Longman, 1971, p. 74 after V. Baker, Bristol University.

If the £15 000 tractor given in the previous example (Table 3.7) is sold after 10 years for £2 472 then the annual depreciation cost will be:

$$\frac{£15\ 000 - £2\ 472}{10} = £1\ 252 \text{ per annum}$$

A useful guide to the likely 'life' of machines is given in Table 3.8.

Table 3.7   Annual depreciation – diminishing balance method
Tractor £15 000 new

End of year	Amount of depreciation during year (at 16.5% per annum) depreciation (£)	Written-down value (£)
1	2 475	12 525
2	2 067	10 458
3	1 726	8 732
4	1 441	7 291
5	1 203	6 088
6	1 004	5 084
7	838	4 246
8	701	3 545
9	585	2 960
10	488	2 472

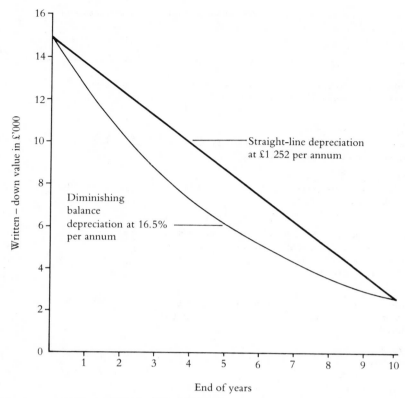

Figure 3.1 Depreciation of tractor by diminishing balance and straight line methods. Purchase price £15 000

Interest charge
Interest on the capital invested in machinery should be charged and included in comparative calculations, since a farmer could invest that money in some other way which would yield him a return. Interest is normally charged on half the capital invested in the machine.

Vehicle taxation and insurance
Annual taxation must be paid on tractors, combines and other self-propelled farm vehicles that regularly use the public highway. All vehicles should be insured, and both these cost items are incurred whether the machines are in regular use or not.

Housing
The annual cost of housing for farm machinery is not easy to calcu-

Table 3.8   Estimated useful life of power-operated machinery in relation to annual use

Equipment	Annual use (hours)				
	25	50	100	200	300
Group 1 Ploughs, cultivators, toothed harrows, hoes, rolls, ridgers, simple potato planting attachments, grain cleaners	12+	12+	12+	12	10
Group 2 Disc harrows, corn drills, binders, grain-drying machines, food grinders and mixers	12+	12+	12	10	8
Group 3 Combine harvesters, pick-up balers, rotary cultivators, hydraulic loaders	12+	12+	12	9	7
Group 4 Mowers, forage harvesters, swath turners, side-delivery rakes, tedders, hedge-cutting machines, semi-automatic potato planters and transplanters, unit root drills, mechanical root thinners	12+	12	11	8	6
Group 5 Fertilizer distributors, combine drills, FYM spreaders, elevator potato diggers, spraying machines, pea cutter–windrowers	10	10	9	8	7
Miscellaneous Beet harvesters	11	10	9	6	5
Potato harvesters	—	8	7	5	—
Milking machinery	—	—	—	12	10

	Annual use (hours)					
	500	750	1 000	1 500	2 000	2 500
Tractors	12+	12	10	7	6	5
Electric motors	12+	12+	12+	12+	12	12

Source: C. Culpin. *Profitable farm mechanisation*. Crosby Lockwood, T.A 2 (1), p. 297.

late, but obviously if a new machine is being purchased, some consideration must be given to storage, and if this involves a new building additional costs will be incurred.

Machinery running costs

These are costs which are only incurred when a machine is actually being used. These items include fuel and oil, repairs and maintenance, and broadly speaking the cost of each item per working hour for a machine doing a particular job is fairly constant.

Fuel and oil

Consumption of fuel and oil will vary somewhat with the particular job being done. Obviously a tractor ploughing all day with a four-furrow plough will consume more fuel than one that spends its time mainly idling.

With fuel and oil costs changing rapidly, revision of the charge used should be made frequently.

Repairs and maintenance

Repairs to farm machinery are necessary to keep the other running costs as low as possible and also to prolong the life of the machine. With high capital replacement cost good maintenance programmes are important. Considering the lifetime of any machine, the repair cost graph is generally considered to be 'lumpy', i.e. not steady, with these items occurring unpredictably and usually in fairly large sums. Many farmers believe there is a strong correlation between the 'ability' of the person who operates the machine and the bill for repairs. It follows, therefore, that the calculation of accurate machinery repair costs per annum is very difficult; however, estimates can be made which provide a useful guide.

Methods of calculating repair costs

Estimated method. An annual fixed charge for repairs can be calculated by taking 5 per cent of the original purchase price of the machine, depending on the age of the machine. In cases where a machine is older or doing a lot of work in a year a higher figure should be used. This is a very approximate method; the same figure being used for all types of machines. The obvious fact that some machines are more expensive to repair than others is ignored. Nevertheless, it is a useful guide for management calculations.

Detailed estimated method. In this method a percentage of the original purchase price is taken and this varies with the anticipated hours of use of the machine. A series of figures are given in Table 3.9.

Calculating the operating costs of farm machinery

Now that each item composing the overheads (fixed costs) and running costs of machinery has been closely examined, it is possible to make detailed calculations of the actual operational costs of machines, being made up of partly fixed costs and partly variable

Table 3.9   Estimated annual cost of spares and repairs as a percentage of purchase price★ at various levels of use

	Lower levels of use per 100 hours	Approximate annual use (hours)				Additional use per 100 hours
	Subtract	500	750	1 000	1 500	Add
Tractors	0.5%	5%	6.7%	8.0%	10.5%	0.5%

		Approximate annual use (hours)				Additional use per 100 hours
		50 (%)	100 (%)	150 (%)	200 (%)	Add (%)
Harvesting machinery, Combine harvesters, self-propelled and engine driven		1.5	2.5	3.5	4.5	2.0
Combine harvesters, p.t.o. driven, metered-chop forage harvesters, pick-up balers, potato harvesters, sugar-beet harvesters		3.0	5.0	6.0	7.0	2.0
Other implements and machines						
Group 1						
Ploughs, cultivators toothed harrows, hoes, elevator potato diggers } normal soils		4.5	8.0	11.0	14.0	6.0
Group 2 Rotary cultivators, mowers, binders, pea cutter-windrowers		4.0	7.0	9.5	12.0	5.0
Group 3 Disc harrows, fertilizer distributors, farmyard manure spreaders, combine drills, potato planters with fertilizer attachment, sprayers, hedge-cutting machines		3.0	5.5	7.5	9.5	4.0
Group 4 Swath turners, tedders, side-delivery rakes, unit drills, flail forage harvesters, semi-automatic potato planters and transplanters, down-the-row thinners		2.5	4.5	6.5	8.5	4.0
Group 5 Corn drills, milking machines, hydraulic loaders, simple potato-planting attachments		2.0	4.0	5.5	7.0	3.0
Group 6 Grain dryers, grain cleaners, rolls, hammer mills, feed mixers, threshers		1.5	2.0	2.5	3.0	0.5

★ When it is known that a high purchase price is due to high quality and durability or a low price corresponds to a high rate of wear and tear, adjustments to the figures should be made.

Source: C. Culpin. *Profitable farm mechanisation*, 2nd edn. T.A 3, p. 299.

Table 3.10   *Operating cost of potato harvester costing £12 500*

Fixed costs	£
1. Depreciation over 8 years (straight-line method)	
$= \dfrac{£12\ 500}{8\ \text{years}}$	1 562.50
2. Interest on capital	
$= \dfrac{£12\ 500}{2} \times 14\%$	875.00
3. Vehicle tax, insurance and housing	—
Total fixed costs	£2 437.50
Running costs	
1. Repairs	
5% of purchase price $= \dfrac{£12\ 500}{100} \times 5$	625.00
2. Fuel and oil (for tractor)	
28 ha ÷ 0.7 ha/hour*	
= 40 hours at £2.40 per tractor hour	96.00
Total running costs	£ 721.00
Operating cost	£3 155.50
Operating cost per hectare (28 ha)	£ 112.70

* Average rate of working in hectare per hour.

costs. Two examples are given: firstly that of a potato harvesting machine purchased new at £12 500 and used to harvest 28 ha of potatoes per annum. The calculation of the operation cost for this machine doing this work has been done by calculating the depreciation of the machine on a 'straight line' basis and repair costs at 5 per cent of purchase price of the machine – see Table 3.10 (source calculated after Norman and Coote, Table 3.7, p. 82).

The second example is the calculation of the hourly operating cost of a tractor costing £15 000 when new, used at three different levels of use in its third year of life – see Table 3.11.

From Tables 3.11 and 3.12 it can be seen that although the total fixed cost per annum increases slightly as the tractor is used more, the fixed cost per hour falls rapidly from £7.98/hour at the 300 hours per annum level to £2.03/hour at the 1 500 hours per annum level. The running costs per hour do fall slightly with greater use, but the fall is nowhere near as great as that of the fixed costs.

When the fixed and running costs are added together to give the operating cost of the tractor, it is important to note that the operating cost per hour falls rapidly between 300 and 800 hours per annum; the fall is not so great at the higher rate of use of 1 500 hours per annum, this is due largely to the spreading of the fixed costs and the higher

Table 3.11   Calculations of hourly fixed and running costs for a tractor at three levels of use

Tractor costing £15 000 new – tractor in its third year of life

	Light use 300 hours/annum Depreciation at 10%			Average use 800 hours/annum Depreciation at 13%			Heavy use 1 500 hours/annum Depreciation at 19%		
Fixed costs									
1. Depreciation									
Diminishing balance	New	£15 000	WDV	New	£15 000	WDV	New	£15 000	WDV
calculation (see	Yr 1	1 500	13 500	Yr 1	1 950	13 050	Yr 1	2 850	12 150
Table 3.6 for	Yr 2	1 350	12 150	Yr 2	1 697	11 353	Yr 2	2 309	9 841
depreciation rates)	Yr 3	1 215	10 935	Yr 3	1 476	9 877	Yr 3	1 870	7 971
∴ Depreciation		1 215			1 476			1 870	
2. Interest $\frac{15\ 000}{2} \times 14\%$		1 050			1 050			1 050	
3. Vehicle tax and insurance		130			130			130	
Total fixed costs		£2 395			£ 2 655			£ 3 050	
Fixed costs (£/hour)		£7.98			£3.31			£2.03	
Running costs									
1. Fuel and oil at £2.40/tractor hour		720			1 920			3 600	
2. Repairs and spares (see Table 3.9 for percentage rates)		at 4% 600			at 7% 1 050			at 10.5% 1 575	
Total running costs		£ 1 320			£ 2 970			£ 5 175	
Running costs (£/hour)		£4.40			£3.71			£3.45	

running costs per hour. The calculations in Tables 3.11 and 3.12 illustrate the fact that fixed costs are incurred irrespective of whether the tractor is used a lot or a little.

Table 3.12   Calculation of the hourly operating cost of tractor at three levels of use (based on Table 3.11)

Use (hours per annum)	Light 300	Average 800	Heavy 1 500
Fixed cost (£/hour)	7.98	3.31	2.03
Running cost (£/hour)	4.40	3.71	3.45
Operational cost (£/hour)	12.38	7.02	5.48

Electricity and contractor's charges
In completing a survey of all the components of machinery costs it must be mentioned that the items of electricity and fuel consumed on the farm are normally grouped in the machinery bracket. Also, strictly speaking, contractors' charges for work done on the farm by an outside contractor are machinery costs and are similarly included. Note, however, for the purposes of gross margin calculations some contract costs are allocatable, e.g. contract-combining cereals, and such items are grouped as variable costs.

Conclusions

The need for an appreciation of the economics involved in the use of farm machinery continues to increase. Although it is easy for the farmer to recognize clearly certain machinery cost items – he can hardly fail to notice the cheques made out for fuel, oil and repairs – he must not overlook the fact that the major costs of operating machinery are depreciation and interest on the capital invested.

FARM LABOUR COSTS

The farm employee of today is a person who needs to have a wide range of abilities and skills. On some farms there are a number of workers, while on other farms there is only the farmer's family or possibly just the farmer himself. In fact, over 50 per cent of the holdings in England and Wales employ no paid labour at all. Whether the size of the farm is large or small, whether the farm system is extensive or intensive, the work involved in the running of that farm ranges from the dull, monotonous routine tasks to the highly skilled operations. Often a farm worker must be capable of undertaking all these jobs proficiently, since where crops and livestock are concerned a great deal depends on attention to detail and jobs being done properly.

Reasons for examining labour costs
The number of workers in the farming industry continues to fall: the figures shown in Table 3.13 clearly show the trend from the 1940s into the late 1960s. Table 3.14 brings the picture into the 1980s still showing the same, albeit slower, trend.

The benefits of farm machinery substitution for labour have not

Table 3.13   Numbers of agricultural workers at June in the United Kingdom ('000) workers)

	Full-time*		Part-time†		
	Males	Females	Males	Females	Total
1946	599	96	197	84	976
1947	611	91	201	77	980
1948	625	90	139	78	932
1949	645	85	135	69	934
1950	639	79	136	64	918
1951	621	70	129	62	882
1952	594	70	132	73	869
1953	578	68	128	68	842
1954	563	64	121	67	815
1955	535	60	119	74	788
1956	510	56	113	75	754
1957	502	55	116	77	750
1958	488	50	114	78	730
1959	480	47	112	80	719
1960	462	43	111	77	693
1961	439	41	107	75	662
1962	420	39	103	71	633
1963	407	37	98	69	611
1964	381	34	97	72	584
1965	355	33	94	69	551
1966	332	31	91	68	522
1967	315	31	76	63	485
1968	296	28	68	58	450
1969	281	27	69	56	433

* Comprises regular whole-time workers and includes members of the Women's Land Army and prisoners of war in earlier years.
† Comprises workers returned in the agricultural censuses as regular part-time and seasonal or casual workers.
Source: Annual review and determination of guarantees, 1970. HMSO, Table J, p. 34. Cmnd. 4321.

been lost on the industry. Farm management planning techniques throughout the 1950s and 1960s have highlighted the many ways in which farmers could adjust to the 'drift' of labour from the land. The response reflected the developments of society in general over a 25-year period. Retaining good employees was a difficulty often highlighted during this period; as the rewards from manufacturing and traditional heavy industries lured many workers from farms.

Since the early 1970s the trends have looked much the same, but, for very different reasons. Technically the industry continued to stride forward. Labour productivity as calculated by the Ministry of Agriculture, Fisheries and Food (MAFF) had an annual increase of 4 per cent during the 1970s. This coincided with an average annual reduction in the labour force for the same period of 4 per cent. Oil prices and the cost of all basic raw materials, in particular those link-

Table 3.14 Number of persons engaged in agriculture* (At June of each year. '000 persons)

		Average of 1972–74	1979	1980	1981	1982	1983 (provisional)
Workers							
Regular whole-time:							
Hired:	male	166	139	133	128	124	122
	female	15	12	12	11	11	11
Family:	male	49	30	30	30	30	30
	female	15	6	5	5	5	5
All male		215	169	163	158	155	152
All female		30	18	17	17	16	15
(Total)		(244)	(187)	(180)	(174)	(170)	(167)
Regular part-time:							
Hired:	male	25	20	19	19	19	18
	female	26	25	25	24	23	22
Family:	male	17	13	13	13	13	12
	female	18	7	7	7	7	7
All male		41	33	32	32	32	31
All female		44	33	32	31	30	29
(Total)		(86)†	(66)	(64)	(62)	(62)	(60)
Seasonal or Casual:							
All male		41	56	57	57	57	56
All female		37	41	43	40	41	42
(Total)		(78)‡	(97)	(101)	(97)	(99)	(97)
Salaried managers§		6	8	8	8	8	8
Total employed		414	358	353	342	339	332
Farmers, partners and directors							
Whole-time		222	215	208	204	203	201
Part-time		74	88	90	91	93	93
(Total)		(296)	(304)	(298)	(295)	(296)	(293)
Total		710	661	651	637	634	625
Wives/husbands of farmers, partners and directors (engaged in farm work)			79	75	75	74	76

* The figures are based on returns in the Agricultural Census but include some estimates for figures not directly obtainable from the Scottish Census results. Wives/husbands of farmers, partners and directors engaged in farm work were returned separately in 1977. Figures for earlier years exclude this category and this is thought to explain the decrease in the number of regular whole-time and part-time female workers from 1977 onwards.

Figures include estimates for all minor holdings (previously called statistically insignificant holdings) in England and Wales not surveyed in the respective June Censuses.

† Includes seasonal or casual workers in Northern Ireland. See footnote ‡.

‡ Before 1975 seasonal or casual workers were not returned as a separate item in Northern Ireland, but were included with part-time workers.

§ Figures relate to Great Britain only.

Source: Annual review of agriculture, 1981. HSMO, Table 4, p. 160. Cmnd 8132.

ed to fossil fuels, have been a big catalyst for change. Many farm businesses already have made considerable reductions in labour costs; redundancy of labour appearing for the first time since the 1930s. Market forces within Europe and the funding of the Common Agricultural Policy (CAP) are continuing the process.

The complexities of the situation are well documented and are by no means peculiar to British agriculture. Most farmers have been forced to examine critically the structure of their business, inflation and interest rates in particular forcing many to 'rationalize' for the first time. However, the fact that good employees, well managed, create farming output and wealth must not be forgotten.

Examining the efficiency of utilization of farm labour

Technical efficiency

This is often considered to be the speed and thoroughness with which a worker does a particular job. Such criteria are rather intangible and, therefore, the calculation of a labour efficiency index is recommended. In Chapter 1, Worksheet 7 (Table 1.12) labour cost per 100 standard man-days was calculated.

The standards used to calculate standard man-days are based on average annual hours of labour required for particular enterprises. It must be emphasized that these are only average figures and these standards themselves will vary with the size of enterprise, size and location of the farm, degree of mechanization, etc. on the farm. They do, however, give a comparative guide between farms of the same type in the same locality and also permit comparisons from year to year.

In addition to calculating labour cost in relation to the theoretical labour requirement of a farm, a labour efficiency index can be calculated when the total standard labour requirement (in man-days) for the enterprises on a farm is obtained. This is then compared with the actual number of man-days available on the farm.

$$\frac{\text{Labour}}{\text{efficiency index}} = \frac{\text{Number of standard man-days required}}{\text{Actual number of man-days available}} \times 100$$

The meaning of the labour efficiency index is fairly obvious. If the index is high, then the labour is being efficiently used compared with average achievements. If the index is low, the efficiency of utilization is poor compared with the average. It must be stressed again that the comparison is with an average and, therefore, subject to a number of limitations, and any replanning of labour use should be based on other efficiency measures as well as this one.

Economic efficiency

Measures of the economic efficiency of labour use were introduced and discussed fully in Chapter 1. Measures of economic efficiency, together with the labour efficiency index, should lead to a fairly sound analysis of the efficiency with which labour is being employed on a farm.

Work study

Work study involves a detailed analysis of the way in which individual tasks are carried out on farms and the time taken to do them. Obviously it is impossible to go into the details of the techniques employed in a book of this type and the reader should consult specialist books on this subject – see Appendix F, (p. 304).

Work study analysis is a logical investigation of work, and the procedure to follow is: select the problem, record the present methods, examine these methods, develop improved methods, install the better methods and maintain them.

In essence, work study techniques either analyse farm jobs with a view to improving methods of work (method study) or measure the time taken to carry out specific jobs which can be compared with average times (work measurement). This latter method is very specialized and of limited use to the average farmer.

Method study is of immediate value to many farmers who can easily make use of it provided they understand the basic principles involved. A number of logical steps have been put forward and method study is simply a logical approach to a particular problem.

When a problem has been selected, it may involve a complete enterprise or part of an operation, e.g. collecting eggs, when the actual work under examination is recorded. A standard chart together with a series of conventional symbols as abbreviations is used to record what actually happens. The types of charts commonly used are (i) flow process charts, and (ii) multiple activity charts.

Flow process charts.   These record either the movement of a man or material and aim at improving the way in which a job is done. The symbols used are as follows:

○ – operation: where something is done or somebody does something, e.g. picking up potatoes.

□ – inspection: where something is inspected for quality or quantity, e.g. checking bags of potatoes on a trailer.

◊ – transport: where something is moved from one place to another or somebody moves from one place to another, e.g. carrying potatoes in a basket to empty into a sack.

▽   – storage: where something is stored, e.g. potatoes put in a clamp.

◯   – delay: where something or somebody is temporarily taken out of circulation, e.g. waiting for the potato spinner to come round again.

A flow process chart for either man or materials can then be compiled.

Multiple activity charts.   These record the activities of more than one person, machine or material. A time-scale is included showing both the sequence of events and the relationship between them as they take place. The standard markings used are:

> Man or machine working
> Man or machine idle
> Man moving from one place to another
> Man holding material or equipment
> Man inspecting

Using the symbols given, a series of columns can be constructed for each man or machine and thus it can be seen from the multiple activity chart what each is doing at any given time, and obviously to see what each is doing in performing an integrated job, e.g. a team of men making silage or milking in a parlour.

When the information is recorded it should be carefully examined and the following sequence of questions posed: What is achieved? Where is it done? When is it done? Who does it? How is it done?

This progressive system of examination will usually indicate the inefficient items and the improved ways of doing jobs can be applied and put to work. Once a new routine is introduced, it must be maintained and a reversion to old ways prevented.

Work study can lead to better use of farm labour, and results achieved, such as a man handling more cows through a parlour, are now well known.

Planning the utilization of farm labour

In planning the utilization of the farm labour force over a season, a labour profile can be constructed. Such a profile shows graphically the seasonal labour requirements of each enterprise on the farm and illustrates the total demand of all enterprises on the farm labour in each month of the year. The procedure for constructing a labour profile for a farm is as follows:

1. Calculate the *standard man-hours* required for each enterprise on the farm, using the figures given in Table 3.15 (These *standard man-hours are standard man-day* figures given in Worksheet 5 (Table 1.10), multiplied by 8.)
2. Calculate the *monthly* requirements in standard man-hours for each enterprise by reference to Table 3.15 which gives the percentage distribution month by month.
3. Then construct a labour profile as shown in Fig. 3.2, clearly hatching (or colouring) to indicate each enterprise.
4. The troughs, or slacker periods, can be used for allocating general farm maintenance work, estate work, repairs to buildings, holidays, etc. Fifteen per cent of the total number of man-hours required on the farm is considered adequate to cover this. Thus, calculate this 15 per cent and distribute it in the 'trough' months on the profile, bringing the slacker months up to the same level.

The monthly standard man-hours calculated using Table 3.15 are given in Table 3.16. For example, the calculation for spring barley in May is as follows:

(a) Standard man-hours per annum for barley:
24 ha × 20 standard man-hours = 480 standard man-hours (from Table 3.15).
(b) In the month of May the requirement for barley is 3 per cent of the annual amount from Table 3.15, therefore:
3 per cent of 480 standard man-hours = 14 standard man-hours

The labour profile for Littledown Farm, given in Fig. 3.2 clearly indicates the times when labour peaks will occur and the slacker periods when estate work, etc. can be carried out. If the number of man-hours available on the farm are plotted, the times of the year when extra man-hours will be needed are easily seen. This may be satisfied by either employing casual labour or paying overtime rates to the regular workers, or a combination of both.

The labour profile is also useful in planning the effects of changes in the scale of enterprises on the seasonal labour demands, as well as the effects on the farm labour of introducing new enterprises and eliminating old ones. Labour profiles can also aid the selection of combinations of farm enterprises which will minimize peaks and create a more even demand for labour throughout the year.

It may be felt that a large number of calculations are involved in preparing a labour profile, but the outcome can often prove to be very enlightening and the effort expended more than worth while.

Table 3.15   *Standard man-hours per annum required by various farm enterprises and the percentage distribution of these requirements on a monthly basis*

Enterprise	Man-hours per hectare per head	Percentage distribution of man-hours per hectare or per head per month											
		Jan.	Feb.	Mar.	Apr.	May	June	July	Aug.	Sept.	Oct.	Nov.	Dec.
Winter wheat	20	—	—	3.3	6.7	—	—	—	23.1	30.6	30.8	5.5	—
Winter barley	20	—	—	3.3	6.7	—	—	23.1	30.6	20.0	10.8	5.5	—
Winter oats	20	—	—	3.3	6.7	—	—	23.1	30.6	25.0	5.8	5.5	—
Spring wheat	20	—	—	30.7	—	3.0	—	—	24.4	25.0	4.0	8.9	4.0
Spring barley	20	—	—	27.7	3.0	3.0	—	—	36.6	12.8	4.0	8.9	4.0
Spring oats	20	—	—	30.7	—	—	—	—	30.0	22.4	4.0	8.9	4.0
Potatoes – maincrop	176	—	—	9.0	18.2	2.4	4.6	4.6	1.1	9.8	37.5	11.4	1.4
Potatoes – early	176	—	3.2	31.5	4.1	2.2	53.6	—	—	—	—	4.1	1.3
Fallow	20	—	12.5	12.5	12.5	12.5	12.5	—	—	12.5	12.5	12.5	—
Rape (winter)	14	—	—	—	—	—	20.0	70.0	—	—	—	—	10.0
Kale (cut/folded)	80/16	—	—	10.0	28.0	30.0	4.0	—	—	14.0	14.0	—	—
Leys (grazed)	8	—	—	19.0	19.0	12.0	19.0	19.0	8.0	4.0	—	—	—
Leys (hay 1st cut)	20	—	—	5.0	—	15.0	75.0	2.5	2.5	—	—	—	—
Leys (silage 1st cut)	20	—	—	5.0	—	75.0	15.0	2.5	2.5	—	—	—	—
Downland grass	8	—	—	19.0	19.0	12.0	19.0	19.0	8.0	4.0	—	—	—
Dairy cows	40	9.3	9.3	9.3	8.2	7.4	7.4	7.4	7.4	7.4	8.3	9.3	9.3
Dairy followers 2+ years	20	12.0	12.0	11.0	5.0	5.0	5.0	5.0	5.0	5.0	11.0	12.0	12.0
Beef cows	16	12.0	12.0	11.0	5.0	5.0	5.0	5.0	5.0	5.0	11.0	12.0	12.0
Fattening beef 18 month	24	15.6	15.6	15.6	7.8	1.60	1.60	1.60	1.60	1.60	12.5	12.5	12.5
Sheep (per ewe)	4	8.0	8.0	24.0	10.0	8.0	10.0	5.0	5.0	5.0	6.0	5.0	5.0
Br. pigs (per sow)	32	8.34% per month											
Fattening pigs	5	8.34% per month											

Table 3.16 *Monthly labour requirements of enterprises, in standard man-hours, for Littledown Farm – Year 2*

Enterprise ha/hd	Man-hours ha or head	Total Man-hours	Jan	Feb	Mar	Apr	May	June	July	Aug	Sept	Oct	Nov	Dec
Winter wheat	50	1 000	0	0	33	67	0	0	0	231	306	308	55	0
Winter barley	30	600	0	0	20	40	0	0	139	184	120	65	33	0
Spring barley	24	480	0	0	133	14	14	0	0	176	61	19	43	19
Com. peas	—	0	0	0	0	0	0	0	0	0	0	0	0	0
M/C pots	8	1 408	0	0	127	256	34	65	65	15	138	528	161	20
Herb seed	—	0	0	0	0	0	0	0	0	0	0	0	0	0
OSR Winter	—	0	0	0	0	0	0	0	0	0	0	0	0	0
OSR Spring	—	0	0	0	0	0	0	0	0	0	0	0	0	0
ARABLE	112	3 488	0	0	312	378	48	65	203	606	625	920	291	39
Leys grazed	130	1 040	0	0	198	198	125	198	198	83	42	0	0	0
Leys hay	10	200	0	0	10	0	30	150	5	5	0	0	0	0
Leys sil.1	58	1 160	0	0	58	0	870	174	29	29	0	0	0	0
Leys sil.2	—	0	0	0	0	0	0	0	0	0	0	0	0	0
Leys sil.3	—	0	0	0	0	0	0	0	0	0	0	0	0	0
Downland grass	20	160	0	0	30	30	19	30	3	0	6	0	0	0
GRASSLAND	218	2 560	0	0	296	228	1 044	552	235	117	48	0	0	0
Dairy cows	130	5 200	484	484	484	426	385	385	385	385	385	432	484	484
Followers	35	700	84	84	77	35	35	35	35	35	35	77	84	84
Beef cows	16	0	0	0	0	0	0	0	0	0	0	0	0	0
Beef 18mth	24	0	0	0	0	0	0	0	0	0	0	0	0	0
Sheep ewes	512	2 048	164	164	492	205	164	205	102	102	102	123	102	102
Sows	106	3 392	283	283	283	283	283	283	283	283	283	283	283	283
Pigs	5	0	0	0	0	0	0	0	0	0	0	0	0	0
LIVESTOCK		11 340	1 014	1 014	1 335	949	867	907	805	805	805	914	953	953
TOTAL		17 388	1 014	1 014	1 943	1 555	1 959	1 524	1 243	1 528	1 479	1 834	1 244	992
MAINTENANCE		2 608.2												
TOTAL		19 996.2												

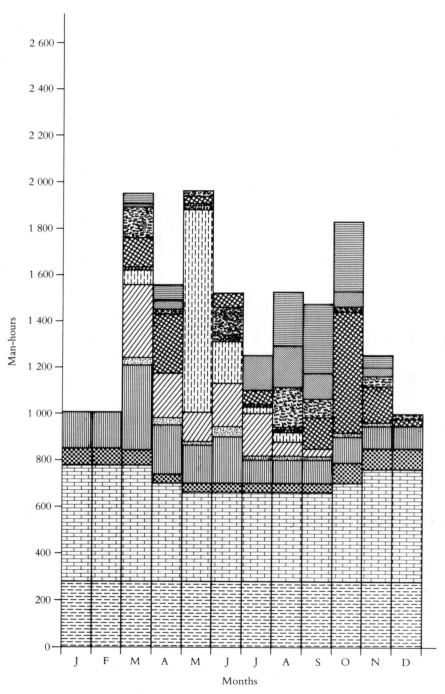

Figure 3.2 Example of a labour profile

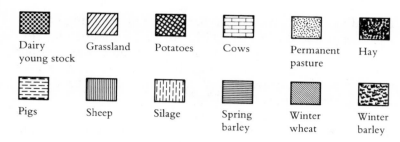

Dairy young stock	Grassland	Potatoes	Cows	Permanent pasture	Hay

Constructing a labour profile for Littledown Farm
Cropping and stocking – Year 2

	Hectares		Average No.
Winter wheat	50	Dairy cows	130
Winter barley	30	Dairy followers	
Spring barley	24	(replacement units)	35
Maincrop potatoes	8	Sheep (ewes and rams)	512
Leys (silage)	58	Pigs (sows and boars)	106
Leys (hay)	10		
Permanent pasture	20		
Total grass leys	130		

FARM BUILDINGS, FIXED EQUIPMENT AND OTHER FIXED COSTS

Once a decision has been made to invest in fixed equipment, then an annual cost will automatically result. It comprises depreciation of the building (or fixed equipment), interest on the capital invested in the building, regular maintenance of the building and insurance on the building.

When considering the depreciation of farm buildings, they should not be considered as long-term investments like some commercial buildings. The 'life' of farm buildings should be taken as 10–15 years, depending upon the function and type of construction of the building. It is generally agreed that it is wrong to regard farm buildings as long-term constructions. 'Shorter life' farm buildings are becoming more common, e.g. pole barns, cow kennels, and timber and alloy rather than concrete and asbestos structures. Like movable machinery, buildings depreciate due to obsolescence, and general deterioration as well as wear and tear. For budgeting it is normal to average depreciation over 10–15 years.

In any calculations involving farm buildings, an interest charge should be included on the capital invested in them. As for farm machinery, a reasonable percentage (say the current bank borrowing rate) is charged on half the capital invested, since the building is written off over this period during which the loan is completely repaid.

Estimating a figure for the maintenance of farm buildings is rather involved. Obviously, maintenance on a building such as a parlour will be greater than for a straw barn. A figure of 1.25 per cent of the capital cost is a useful guide.

The premium for the insurance of farm buildings will vary with the uses and purposes of the building. The insurance premium will be higher where the risk is greater, e.g. buildings near a source of heat.

Rent

Rent is the charge made by a landowner to a tenant for the 'hire' of the land, buildings, farmhouse and cottages. There is keen competition for farms which become available for tender. In the farm business analysis of an owner-occupied farm, a rent is imputed so that comparisons can be made more accurately.

General farm overheads

In all farm accounts there will be a number of fixed cost items which are of a general nature. These may include the farm water rate, general farm insurances, office expenses including telephone, stationery and postage, and professional charges. Although these items as a group may seem to be small, they must not be overlooked.

GENERAL CONCLUSIONS

The cost items classified as fixed costs are frequently the major proportion of farm costs. Generally speaking, farmers have not paid enough attention to these items in the past and have tended to concentrate on reducing variable costs such as feed consumed or fertilizers spread, being items that are more easily controlled. However, if these so-called fixed costs are not carefully controlled, they alter imperceptibly and thus become anything but fixed. The likely consequence is too well known: a smaller profit margin.

4
THE ECONOMICS OF AGRICULTURE

The importance of regarding farming as a business cannot be overemphasized. Anyone who sets out to make a profit from farming must recognize his farm as a business in exactly the same way as other entrepreneurs regard their businesses. Whatever the business, farming or otherwise, certain basic economic principles underlie that business, and these are, in essence, common sense applied according to the rules of logical thought. A knowledge of these principles may, however, help to maintain the success of a business or help to avert its failure.

Farmers, like all businessmen, are continually confronted with the problem of choice relating mostly to the best use of their resources – land, labour and capital. How should each be deployed in the farm business so that the objective for running that business can be achieved? An understanding of the basic economic principles which underlie farming can help a farmer, or farm manager, to make his business successful. However, the farmer must remember that it is only by the application of these principles that he will be able to make better use of his resources.

Some of the basic principles of economics relating to agriculture will be considered in this chapter.

SUPPLY AND DEMAND

An understanding of the interrelationships between supply, demand and price is important in any business including farming. Stated in the simplest of terms, price will be influenced by the demand for a product and its availability. In a situation of perfect competition (i.e. no guaranteed prices, subsidies, etc.), if the supply of a commodity rises with the demand for it, then price will remain fairly even. If the demand for a commodity increases but supply remains fairly even, then the price of that commodity will rise. When supply of a product rises but demand remains fairly even, then the price of the product will fall; conversely, if the supply of a product falls then the price of the product will rise when demand remains constant. In the days of 'free competition' in British agriculture, when farmers were directly subject to the forces of supply and demand, most farmers were painfully aware of the consequences of supplies exceeding demand. Low milk prices, clamps of rotting potatoes in the early summer and the smell of rotting onions at the roadside were clear evidence of supply having exceeded demand. On the other hand, high prices for potatoes and pigs, where demand exceeded supply, and rock-bottom prices when supply exceeded demand, gave rise to fluctuations in quantities produced over the years.

These fluctuations still occur, though to a lower degree due to the immediate post-war period measures of guaranteed prices and assured markets and the more recent implementation of the Common Agricultural Policy. Although certain products, e.g. horticultural crops, do not receive the protection afforded by a 'protected market', broadly speaking most farmers nowadays are fairly well insulated from the direct impact of the laws of supply and demand and, therefore, need not live in fear of 'the bottom dropping out of the market', as was often the fear of their forefathers.

Although farmers' prices may be protected irrespective of quantities of products produced, some attempts have been made to regulate supplies of products. In contrast with some other industries, control of the quantities of output from agriculture is very difficult. Variations in levels of output are inevitable since so many factors are involved which are outside man's control. However, the Potato and Milk Marketing Boards attempt to limit production by means of a quota system and the British Sugar plc operates a system of contracts based on hectares grown for sugar-beet. Even though there are these attempts to regulate supply the national output of these two products varies considerably from year to year depending on the seasons, hence the recent introduction by the MMB of seasonality payments.

In conclusion, it is fair to say that although the present Common Agricultural Policy does provide a cushion for the farmer against the direct impact of supply and demand forces, fluctuations in supply and demand, experienced since man first started to farm, are still very evident.

THE LAW OF DIMINISHING RETURNS

The law of diminishing returns is essentially very simple. It states that yields of crops and stock do not increase in direct proportion to increases in inputs, but rather, after a certain level of yield, as levels of an input are increased, the rate of increase in yields diminishes.

The effect of the law of diminishing returns is clearly shown by the theoretical figures given in Table 4.1, indicating the response of winter wheat to various levels of nitrogen fertilizer applied as a top dressing in the spring.

From Table 4.1 it can be seen that the response of the winter wheat to the nitrogen fertilizer varies at different levels of its application. The response of the wheat at lower levels of nitrogen application is high; at the higher levels of nitrogen application the response decreases and by the time 175 kg N/ha are applied, the result is, in fact, a depression of yield because the technical limit of the crop has been exceeded and lodging or disease may be present. The response increments are shown in Table 4.1 column (c). In the early stages increasing returns occur; then diminishing returns result and finally the negative response occurs at the 175 kg N/ha level.

The figures in Table 4.1 clearly show that after an initial phase of increasing returns, diminishing returns result. The responses are plotted as a graph (see Fig. 4.1).

It is important for farmers to remember that diminishing returns will apply to all production processes in agriculture – feeding dairy cows as well as applying nitrogen to grass and cereals. Having established the fact that diminishing returns will occur in a production process, the next obvious question is how much of a

Table 4.1   Response by winter wheat to different levels of nitrogen applied in the spring

Rate of nitrogen applied (kg N/ha)	Yield of grain (tonnes/ha)	Marginal increase in yield (tonnes/ha)
(a)	(b)	(c)
—	3.8	—
25	4.6	0.8
50	5.5	0.9
75	6.2	0.7
100	6.8	0.6
125	7.0	0.2
150	7.1	0.1
175	7.0	−0.1
200	6.8	−0.2

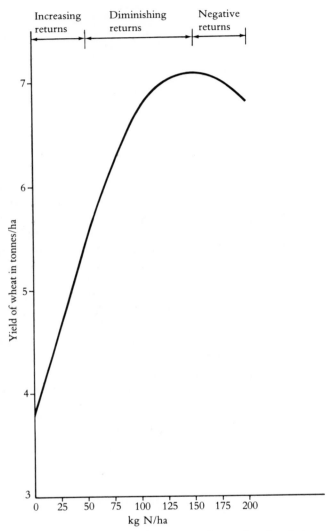

*Figure 4.1   Response of winter wheat to different levels of nitrogen
fertilizer applied – showing diminishing returns*

particular input should be employed in any production process. To
answer this question marginal analysis must be explained.

Marginal analysis

Marginal analysis is concerned with the changes that occur in a production process when further increments of an input are employed. If the figures given in Table 4.1 are taken and the nitrogen costed at 37 p/kg and the wheat grain valued at £121 tonne, then the figures given in Table 4.2 result.

From Table 4.2 it can be seen quite clearly that at the lower levels of nitrogen application the extra (marginal) revenue (column (d)) from the wheat considerably exceeds the extra (marginal) cost (column (e)) of the increment of nitrogen fertilizer applied, e.g. by increasing the level of nitrogen per hectare from 25.0 to 50 kg, the extra wheat produced was worth £108.90 while the cost of the 25.0 kg of nitrogen applied to produce this increase in yield was only £9.25. Towards the other end of the scale, when the nitrogen fertilizer application was increased from 150.0 to 175.0 kg, the marginal revenue was − £12.10 while the marginal cost was £9.25 − obviously not a profitable proposition.

In any production process, if profit margins are to be maximized, then the optimum point to which inputs should be employed is where marginal revenue equals marginal cost. In this particular example (see Table 4.2) the amount of nitrogen fertilizer that should have been applied was somewhere between 150.0 and 175.0 kg N/ha. At 150.0 kg N/ha the marginal revenue (£12.10) was greater than marginal cost (£9.25), and at 175.0 kg N/ha the marginal cost (£9.25) exceeded marginal revenue (−£12.10).

Marginal analysis permits the location of the point in a production process where marginal revenue equals marginal cost. When this position has been located, then the question raised earlier as to how much of an input should be employed in a production process can be answered − assuming that capital is

Table 4.2 *Response by winter wheat to different levels of nitrogen applied in the spring*

Rate of nitrogen applied (kg N/ha)	Yield of grain (tonnes/ha)	Marginal increase in yield (tonnes/ha)	Marginal value of* increases in yield of grain	Marginal cost of nitrogen (£/ha)†
(a)	(b)	(c)	(d)	(e)
—	3.8	—	—	—
25.0	4.6	0.8	96.80	9.25
50.0	5.5	0.9	108.90	9.25
75.0	6.2	0.7	84.70	9.25
100.0	6.8	0.6	72.60	9.25
125.0	7.0	0.2	24.20	9.25
150.0	7.1	0.1	12.10	9.25
175.0	7.0	−0.1	− 12.10	9.25
200.0	6.8	−0.2	− 24.20	9.25

* Wheat at £121/tonne.
† Nitrogen at 37 p/kg.

Table 4.3   *Responses by winter wheat to different levels of nitrogen fertilizer applied in the spring –*
margin of wheat sales minus nitrogen cost at different levels of nitrogen application

Nitrogen (kg)	Yield in tonnes/ha	Value of grain at £121/tonne	Cost nitrogen at 37 p/kg N	Margin of wheat sales minus nitrogen cost
(a)	(b)	(c)	(d)	(e)
25.0	4.6	556.60	9.25	547.35
50.0	5.5	665.50	18.50	647.00
75.0	6.2	750.20	27.75	722.45
100.0	6.8	822.80	37.00	785.80
125.0	7.0	487.00	46.25	800.75
150.0	7.1	859.10	55.50	803.60
175.0	7.0	847.00	64.75	782.25
200.0	6.8	822.80	74.00	748.80

Note: The optimum level of nitrogen inputs is between 150.0 and 175.0 kg N/ha, where the margin of wheat sales minus nitrogen cost is greatest. After this point the margin decreases.

available and profit margins are to be maximized.

Some would try to argue that this marginal concept is too theoretical and would, therefore, dismiss it as being irrelevant to farming. This is dangerous; obviously the principle applies in farming as in any other business – too high levels of input can be employed. It follows, therefore, that the doctrine of maximizing output (i.e. produce up to the level of the technical limit) does not make economic sense and will consequently affect profit margins.

The effect on final profit margins of increasing inputs beyond the point where marginal revenue equals marginal cost can be shown by calculating a margin of 'wheat sales minus nitrogen cost' (this is similar to the efficiency measure calculated in Ch. 1 – Worksheet 7, Table 1.12). Taking the figures given in Table 4.2, margins of wheat sales minus nitrogen cost have been calculated and are presented in Table 4.3.

The optimum level of nitrogen input so as to maximize margin of wheat sales minus nitrogen cost is the same point as was located in Table 4.2, i.e. between 150.0 and 175.0 kg N/ha. Where higher levels of nitrogen fertilizer are used, although the total yield may increase, the margin decreases. This conclusion is valid in the circumstances given but may, of course, be modified by technology. A very good example of this is illustrated in Fig. 4.2 where the effect of fungicides in addition to fertilizer levels is considered. Here, of course, the margin is affected by the additional cost of fungicide required to bring about the increased response to higher levels of nitrogen. This and other aspects of a higher technology approach to the growing of cereals is covered more fully in Chapter 8.

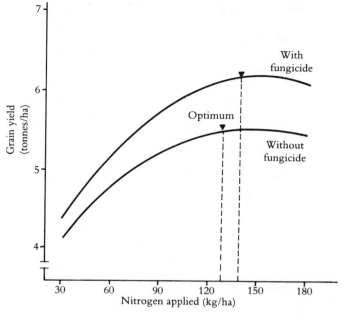

Figure 4.2   Effect of nitrogen and fungicides on winter barley yields (P. Needham, 'Winter barley nitrogen needs', Arable Farming, March 1980)

Average returns

Farmers are usually very much concerned with averages – average levels of outputs, average levels of costs and so on. Now that the concept of marginal analysis has been explained and it has become evident that to maximize profit margins the optimum level of input to aim at in any production process is that point where marginal revenue equals marginal cost, it is important to examine the concept of average levels of results.

If the data used earlier (Tables 4.1 and 4.2) are re-examined, average levels of responses can be calculated for the various levels of nitrogen fertilizer inputs – these are given in Table 4.4. In column (c) it will be seen that the best average level of response made by the winter wheat to the nitrogen fertilizer applied in the spring was obtained at the lower level of nitrogen application. As larger amounts of nitrogen were applied the average level of response fell – because of the effect of the law of diminishing returns.

It follows, therefore, that where maximum profit margins are being sought, the optimum level of input can only be determined by reference to marginal analysis, and averages, by themselves, can be misleading.

Conclusions on marginal and average analysis

1. As levels of an input are increased in a production process, a certain level of yield is attained after which any further increases in input result in diminishing increases in output.

2. If profit margins are to be maximized, the optimum level of input to employ in a production process is where marginal revenue equals marginal cost and not where the highest average level of response is achieved. This optimum level of input will obviously be affected by changes in price of input and value of output.

3. Since the greatest response per unit of input is obtained in the early stages of the production process then, where capital is limited, it will be better to apply small amounts of an input over the whole enterprise rather than the optimum amount to only part of the enterprise (i.e. it is better to apply 75.0 kg/ha of nitrogen fertilizer on all the winter wheat rather than an optimum amount of, say, 150.0 kg of nitrogen fertilizer on some of the winter wheat and none on the remaining area.

4. Maximum profit margins will not be realized by maximizing output, i.e. by producing the greatest possible output. Maximum profit margins will always be short of the 'maximum output' or 'technical limit' of a production process – unless, of course, the input being employed costs nothing.

Average and marginal returns on capital

Farmers and managers should clearly distinguish in their minds between average and marginal returns on capital. Average returns

Table 4.4   *Average response by winter wheat to different levels of nitrogen fertilizer applied in the spring*

Rate of nitrogen fertilizer applied (kg N/ha)	Yield of grain (tonnes/ha)	Average grain yield per 12.5 kg/N (tonnes/ha)
(a)	(b)	(c)
—	3.8	0.184
25.0	4.6	0.184
50.0	5.5	0.110
75.0	6.2	0.083
100.0	6.8	0.068
125.0	7.0	0.056
150.0	7.1	0.047
175.0	7.0	0.040
200.0	6.8	0.034

relate to the return on all the capital invested in an enterprise while marginal returns relate to the return on an extra (added or marginal) sum of capital. The figures in Table 4.5 may help to illustrate this difference.

In Table 4.5. results are given for three farm enterprises on the same farm. The average capital invested in each enterprise (in buildings, stock, equipment, etc.) is £50 000. The present returns are such that the average percentage return on the £50 000 average capital invested in each enterprise is 10 per cent from pigs, 5 per cent from poultry and 20 per cent from cows. Each enterprise can be extended and a sum of £10 000 is being considered for investment in one of the enterprises. The expected results are budgeted and the anticipated return (marginal return) on this £10 000 is £3 000 (30 per cent) from pigs, £1 000 (10 per cent) from poultry and £500 (5 per cent) from cows. (This may be due to the fact that most of the £10 000, if invested in the cow enterprise, would need to go into buildings and equipment while most of the £10 000, if invested in the pigs' enterprise, could go into stock – the present buildings being suitable and containing spare pig space.) The total return (average return) on the total £60 000 would be 13.3 per cent from pigs, 5.8 per cent from poultry and 17.5 per cent from cows.

If the average return on capital was considered without reference to the marginal return figures, then the indication would be to invest the extra £10 000 in the cow enterprise, since at both the £50 000 and £60 000 levels of investment the cows yield the greatest average percentage return on capital. This is, of course, misleading since the greatest marginal return on capital comes from the pigs' enterprise at 30 per cent, and so the £10 000 should be invested in the pigs' enterprise. Average figures, taken in isolation, can obviously be misleading.

Table 4.5   Average and marginal returns on capital in different enterprises

	Pigs	*Poultry*	*Cows*
Capital invested	£50 000	£50 000	£50 000
Return on £50 000	£ 5 000	£ 2 500	£10 000
∴ Average return	10%	5%	20%
Increase capital invested by	£10 000	£10 000	£10 000
Return on extra £10 000	£ 3 000	£ 1 000	£ 500
∴ Marginal return on extra £10 000 invested =	30%	10%	5%
Total return on £60 000	£ 8 000	£ 3 500	£10 500
∴ Average return on £60 000	13.3%	5.8%	17.5%

Equimarginal returns and opportunity cost

From the earlier considerations of maximizing profit margins it was assumed that farmers had adequate capital to employ inputs up to the level where marginal revenue equals marginal cost. If, however, capital is limited then the concept of equi-marginal returns is a relevant principle.

In essence, the principle of equi-marginal returns means that the last £1 spent on an enterprise or factor of production will yield a marginal return exactly equal to the last £1 earned from all other enterprises or factors of production. This is common sense: if £1 spent buying feed will return more than £1 spent buying fertilizer, then the additional feed should be purchased up to that point where the last £1 spent on feed will return exactly the same as the last £1 spent on fertilizer.

Underlying the principle of equi-marginal returns is the concept of opportunity cost. Opportunity cost evaluates the product that was not produced because resources were used for some other purpose. Suppose, for example, that a farmer can grow wheat or barley on a field on his farm.

Budgeted outputs and costs for these two crops are given in Table 4.6.

The comparative margin in favour of wheat is £120, this being the difference in their budgeted margins. If barley is grown in place of wheat, the opportunity cost of making this choice is £550, this being the margin foregone from the wheat crop. Conversely, if wheat is grown in preference to barley, the opportunity cost of so doing is £430, i.e. the margin foregone from the barley crop.

COMPARATIVE ADVANTAGE OR COMPARATIVE COSTS

This economic principle explains the reason why any economic unit, whether a farm, county or regions, concentrates on the production of those items for which its relative advantage is the greatest (or its relative disadvantage is least). It is the basic reason

Table 4.6   *Budgeted costs and outputs of winter wheat or winter barley on a given field*

	Wheat (£)	Barley (£)
Output	740	600
Variable costs	190	170
Margin	550	430

why arable cropping predominates in the east of England and grass production is common in the west. The principle can be simply explained by reference to two farms both in the same area each growing 200 ha of cereals in their cropping programme, but because of different soil types, the following average levels of cereals yields are obtained:

	Farm A per ha (tonnes)	Farm B per ha (tonnes)
Oats	5.0	3.0
Barley	4.25	3.75

From these average yield figures it can be seen that Farm A has a comparative advantage in favour of oats (the land will yield more oats per hectare than barley). Farm B has a comparative advantage in favour of barley (the land will yield more barley per hectare than oats). The tendency, therefore, will be for Farmer A to specialize in oat-growing and for Farmer B to grow barley. The fact that Farmer A has an absolute advantage over Farmer B in growing both oats and barley (i.e. the yields are higher than on Farm B) does not affect the principle of comparative advantage.

In deciding whether or not to specialize, both farmers would reason along the following lines: Farmer A must sacrifice 4.25 = 1.18 tonnes of oats if he wants 1 tonne of barley (because the oats on his farm yield $\frac{5.0}{4.25}$ tonnes/ha, but the barley only yields 4.25 tonnes/ha). Farmer B, on the other hand, must sacrifice $\frac{3.75}{3.0} = 1.25$ tonnes of barley, if he wants 1 tonne of oats. It follows, therefore, that it will be to each farmer's advantage to specialize, especially if Farmer A can acquire a tonne of barley for less than 1.18 tonnes of oats, and if Farmer B can acquire 1 tonne of oats for less than 1.25 tonnes of barley.

In addition to the advantages of each of the farmers that result from specialization, the total output that results from specialization is greater (? an advantage to the national economy). The figures given in Table 4.7, Case (ii) shows this, where Farmer A grows only oats and Farmer B grows only barley. The result of this specialization is a total output of 1 750 tonnes of grain from the two farms, compared with only 1 600 tonnes when each grew 100 ha of each crop.

Clearly then, the resulting total output is greater, and this is explained by the principle of comparative advantage where each farm specializes in growing that crop which yields best under its own particular conditions.

Table 4.7   The principle of comparative advantage – the case for specialization

Case (i): Farmers A and B growing 100 ha each of barley and oats

Area (ha)	Farm A tonnes/ha	tonnes	Farm B tonnes/ha	tonnes	Total (tonnes)
Oats: 100	at 5.0 =	500	at 3.0 =	300	800
Barley: 100	at 4.25 =	425	at 3.75 =	375	800
					1 600

Case (ii): Farmers A and B specializing

Area (ha)	Farm A tonnes/ha	Farm B tonnes	Total tonnes/ha	tonnes	(tonnes)
Oats: 200	at 5.0 =	1 000			1 000
Barley: 200			at 3.75 =	750	750
					1 750

Specialization

Consideration of the principle of comparative advantage has led on to the question of specialization on farms. This involves the concentration and efforts of a farm into one or two specific enterprises on the farm. There are a number of advantages in specializing.

Labour utilization may well be better on farms which specialize; skilled labour can often be employed for specific jobs. Similarly, specialization may lead to better machinery use. Managerial efforts can be concentrated into one or two particular enterprises more easily than over a whole range of different ones and so make better use of specialist machinery. Economically, specialization also offers the advantage of reducing overheads; fixed costs per hectare tend to be lower on larger farms – being one of the advantages of scale.

Diversification (non-specialization)

This is the opposite of specialization and is often called mixed farming. Despite the adage 'mixed farming and muddled thinking' there are a number of positive advantages in running a number of enterprises in a farm business. Risks are spread by diversification – not all the eggs in the same basket. Although setbacks may occur, the impact is not so great as where there is a high degree of specialization.

Another advantage of diversification is the utilization of by-products from other enterprises, e.g. beef animals utilizing pea-haulm silage, pigs eating chat potatoes. Furthermore, many farms have a range of buildings, and if the farm carries a number of enterprises this may mean better use is made of these buildings.

In summary, the arguments for and against specialization or diversification essentially revolve around the nature of the farmer himself and his ability to control the enterprises on his farm so as to produce a high enough level of gross margin to cover his fixed costs and to leave a reasonable profit margin at the end.

TYPE OF ENTERPRISE

Any consideration of the economic principles relating to farming would not be complete without reference to the interrelationships of enterprises within a farm business. Basically, farm enterprises can be classified as follows:

1. Complementary enterprises
These are enterprises which aid or contribute towards the success of each other, e.g. leys and cereal production, cheese-making and whey feed to pigs, pigs being fed chat potatoes.

2. Supplementary enterprises
These are enterprises which do not compete with other enterprises but may use up superfluous resources available on the farm, e.g. pigs and poultry enterprises using spare labour and buildings.

3. Competitive enterprises
These are extremely well known, especially on grass farms, since these enterprises compete with each other, e.g. sheep and dairy cows competing for grass, dairy cows and dairy followers competing for grass on the same farm.

Any business-management appraisal must consider a farm business as a whole and the interrelationships between enterprises in that business must not be ignored, neither should individual enterprises be examined in isolation. When the farm business is regarded as a whole, then the basic principles of economics outlined in this chapter can be applied and their likely effects anticipated since basic principles of economics will influence every farm business.

5 CAPITAL IN AGRICULTURE

The purpose of this chapter is to remove some of the mystique that surrounds capital and enable the reader to identify and measure types of capital, be aware of how to acquire finance and maintain, if not increase, his capital through good financial management.

Capital is recognized as one of the three basic factors of production along with land and labour. Like these other factors, capital has its own peculiar characteristics and if the business is to be successful the principles of best resource use, touched upon in Chapter 4, must be applied to it. According to the economist, capital represents a stock of resources available to be used to satisfy the future needs of the business – e.g. buildings, machinery, livestock, fertilizers, seeds, etc. This view does not conflict with the farmer's idea of capital being the monetary equivalent of all the productive resources. However, regardless of which of the above views is preferred, it is likely that, when the stock of capital in a business is not deemed sufficient to meet future or current needs, its importance is readily recognized. Such a situation may have arisen, among other reasons, out of poor business performance or overtrading. The possibilities open to the farmer, faced with a shortage of capital, may lie in changing the financial structure of the resources, i.e. by selling stored grain and releasing cash for working capital, or, if the scale of resources presents difficulties, then the solution may lie in the acquisition of a loan to provide the necessary finance.

Money provides the means whereby the restructuring or the addition of extra capital to the business may take place. It is the use of money that enables the capital resources to exhibit the characteristic of flexibility, which is viewed by bankers and others who understand capital as a characteristic to be used judiciously and to advantage and by others with deep suspicion. This latter attitude need not be the case if a little study and common sense is applied to the subject

It is necessary to add a cautionary note here. Not only must the manager be fully conversant with his business but he must also be aware of circumstances beyond the farm gate which in the various guises of inflation, interest rates, taxation and EEC policy will have an effect upon his business. It may be, of course, that he will not be aware of the ramifications of all these features and, therefore, a willingness to use the specialist skills of the accountant, banker, local management adviser and solicitor may well prove to be prudent.

MEASURING CAPITAL – THE FARM BALANCE SHEET

Capital invested in the farm business can be considered in two basic categories:
1. Landlord's capital;
2. Tenant's capital.

Landlord's capital
comprises investment in the land itself, in roads, buildings and improvements.

Tenant's capital
is that which is invested by the tenant in a farm and comprises all those items necessary for running the farm business which are not provided by the landlord, i.e. machinery, tenant's fixtures (buildings and fixed equipment provided by the tenant with the agreement of the landlord), livestock, stores, tenant right and cash.

Owner-occupier's capital embraces both landlord's capital and tenant's capital under the one heading.

The farm trading account (Ch. 1, Table 1.3) showed the margin obtained from a year's trading, and also showed the tenant's opening and closing valuations. In order to assess the capital position of the farmer at the end of the trading year, further information is required, i.e.:
(a) how much he owes (sundry creditors);
(b) how much is owing to the farm (sundry debtors);
(c) the amount of cash at the bank and in hand;
(d) any outstanding long-term loans;
(e) any other assets or liabilities

This information is not shown in the trading account, but will appear in the balance sheet. A balance sheet can be drawn up at any time and its basic layout is as follows:

LIABILITIES		ASSETS	
Sundry creditors	Liquid	Cash in hand	
Bank overdraft	liabilities	Cash at bank	
		Sundry debtors	
		Valuation of crops and saleable stores	Liquid assets
		Livestock for sale	
		Shares and other realizable investments	
		Valuation of farm buildings	
Loans, mortgages, etc.	Fixed liabilities	Fixed equipment	
		Machinery and livestock not for sale	Fixed assets
		Land and houses	
Balance being	Net capital		
	Total assets		Total assets

It is conventional in the balance sheet to list the assets according to the degree of liquidity, i.e. with the most liquid asset (cash) being shown at the top and the least liquid (land) being placed at the bottom. If the columnar layout is preferred for the balance sheet then the entries would remain as above, but with the liabilities being placed under the column of assets.

The balance sheet can be drawn up either to show the net capital of the farm business or to show the net capital of the proprietor. Shares and investments outside the farm business will only appear on the balance sheet in the latter instance.

Functions of the balance sheet

1. To indicate the net capital or net worth of the business or individual on a given date.
2. To show the distribution of net capital between partners in a business.

3. To indicate the liquidity of the business at a given date.
Before the balance sheet can be discussed further, some terms must be clearly defined:

Net capital or net worth	= Total assets − total liabilities.
Solvency	= The state of financial affairs which exists when net capital is shown on the balance sheet, i.e. when total assets exceed total liabilities.
Insolvency	= When total liabilities exceed total assets.
Liquidity	= Liquid assets − liquid liabilities. This is a measure of the amount of 'ready cash' that can be raised from the business at a given time.
	It is the difference between realizable assets and immediate commitments, but is by no means synonymous with 'solvency', since it is possible to be solvent yet unable to raise ready cash.
Equity	= The capital owned by an individual expressed as a percentage of the total assets of the business. It is a measure of the farmer's personal investment or 'stake' in the farm business.

N.B. It is important to distinguish between 'profitability' and 'solvency'. Although a business may show profits which are acceptable by comparative standards, it will only remain solvent if it can retain a portion of its profit to maintain or increase net capital.

Where 'drawings' exceed 'profits' then the level of net capital will diminish, and if this continues the business will eventually become insolvent.

The income generated by capital invested in a farm business must, therefore, provide for the following:
1. Living expenses of the farmer and his family;
2. Taxation;
3. Interest on capital outstanding;
4. Private drawings;
5. Repayment of loan capital.

Living expenses, taxation, interest and private drawings will all diminish the net capital position.

Repayment of loan capital will leave the net capital position unaltered, since this results in a corresponding reduction in the loan liability on the balance sheet, but the necessary liquidity must be available to allow such repayments to be made on schedule.

In order to show the distribution of capital between partners in a business a capital account is drawn up. This also serves to prove

Table 5.1   Littledown Farm – balance sheet statement as at end of Year 2

	£	£
Capital employed		
Balance at start of Year 2		297 141
Profit		15 181
		282 412
Personal drawings		9 152
		301 170
Represented by:		
Fixed assets		
Machinery and tenant's equipment	110 203	
Breeding livestock	79 270	
Work in progress (fixed element of tillages)	10 762	200 235
Current assets		
Debtors	13 338	
Non-breeding livestock	23 800	
Harvested crops in hand	69 675	
Tillages	9 818	
Feed, forage and fertilizer	37 860	
Cash in hand	350	
	154 841	
Current liabilities		
Creditors	6 500	
Bank overdraft	35 406	
	41 906	
Net current assets		
Financed by		112 935
Long-term liabilities		12 000
Net capital		301 170

the account by reconciling opening and closing net capital with the trading account profit and drawings as shown in Table 5.1.

Summary of balance sheet

	£
Total assets	355 076
Total liabilities	53 906
Net capital	301 170

Therefore, the business is solvent.

Joint equity of farmer and his wife in business:

$$= \frac{\text{Net capital}}{\text{Total assets}} \times 100 = \frac{301\ 170}{355\ 076} \times 100 = 84.8 \text{ per cent}$$

Since this business is farmed in partnership by the farmer and his wife and the share of equity is 50 : 50, it is possible to identify their separate shares and equity in the business as follows:

Partner A $\frac{150\ 585}{355\ 076} \times 100 = 42.4$ per cent

Partner B $\frac{150\ 585}{355\ 076} \times 100 = 42.4$ per cent

In this case the equities are equal, but in other circumstances would follow the agreed share of equity.

N.B. The net capital rises by £6 029 during the year since this is the amount by which the profit generated by the farm exceeds the total drawings of £9 152. This increase in net capital is divided between the partners as follows:

Partner A – Plus £3 014.5
Partner B – Plus £3 014.5

£6 029

The drawing on the business of £9 152 are made up as follows:

	£
Private drawings	6 862
Taxation (on Year 1 profits)	750
Notional benefits (produce consumed, house rent, private car)	1 540
	9 152

In this example is should be noted that the net capital has increased only marginally (an increase of 2.0 per cent) due to the level of drawings from the business in relation to the farm profit. This reflects the situation today for many farmers whose drawings are not excessive, but for whom farm profits have shown a steady decline in contrast to steadily rising costs. Indeed, this farm's profit (see Ch. 1 – Table 1.11, Worksheet 6) compares very favourably with the standard comparative data.

Liquidity

The liquidity of the business can be assessed either as a figure or a ratio. If we first look at the balance sheet for Year 2 (see Table 5.1) end we see that if the farmer met all his current liabilities out of current assets, then he would have net current assets of £112 935 Clearly, the farmer has no problems if one relates this figure to the scale of the business. If we look at the relationship between current assets and liabilities, we can obtain a measure of the liquidity using the current liquidity ratio:

$$\text{Current liquidity ratio} = \frac{\text{Current assets}}{\text{Current liabilities}} = \frac{154\ 841}{41\ 906} = 3.7{:}1$$

This shows that the current liabilities are covered three point seven times by current assets. This represents a wide safety margin, wider than that considered reasonable by the banks who, generally speaking, would be happy with a 2 : 1 ratio. However, one might argue that part of the reason why it is high is because the year of 31 December almost guarantees a high crops in store figure.

Equity
In this case the equity owned by the partners is high and may be calculated as follows:

$$\text{Equity} = \frac{\text{Net capital}}{\text{Total assets}} \times 100 = \frac{301\ 170}{355\ 076} \times 100 = 84.8 \text{ per cent}$$

Table 5.2   Funds flow for Littledown Farm – Year 2

	£	£
Profit	15 181	
Add:		
Depreciation – tenant's fixtures	1 878	
machinery	19 500	
Decrease in valuations	—	
Increase in creditors	1 306	
Decrease in debtors	—	
Capital sales	4 000	
Capital grants	—	
Capital introduced	—	
Private income/transfers in	—	
Total		41 865
Less:		
Increase in valuations	24 397	
Decrease in creditors	—	
Increase in debtors	876	
Capital expenditure – machinery	14 000	
– other	3 000	
Loan repayments	—	
Capital withdrawals	—	
Private expenditure	6 862	
Notional benefits	1 540	
Tax	750	
Transfers out	—	
		51 425
Surplus/deficit (annual cash flow)		−9 560
Opening bank balance	25 846	
Closing bank balance	−35 406	

The risks and rewards associated with different levels of equity are covered in the next section on gearing.

It is important to note that a balance sheet is only drawn up on one day and, therefore, only represents a 'snapshot' picture of the capital in the business. More important to the farmer is the trend shown by a number of balance sheets. In Appendix A the balance sheet for year-end 3 is shown and comments on the trends shown accompany it.

One aspect of the business that is important both to the farmer and to anyone lending him money is a statement showing where the money has gone in the course of a year and explains why in spite of making a profit the overdraft has risen to £35 406 from £25 846. This is variously called 'funds flow' or 'source and disposition of funds'. The funds flow for Littledown Farm is shown in Table 5.2.

Capital gearing

Where a business is run both on owner's or proprietor's capital together with loan capital, this is a means of expressing the proprietor's equity as a ratio (see Table 5.3).

The gearing ratio is easily determined from the balance sheet and can be of value in making a quick appraisal of the proprietor's likely position under different rates of return on the total capital invested in the business.

When the return on total capital in the business is greater than the interest charged on borrowed capital, then the proprietor's net worth will increase if all profits are reinvested, and the margin after paying interest charges will be high when expressed as a percentage of the proprietor's capital. Under these circumstances the higher the gearing the more profitable the business will be to its proprietor.

But if the overall return on capital is lower than the rate of interest charged on loan capital, then the proprietor's net worth will quickly be eroded when the gearing is high, but may be maintained

Table 5.3   Example of capital gearing ratios

	No gearing	Low gearing	High gearing
Loan capital (A) £	—	40 000	120 000
Proprietor's capital (B) £	200 000	160 000	80 000
Total assets £	200 000	200 000	200 000
Level of equity	100%	80%	40%
Capital gearing B : A	—	4 : 1	1 : 1.5

Table 5.4   The cases for high and low capital gearing

	No gearing	Low gearing	High gearing
Gearing ratio	—	4 : 1	1 : 1.5
Total assets	200 000	200 000	200 000
Situation 1			
Assuming 15% return on total capital invested			
Profit before deduction interest	£30 000	30 000	30 000
Less interest on loan capital at 12%	—	4 800	14 400
Profit after deducting interest	£30 000	25 200	15 600
Profit expressed as % of proprietor's capital	15	15.75	19.5
New level of equity if all profit reinvested (%)	100	92.6	47.8
Situation 2			
Assuming 5% return on total capital invested			
Profit before deducting interest	£10 000	10 000	10 000
Less interest on loan capital at 12%	—	4 800	14 400
Profit after deducting interest	£10 000	5 200	−4 400
Profit expressed as % of proprietor's capital	5	3.25	—
New level of equity if all profit reinvested (%)	100	82.6	37.8

at a low level of gearing as the extension of Table 5.3 illustrates – see Table 5.4.

High gearing may well be justified if the asset is expected to generate a high return, e.g. a machine for contracting. Where the asset can only be expected to generate a moderate or low return, e.g. buying land, then a policy of high capital gearing could well have serious consequences.

Measuring return on capital in the farm business

Figures of percentage return on capital are frequently quoted, but unless a clear definition is made as to (a) the form of return, and (b) the type of capital invested, then such measures can only be extremely misleading.

In order to appraise investment of capital accurately it is necessary to make valid comparisons between the returns made on capital by different enterprises or alternative investments. It is therefore absolutely essential, as with all efficiency factors, to compare like with like.

In expressing return on capital, the following margins could be used:
1. Net margin or management and investment income;
2. Net cash flow.

At the same time, the capital employed could be expressed as follows:
1. Tenant's capital;
2. Landlord's capital;
3. Owner-occupier's capital;
4. Initial capital – the capital required to start a business or to initiate a change of policy;
5. Average capital – half initial capital in machinery, buildings and depreciating assets + value of livestock and share of working capital (see The pigs enterprise, Ch. 7, p. 220).
6. Fixed capital – that which is tied up in land, buildings, fixed equipment and breeding livestock, and not easily realizable;
7. Working capital – the capital required to finance the production cycle, e.g. to provide seed, fertilizers, feedingstuffs, fattening stock and to cover labour and fixed costs. The absolute amount depends on the length of the production cycle;
8. Marginal capital – the extra capital required to initiate or change a policy.

By using the formula:

$$\text{Percentage return on capital} = \frac{\text{Margin} \times 100}{\text{Capital employed}}$$

it is now possible to calculate thirty-two possible ways of expressing return on capital – all of them different and none of them of any value unless used in the right context and compared with figures calculated on the same basis. The need for care in interpreting such measures will now be obvious.

The rates of return most frequently used and generally accepted are:

$$\frac{\textit{Return on initial}}{\textit{capital}} = \frac{\text{Management and investment income} \times 100}{\text{Initial capital}}$$

This is used in appraising the return on a long-term investment and is of particular value where the asset itself does not depreciate.

$$\frac{\textit{Return on average}}{\textit{capital}} = \frac{\text{Management and investment income} \times 100}{\text{Average capital}}$$

This is the most appropriate measure when assessing the return on a depreciating asset, e.g. a machine, the margin being expressed as a percentage of half the initial capital when the asset is completely written off.

This will, of course, always give a higher percentage return than the rate of return on initial capital.

$$Marginal\ return\ on\ marginal\ capital\ = \frac{Budgeted\ margin \times 100}{Marginal\ capital}$$

This may in some cases be the same as
$$\frac{Gross\ margin \times 100}{Marginal\ capital}$$

The use of marginal return on capital was explained more fully in Chapter 4.

$$Return\ on\ tenant's\ capital = \frac{Management\ and\ investment\ income \times 100}{Tenant's\ capital}$$

This measure is most frequently used where farm performance is being evaluated (see Ch.1). However, the basis upon which the machinery value is calculated will have an effect upon the final answer. Usually, the figure for machinery will be an historic cost, but if based on current replacement costs will reduce the percentage return on tenant's capital. Providing the comparison made is with 'like' within a year and from year to year then no risk of misinterpretation should occur.

APPRAISING CAPITAL INVESTMENT

In Chapter 2 consideration was given to *budgeting* as a means of establishing the likely effect of changes in the farm business upon future profitability. However, the rate of return on the capital invested in the various propositions was not examined critically. Where a number of alternative projects present themselves or where the financial circumstances, such as high interest rates, call into question the worthwhileness or feasibility of an investment then a more detailed appraisal may be appropriate. The methods or method employed should ideally satisfy the following requirements:

(a) Valid comparisons should be possible even where projects differ in the amount of capital required, the timing of the capital outlay or of the income arising from the investment.
(b) A statement of the worthwhileness and financial feasibility of the project. In the case of the latter, problems may arise where loans have been made and in these circumstances it is important to know if the project will generate sufficient money to meet the demands of interest repayment, to say nothing of principal repayment, or any other demands, i.e. tax and living expenses.

Projects may, of course, show a high return on capital and yet be unable to meet critical repayments at the right time. Such projects are not feasible.

The three main methods available are:

1. Payback;
2. Rate of return;
3. Discounted cash flow.

Payback

The payback period is the time taken to recover the capital outlay and is calculated by accumulating forward the annual net cash flows *(before charging depreciation) until they equal the capital input.*

Rate of return

This is the annual net cash flow, after charging depreciation, expressed as a percentage of the capital outlay. Problems arise in relation to the capital inasmuch as sometimes the initial capital is used and sometimes the initial capital is halved to arrive at a figure representing average capital. Clearly, the answers from either method are going to vary considerably. If the annual net cash flow (after depreciation) is £900 for an initial investment of £10 000 the return on initial capital will be 9 per cent, and on the 'average' capital 18 per cent. If the farmer has a minimum requirement for a 16 per cent return on capital then the method will determine whether or not the project is acceptable.

Table 5.5   An investment appraisal using payback as the criterion

Year	Capital invested (£)	Annual net cash flow (£)	Cumulative net cash flow (£)
0	20 000	—	—
1		3 000	3 000
2		4 000	7 000
3		3 500	10 500
4		3 500	14 000
5		5 000	19 000
6		4 500	23 500

Note: In the above example, payback occurs in the sixth year of the project.

Table 5.6   *An investment appraisal using rate of return as the criterion*

Year	Capital invested £	Annual net cash flow £	Cumulative net cash flow £
0	20 000	—	—
1		3 000	3 000
2		4 000	7 000
3		3 500	10 000
4		3 500	14 000
5		5 000	19 000
6		4 500	23 500
7		4 000	27 000
8		4 000	32 000
9		3 000	35 000
10		5 000	40 000

The following simplified examples, shown in Table 5.5 and 5.6 demonstrate these two techniques.

Total accumulated net cash flows =   40 000
Less original capital (reflecting depreciation) = 20 000
                                                                         ────────
                                                                          20 000

Average annual net cash flow = $\dfrac{20\,000}{10}$ = 2 000

∴ Return on initial capital = $\dfrac{2\,000}{20\,000} \times 100 = 10$ per cent

Note: If, as pointed out earlier, the initial capital in Table 5.5. were to be halved to represent average capital then the return on average capital would be:

$\dfrac{2\,000}{10\,000} \times 100 = 20$ per cent

In Table 5.4 the payback method is used to evaluate the project in question, and if this is the only criterion then no difficulties are presented. However, this method does not take account of income generated in the years after payback nor does it attempt to show return on capital. Neither method, in Tables 5.4 and 5.5, includes any accurate assessment of feasibility, although it could be argued that the payback method attempts this on the basis that the shorter the payback period the lower is the risk that the project will not be feasible. Neither method takes any account of the timing of the net cash flows, giving the same value to profit arising in Year 1 as to that in the last year of the project.

Most of the above disadvantages can be avoided by the use of the discounted cash flow technique. On its own the discounting of cash flows allows only for the worthwhileness of a project to be assessed, but the technique allows taxation allowance, interest and tax payments to be taken into account and the variable cash flows to be given a weighting according to their timing.

DISCOUNTED CASH FLOW CALCULATIONS

A viable investment in the farm business must during its life repay its initial capital and also generate a yield equivalent to or better than that which could be obtained by investing elsewhere at compound interest.

Since capital always has a value or opportunity cost, it must be regarded as a constantly growing or moving commodity. Discounted cash-flow techniques are, therefore, used to appraise the return on an investment over a period of time and are based upon compound interest.

The principle of 'discounting' or, conversely, of 'compounding' can be explained as follows:

If £1 is invested for 5 years at 10 per cent compound interest, it will at the end of that period be worth £1.611. The growth of £1 over 5 years at 10 per cent compound interest can be shown as follows:

The value of £1.0 at the end of 1 year is £1.1 $\quad$ = £1.000
The value of £1.0 at the end of 2 years is $(£1.1)^2$ = £1.210
The value of £1.0 at the end of 3 year is $(£1.1)^3$ = £1.331
The value of £1.0 at the end of 4 years is $(£1.1)^4$ = £1.464
The value of £1.0 at the end of 5 years is $(£1.1)^5$ = £1.611

One could, therefore, say that the present value of £1.611 receivable in 5 years' time at 10 per cent compound interest is £1.00, or that £1.611 discounted for 5 years at 10 per cent will be worth £1.00.

The present value of £1 receivable at a future date is clearly less than £1 and can be calculated as follows:

Present values of £1 discounted at 10 per cent are:

In one year $\quad \dfrac{£1}{1.100}$ = £0.9091 (multiplying factor)

In two years $\quad \dfrac{£1}{1.210}$ = £0.8264 (multiplying factor)

In three years $\dfrac{£1}{1.331}$ = £0.7513 (multiplying factor)

In four years $\dfrac{£1}{1.464}$ = £0.683 1 (multiplying factor)

In five years $\dfrac{£1}{1.611}$ = 0.620 7 (multiplying factor)

The present value of £1 received in 5 years at 10 per cent is £0.6207. This means that £0.6207 if invested now at 10 per cent compound interest will be worth £1.00 in 5 years' time.

Since these calculations are cumbersome, tables are published in Appendix B (p. 294) from which it is possible to obtain these appropriate discount factors and reciprocals.

If a forward budget indicates the likely net cash flows from a given investment, then two measures may be used in appraising the profitability of the investment using discounted cash flow techniques.

The two methods are:
1. The net present value of the investment;
2. The discounted yield of the investment.

The net present value is the capital gain or growth that can be obtained from an investment after discounting the net cash flows at a predetermined rate of compound interest and deducting the initial capital. If an investment shows a positive net present value it is therefore deemed to be worth while.

The discounted yield is the rate of compound interest that will equate the present value of the net cash flows of a project over a given period back to the value of the initial investment. It is, in other words, the equivalent rate of compound interest earned by the investment during its life.

The net present value of the project is found by calculating the present value of the forecast incomes after discounting them at a given rate. The rate of compound interest or discount factor could be:
(a) the opportunity cost of the capital, i.e. the rate of interest at which the farmer is prepared to invest off the farm;
(b) the lowest acceptable return for on farm investment; or
(c) the current bank overdraft or loan interest rate.

The example given in Table 5.7 will illustrate this technique using the same basic net cash-flow data as used in the payback and rates of return examples shown in Tables 5.4 and 5.5 respectively. The discount rate taken will be 12 per cent.

Since the net present value is positive the investment is worthwhile and clearly produces a return which at compound interest is greater than 12 per cent. The calculation of net present value is of greatest value when the possibility of alternative projects exists since the most worthwhile project can be chosen by the size of the net

Table 5.7 *Discounted cash flow for a proposed project*

Year	Net cash flow (£)	Discount factor at 12% (see Appendix B1) (£)	Present value of forecast NCF (£)
1	3 000	0.893	2 679.00
2	4 000	0.797	3 188.00
3	3 500	0.712	2 492.00
4	3 500	0.636	2 226.00
5	5 000	0.567	2.835.00
6	4 500	0.507	2 281.50
7	4 000	0.452	1 808.00
8	4 500	0.404	1 818.00
9	3 000	0.361	1 083.00
10	5 000	0.322	1 610.00
Total	40 000	—	22 020.50

	£
Present value of cash flow	22 020.50
less Initial capital	20 000.00
Net present value of investment	2 020.50

present value, providing, of course, that the same discount factors are applied to each alternative. However, in this case there are no alternative projects, but the discounted yield of the project can be established.

The discounted yield is the rate of compound interest that will discount the net cash flows to the value of the investment over a period of years.

If the net cash flows are constant or fluctuate around a mean, this involves a simple calculation to find the appropriate discount factor:

$$\text{Discount factor} = \frac{\text{Initial capital}}{\text{Annual net cash flow}}$$
$$= \frac{20\ 000}{4\ 000} = 5.00$$

By referring to the table for calculating the present value of a future annuity (see Appendix B2 (p. 294) this factor is found to correspond to a return of just over 15 per cent, i.e. almost exactly half-way between the return on initial capital and the return on average capital.

When the cash flows are not constant but fluctuate from year to year, then a discount factor based on the average net cash flow is unreliable and the full discounted cash flow calculation must be made. Finding the actual discounted yield is in practice largely a matter of trial and error. However, since it is known that the discounted yield is greater than the rate of return on initial capital and less than the rate of return on average capital, the actual discount rate can be obtained by interpolation.

This can be calculated as shown in Table 5.8.

Where the net cash flows are fairly constant or fluctuate around a predictable mean, then the discounted yield is approximately half-way between the rate of return on initial capital (RRIC) and the rate of return on average capital (RRAC).

The question of which method to use, the net present value or discounted yield, depends upon the circumstances. The calculation of a positive net present value means that the project is worth while, and if a number of alternative or competing projects are being considered then the project can be ranked in order of worthwhile-ness according to the size of the net present value. For single projects the discounted yield may be compared with the cost of capital to determine worthwhileness. Even if the discounted yield exceeds the cost of the capital the project may be rejected if the excess is not considered a fair reward for the degree of risk involved.

Table 5.8   Calculation of discounted yield

Year	Net cash flow (£)	Discount factor at 12% (£)	Present value (£)	Discount factor at 20% (£)	Present value (£)
1	3 000	0.893	2 679.00	0.833	2 499.00
2	4 000	0.797	3.188.00	0.694	2 776.00
3	3 500	0.712	2 492.00	0.579	2 026.50
4	3 500	0.636	2 226.00	0.482	1 687.00
5	5 000	0.567	2 835.00	0.402	2 010.00
6	4 500	0.507	2 281.50	0.335	1 507.50
7	4 000	0.452	1 808.00	0.279	1 116.00
8	4 500	0.404	1 818.00	0.233	1 048.50
9	3 000	0.361	1 083.00	0.194	582.00
10	5 000	0.322	1 610.00	0.162	810.00
			22 020.50		16 062.50

Interpolation

	£
Present value at 12%	22 020.50
less Present value at 20%	16 062.50
	5 958 00
Present value at 12%	22 020.50
less Capital	20 000.00
	2 020.50

$$\frac{2\ 020.50}{5\ 958.00} \times 8 = 2.71$$

Discounted yield = 12% + 2.71 = 14.71%

INVESTMENT APPRAISAL IN PRACTICE

The assessment of worthwhileness and feasibility relies very heavily upon the projection of cash flows, in or out of the business, which are created by the project. The term 'cash flow' is to be taken literally since the calculation of either net present value or discounted yield allows for the covering of the capital outlay and, therefore, depreciation charges should not be included directly when calculating cash flows. Depreciation will, of course, be used in estimating likely tax payments before arriving at the net cash flow figure in any one year. Capital payments on land, buildings and machinery, etc. must, therefore, be itemized separately because of the different ways in which these items may be written down for tax purposes. Working capital items should be calculated quarterly or monthly in the build-up to the annual net cash flow, in order to identify peak capital requirements.

Where a project is developing at the expense of another enterprise, i.e. dairy cows partially replacing cereal production, then it would be necessary to deduct the cash flows lost from the cereals from the cash flows generated by the dairy cows. Similarly, if a new or more expensive machine is to be purchased the money obtained from the sale of the old machine must be deducted from the cost of the 'new' machine.

It is normal when assessing worthwhileness not to deduct the interest charges on borrowed capital from the net cash flow, although like depreciation it will have been taken into account in calculating tax payments.

Some projects will still have at the end of the appraisal period some equipment, stock or buildings which will have a cash value. This value ideally should be included in the final year cash flow, but care should be taken when dealing with, say, 10-year-old buildings, whereas livestock such as breeding females may easily be estimated using current values.

Little has been said about the effects of inflation. There are basically two reasons for not doing so. The first aspect is that if a number of projects are under consideration then it is clear that inflation will affect them all. Secondly, whether it will affect them all equally is not known and is, therefore, unpredictable. Farm business management endeavours to quantify those things that fall within reasonable parameters of predictability, not without. The fact that inflation will create many consequences is not at issue, but the investor must be aware that with the passage of time the repayment of £1 borrowed will be effected in later years with a £1 that has far less purchasing or investment potential – a factor that must weigh in his favour.

Discounted cash flows can deal realistically with variable cash flows and complicated projects involving varying finance requirements over different periods of time. However, the method will not produce a good answer out of suspect cash-flow data, but it does bring into focus those areas that, in the budgeting, are particularly sensitive. In the past people have, understandably, been put off by the amount of calculation required to complete a net cash flow, discount and then interpolate. Today, programmable calculators can take all the drudgery out of the task to say nothing of the potential these have, together with micro-processors and mini-computers, for exploring alternative projects and a variety of sensitivity levels.

SOURCES OF CAPITAL

The main sources of capital financing for the agricultural industry may be summarized in the following.

Accumulated profits from within the industry itself

This is the money generated by the employment of the capital and other resources in the farm business. Not all of the profit generated is normally available since some of it is deducted to finance personal spending and meet tax payments. Additionally, the residue left in the business may not always be in a liquid or readily available form so, although the business may be in a healthy state by any applied criteria, there may be a short-term need for working capital to finance the production cycle.

Outside investors

This source may be supplied by private individuals, who for many reasons, wish to invest in a farm business, or by public shareholders' capital. However, only a very small percentage of the holdings in the United Kingdom are in the hands of limited companies, since farm businesses have historically tended to centre around the family farm. An advantage of this source is that the cost to the business may be realized as a share of the profits – a very useful arrangement when lean years are encountered and the share is proportionately reduced. Compare this with the business committed to meet interest and principal repayments during a lean period.

Grant aid

From 1 October 1980 the Farm Capital Grant Scheme (FCGS) which came into effect on 1 January 1974 was replaced by the Agriculture and Horticulture Grant Scheme (AHGS).

The Farm and Horticulture Development Scheme (FHDS), which also started on 1 January 1974, ceased to operate on the 18 April 1982 being superseded, from 1 October 1980, by the Agriculture and Horticulture Development Scheme (AHDS). Grants available under this scheme are known as development grants.

In the case of both of the above new schemes no claims will be accepted by the Ministry after 31 December 1985 and farmers and growers may apply for either development grants or investment grants but not for both.

It can be seen that grant aid can be subject to frequent revision and the Agricultural and Development and Advisory Services (ADAS) should always be consulted as to the availability of government aid for any proposed project.

Own funds

These are personal funds generated, or inherited, apart from the farming business, and as such cost nothing in real terms to the business, although one could levy the opportunity costs of investing the money elsewhere.

Borrowed funds

There is an increasing need and demand for credit facilities by the farming industry which has been accentuated by a drop in real incomes and a need to modernize and restructure the business. The latter need is not least associated with the intention of protecting the future profit levels of the business and the maintenance, if not improvement, in living standards of the farmer and his family.

From time to time attempts are made to draw up a balance sheet depicting the assets and liabilities of the agricultural industry.

Although the figures themselves may not satisfy the purist the trends are interesting. In the early 1970s, the industry borrowed around 10 per cent of its total assets. Since then the actual amount borrowed has grown substantially, and although the value of the assets has grown, the result is that the industry is currently borrowing around 11 per cent of the value of its total assets. In effect the net capital of the industry has grown at a slightly slower rate than the need for borrowing.

Before the principles of borrowing and sources of funds are considered it must be remembered that every £1 borrowed must be repaid and repaid with interest.

There are certain fundamental principles in relation to borrowing which must be clearly understood. These can be summarized in the following.

Rules of borrowing
1. The loan must show a profit – do not borrow for the purpose of providing amenities.
2. Be sure that interest and capital can be repaid out of profits while maintaining a working level of liquidity.
3. Plan and budget realistically, allowing a judicious margin for variations to plan.
4. Consider all possible alternative sources of credit.
5. Never borrow to bolster a dying or failing enterprise.
6. Aim to repay the loan during the life of the asset for which it is borrowed, e.g. if borrowing to buy a tractor make sure that the money is repaid before the tractor needs replacing.
7. Borrow from the smallest number of sources.
8. Agree on sound arrangements for repaying the loan. If possible, make special arrangements for repayment privileges to enable the loan to be paid off in a shorter time than that originally planned, should the borrower be in a position to do so. Also, make provision for reduced repayments under extenuating circumstances. Arrange if possible an automatic system of repayment such as by banker's order or by direct debit.
9. Make all arrangements the subject of a written agreement.

A prospective lender, often the bank manager, will want to be in a position to judge the respective merits of each lending situation. The inexperienced customer may not be aware of the appraisal and criteria employed and, therefore, does not tailor his case to best advantage. The good presentation of a doubtful business proposition will not turn it into an acceptable one, but the bad presentation of a potentially acceptable case may lead, through lack of confidence on the lender's part, to its rejection.

The lender will be primarily concerned with the following factors when considering a proposal:

(a) Who is the person?

What is his/her ability measured through their 'track' record? Very importantly, how is their integrity rated?

(b) What is the purpose of the loan?

A knowledge of what the loan is for will enable the lender to match the loan with the appropriate finance. Financing a longer-term type of project with short-term funds may well create undue financial strain and the converse may well be more expensive for the borrower.

(c) How much is needed and for how long?

The amount required is important in relation to the borrower's own funds. The borrower may well have to show how the level of loan requested was arrived at – often by means of forecast cash flows.

(d) What is the source of repayment?

The borrower should be able to demonstrate how the borrowing will improve the profits of the business and how the cash flow will produce the cash needed to pay interest and repayment of the capital, to say nothing of increased tax liability through improved profits.

The business should be able to withstand setbacks without the liquidity and solvency of the business being put in jeopardy, i.e. that the 'gearing' is reasonable.

(e) Security.

Many overdraft facilities are provided without security (unsecured) purely on the basis of the capital resources of the farm. Security may well be required over and above that referred to in (d) relating to the 'gearing' of the business. Such security should be viewed as insurance to support a viable business, not to bolster a failing one.

Any prospective lender operating with a modicum of professionalism will have considered the above factors, not only out of self-interest but also out of a general sense of responsibility towards the borrower who may well not appreciate the implications of the proposal. Cash flows have already been referred to, but the lender will almost certainly have 'read' the applicant's balance sheet in order to assess the client's capital position and ability to withstand as yet unknown possible setbacks. Table 5.9 illustrates a simple example of what may go wrong. Here the example illustrates that the borrower's equity may well be as important as his absolute net worth.

In this case two prospective borrowers A and B each have the same net worth, but A has only a small stake in his business so that

Table 5.9   The equity and net worth of two prospective borrowers

	Initial situation		Situation after a 10% setback of assets	
	A (£)	B (£)	A (£)	B (£)
Assets	110 000	15 000	99 000	13 500
Liabilities	100 000	5 000	100 000	5 000
Net capital	10 000	10 000	−1 000	8 500
Equity	9.09%	66.67%	Nil	62.97%

when a 10 per cent setback occurs to the value of both their assets, A is left insolvent, whereas B's equity is only marginally reduced.

As a prospective borrower, then, A is by far a greater risk than B, although his business is much larger and superficially more impressive.

A prospective borrower who has insufficient security of his own may find a guarantor to secure the loan on his behalf. The guarantor undertakes to carry the risk of the loan and to repay the capital, should the borrower find himself unable to do so.

CREDIT FACILITIES

Credit available for agriculture can be considered as falling broadly into three different categories based on the approximate period of repayment and the nature of the assets acquired.

Table 5.10   Credit categories showing the purpose and the source of lending

	Long-term, over 10 years	Medium-term, 3–10 years	Short-term
Purpose	Mainly for: Land purchase Long-term improvements, i.e. land drainage	Specialist buildings Machinery and equipment Breeding stock/production herds	Seasonal finance, 'bridging', working capital, generally meeting a shortfall in liquidity
Source	Agricultural Mortgage Corporation Lands Improvement Company Insurance companies Private mortgages Banks	Banks Central Council for Agricultural and Horticultural Co-operation Hire-purchase companies Leasing companies	Banks Merchants Co-operatives or marketing organizations Creditors

The categories shown in Table 5.10 are not rigid, and therefore it must be remembered that 'overlapping' of the boundaries can and does occur. It can be seen from this table that the sources of finance are not exclusively reserved for a particular purpose, and it is for this reason that the sources will be dealt with as separate entities. It is up to the reader to link the purpose with the appropriate source using Table 5.10.

Sources of credit

Agricultural Mortgage Corporation (AMC)

The AMC is government backed and will offer mortgages on freehold agricultural properties in England and Wales for periods normally between 5 and 40 years. The mortgage offered is usually limited to two-thirds of the value of the property as established by the AMC's valuer. The borrower has a choice of fixed and variable rates of interest and lending facilities which include a wide range of repayment methods designed to meet most borrower's individual requirements. The AMC will not lend money for crops and stock. Providing that payments are prompt and that the terms of the mortgage contract are met then the loan cannot be called in.

In order to obtain a loan the borrower must satisfy the AMC that he is suitably qualified and that sufficient capital is available for the cropping and stocking of the farm. When applying for a loan the applicant should include accounts showing past performance, details (including a map) of the property to be purchased, together with forward budgets and cash-flow projections. The latter should show how the loan is to be serviced and any contingencies to be met.

If a loan is obtained then the borrower is normally expected to make two half-yearly payments of principal and interest combined. The loan is normally expected to run to full term, but the borrower may foreclose a loan upon payment of a redemption fee to cover for any possible loss of interest incurred by the Corporation. Table 5.11 gives examples of annual payments per £1 000 borrowed on annuity-type loans at different rates of interest (the rate at 16 March 1984 was 10.5 per cent on variable-rate loans and 13 per cent on fixed-rate loans).

The Lands Improvement Company

This Company was set up under the Improvement of Land Acts of 1861 and 1899. The Company is able to lend money on the security of a first or subsequent mortgage on agricultural land.

Table 5.11   Examples of annual payments per £1 000 borrowed on annuity-type loans from the Agricultural Mortgage Corporation at three different rates of interest

Term of years	Gross payment per annum (£)	Average capital repayment per annum (£)	Average interest payment per annum (£)
10%			
40	102.06	25.00	77.06
30	105.66	33.33	72.33
25	109.56	40.00	69.56
20	116.56	50.00	66.56
15	130.12	66.67	63.45
10	160.50	100.00	60.50
16%			
40	160.34	25.00	135.34
30	161.60	33.33	128.27
25	163.50	40.00	123.50
20	167.74	50.00	117.74
15	177.66	66.67	110.99
10	203.72	100.00	103.72
20%			
40	200.10	25.00	175.10
30	200.66	33.33	167.33
25	201.72	40.00	161.72
20	204.52	50.00	154.52
15	212.16	66.67	145.49
10	234.92	100.00	134.92

Note: In the earlier years, payments consist mainly of interest; the proportion of the gross annual repayment represented by capital increases as the period progresses.

Source: Nix 1983, p. 123–4

Loans of not less than £25 000 over a period of 2–10 years are normal, although longer repayment periods may be negotiated. The maximum loan, as with the AMC, is limited to two-thirds of the Company's valuation. The loan, however, may be used for a wider range of purposes, i.e. land purchase, the building and improvement of farm buildings, houses, drainage, fencing, roads, tree planting, repayment of other borrowings and capital transfer tax. Any items eligible under the government's development or investment grants are also eligible for a loan from the Company.

As with AMC loans, these may not be recalled unless the contract is not met, but early foreclosure is possible upon a payment of a redemption fee.

Life insurance companies
Some companies will provide a mortgage for up to 60 per cent of their valuation of the property. These companies normally insist on

the borrower covering his loan with an endowment policy. This tends to be an expensive form of borrowing, but does ensure that, in the event of the borrower's death, his dependants will be protected. A borrower could, of course, arrange suitable life cover for any other type of borrowing. This arrangement may be insisted upon by some lenders in the interests of the borrower's dependants.

Private mortgages

These are loans made by relatives and friends, and may or may not have been formalized by a written contract, although the latter case is to be recommended in the interests of both parties. The attraction of the loans is that they will normally carry interest charges (if any) below the normal commercial rate. Payment of the capital is on a basis mutually agreeable to both parties and may be very flexible. The death of the lender may mean that the loan has to be repaid in full, and a commercial loan taken out to cover such an event may prove difficult in some circumstances. It would, therefore, be wise with all private arrangements to draw up and comply with a capital repayment schedule while enjoying the benefits of low or minimal interest charges. The significance, however, of this particular source of credit is on the decline when compared with other sources.

Hire-purchase companies

This is almost invariably a comparatively expensive form of borrowing for two reasons. Interest rates are usually higher than those charged by banks, and interest is calculated for the period of the loan upon the basis of the principal and not the diminishing balance. This method of calculation is called *flat rate*.

An example is given in Table 5.12 where £8 000 is repaid in 2 years in Case A via hire-purchase repayments of 24 equal instalments of interest and capital, and in Case B via a bank loan where repayment of the capital of £1 000 is made every quarter and the interest calculated on the diminishing balance.

Table 5.12 *Borrowing on hire-purchase compared with a bank loan*

	Sum borrowed (£)	Length of loan	Rate of interest (%)	Interest paid (£)
Case A	8 000	2 years	12	1 920
Case B	8 000	2 years	16	1 440

Note: In Case A the interest is calculated flat rate, i.e.

$$\frac{£8\ 000 \times 12}{100} \times 2 \text{ years} = £1\ 920$$

In Case B the interest is calculated on the diminishing balance basis as follows. At the start of the loan period, £8 000 is outstanding. At the end of the first quarter £1 000 principal is repaid and the interest is calculated accordingly:

$$\frac{£8\ 000 \times 16}{100} \times \frac{3}{12} \text{ (3 months)} = £320$$

At the end of the second quarter the interest payment will be:

$$\frac{£7\ 000 \times 16}{100} \times \frac{3}{12} = £280$$

The calculations continue in this manner until all the interest payments are known, which in Case B total £1 440.

Central Council for Agricultural and Horticultural Co-operation (CCAHC)

The CCAHC was formed in 1967 with the aims of promoting, developing, organizing and co-ordinating co-operation in the agricultural and horticultural industries. A scheme of grants for costs and capital items associated with co-operation are catered for such as: feasibility studies; costs of formation of co-operatives; managerial salaries and expenses; training and grants on co-operatively owned items. The latter can attract grants of 15–25 per cent of the cost.

Machinery syndicates, notably successful in many areas, have access through locally formed committees to grants and cheap credit guaranteed by the Agricultural Credit Corporation (ACC).

As with development and investment grants, changes do occur and details should be sought, in this case, from the CCAHC.

Note: The ACC is not directly a source of finance, but does help agricultural and horticultural groups to obtain bank credit by standing as guarantor. If this is done through the CCAHC, there is no fee, and a charge of around 2 per cent per annum of the amount of the guarantee is made. The ACC may act as guarantor for a part or the whole of the borrowing depending on the circumstances.

Leasing companies

Although not strictly speaking a source of credit, the use of a leasing company does enable a farmer to obtain items of capital equipment. The cost of leasing is usually cheaper than hire-purchase and only occasionally cheaper than bank borrowing. This is because the leasing company retain ownership of the item being leased and, therefore, claim the capital allowances from the Inland Revenue. The value of these allowances is built into the cost of leasing during the primary period. At the end of the primary period a new lease may be negotiated, at a nominal rent, or the lease ended. If the capital item is sold it should technically pass to a third party, say, a dealer, unless the item was on a leasing/purchase agreement.

Note: Grants are not available on leased items nor will these items appear as an asset on the farmer's balance sheet.

Co-operatives and marketing organizations

Few co-operatives have the facilities for offering credit to farmers. Some co-operative marketing organizations (e.g. the British Wool Marketing Board) do, however, allow forward payments to be made on produce which has yet to be sold and which is being held in store on the farmer's behalf.

Merchant's credits

This is mainly accounted for by a surcharge on the sale price or by loss of discount on a delayed payment. The interest charged here can be very high and, although some may consider it excessive, it is the merchant's way of ensuring that his bills are paid on time. Cheaper credit can usually be negotiated between a farmer and his merchant, provided that a properly organized plan of buying and selling can be arranged in advance and that any such agreements made are strictly honoured by both parties.

Many merchants will offer attractive purchasing terms if a farmer operates a direct debit scheme with the merchant.

Sundry creditors

Anyone supplying goods or services without receiving immediate payment is supplying credit. Farmers seem to be notoriously bad at settling accounts unless they carry a surcharge or discount rebate. Agricultural contractors in particular appear to suffer from this form of calculated oversight.

Banks

This particular source of credit has been left until last because of its all-embracing flexibility, as shown by Table 5.10, since it caters for all the categories depicted. This flexibility is well illustrated by the diagram shown in Fig. 5.1.

This flexibility is a major characteristic of bank lending, but there are other characteristics which make such a source of credit attractive to the borrower. In the case of the overdraft, these are:

(a) interest is charged, on a daily basis, only upon the amount of money actually being used by the borrower. This makes an overdraft one of the cheapest forms of credit available – interest being charged at a small percentage over 'base rate';
(b) no lower minimum level is put on the borrowing;
(c) it is simple to operate;
(d) allows the borrower flexibility in its application;
(e) security is often not required;
(f) technically the overdraft is renewed annually, but it is unusual for renewal not to be forthcoming.

However, an overdraft is subject to fluctuations caused by government or Bank of England monetary policy and is technically repayable on demand by the bank. This latter action would only occur in extreme circumstances (of a national or personal nature).

If an overdraft requirement persists at a given level from year to year, often called 'hard core' borrowing, then it may make sense for the borrower to restructure his credit and take out a medium-term loan together with an overdraft. A medium-term loan has a number of advantages:

(a) it is possible to negotiate a fixed interest rate, thus removing the

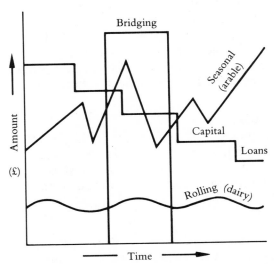

Figure 5.1 The varying requirements financed by credit from banks

element of fluctuation (this may be disadvantageous if interest rates drop);

(b) having negotiated a loan with the bank the amount is not subject to control from outside agencies, i.e. the government or the Bank of England;

(c) repayment of the loan can be linked to the cash flow of the business and even a moratorium may be negotiated on the principal in some circumstances.

Generally speaking, loans are usually more expensive than an overdraft and the bank manager will almost certainly be looking to the balance-sheet ratios in order to ensure that the risk of over-borrowing is not a real danger and that the business is secure should events not turn out as predicted. Again, as with sources of credit dealt with earlier in this chapter, early repayment may require a redemption fee to be paid.

Historically, banks have been particularly associated with lending of a short- to medium-term nature. In recent years, however, this has changed and the more progressive banks will lend money for land purchase and business expansion schemes for up to 20 years. One major clearing bank currently offers a 20-year Farm Purchase Loan Scheme.

More recently loans from the bank have become one step removed by the introduction of credit, for a wide range of commodities, through a nominated retailer. In view of the case with which borrowing may be obtained in this way, caution must be exercised by the borrower in order to avoid over-borrowing. This is not made any easier by the removal of the need to maintain direct contact with the bank manager. Repayment of this credit may extend for up to 3 years.

One source of credit through the bank that has not yet been mentioned is Eurocurrency funds. These can be provided by any bank branch and can, when interest rates on sterling are high, look very attractive. Although the interest rates may be attractive in real terms the risk lies in the relative strengths of the currencies. Since repayment has to be in the original currency borrowed, a business could be financially embarrassed if a borrowing was effected when the interest rates were attractive and the £ high, and if this was followed by a prolonged period when the strength of the £ dropped. If a borrower wishes to take advantage of such a source of potentially cheap credit without exposing himself to undue risk then it may well be sensible to use some Eurocurrency together with a 'normal' borrowing for a proposition.

Since negotiation of bank credit is usually a personal matter between a farmer and his local bank manager, a great deal of importance is attached to the borrower's reputation and integrity.

It is, therefore, extremely important that such agreements – often only verbal – should be honoured and borrowings paid back on time and not allowed to drag on. The manager's permission and approval should always be sought if it is intended to overdraw on a bank account, however short the period, and however great the security.

PLANNING CAPITAL INVESTMENT

One advantage of capital as a resource is its fluidity and adaptability for different purposes. Capital invested in the farm business suffers from two general restrictions: (i) the slow rate of turnover of most farm enterprises; and (ii) the high proportion of fixed costs.

Both these factors limit the possible return on capital. Slow rates of turnover require high margins from each production cycle if the overall rate of return is to be adequate, and high fixed costs will impose restrictions on the business, usually committing it to a narrow range of alternative enterprises.

In planning investment a fundamental aim must always be to keep capital as fluid and as mobile as possible, by keeping the largest possible proportion in productive or working capital which will be capable of earning a return and remain realizable. At the same time the proportion of capital invested in buildings and fixed equipment should be minimized since it is committed for long periods and cannot show a direct return.

When investing capital in the farm three considerations must be made:
1. What will the capital cost be?
2. What must the capital earn if solvency and liquidity are to be maintained?
3. What is the opportunity cost of the capital? i.e. how much could it earn if invested elsewhere at a similar level of risk?

The cost of borrowing capital has already been discussed.

The margin from a farm business or from an investment must be sufficient to cover the following commitments if the business is to remain solvent:
(a) living expenses;
(b) payment of interest on capital;
(c) repayment of borrowed capital;
(d) reinvestment;
(e) taxation.

These aspects and the ways in which they may be dealt with are well illustrated in Appendices A1–8: Capital budget for Littledown Farm.

Opportunity cost of capital

When tying up capital in a farm business it is advisable to consider the opportunity cost, i.e. the income that the capital might generate if invested elsewhere. Income from investments outside one's own business would be regarded as 'unearned' and would be taxable at the full rate. Alternative investments outside agriculture will vary in their return according to:

(a) the risk involved, i.e. the security of the capital;

(b) the length of the loan;

(c) the amount of expected growth of the investment.

Examples of such investments

1. *Building societies* – completely secure; no growth of capital; 4.5–5 per cent after tax deducted by the building society; tax is not reclaimable.
2. *Corporation and council loans* – secure; up to 9.5 per cent interest (gross); tax deducted at source but is reclaimable; no growth of capital.
3. *First mortgage debenture stocks* – secure; up to 9.5 per cent depending on length of loan; no growth of capital.
4. *Unsecured notes* – a higher rate of interest than first mortgage debenture stocks but less security; no growth.
5. *Shares* – less secure; chance of growth; interest or dividend usually proportional to risk; transferable; preference shares the safest.
6. *Unit trusts* – a form of share, but with a wide spread of investment in a large number of different businesses; growth reflecting general trend of share market and property values; interest only moderate and fully taxable.

Before seriously considering investment outside the farm business it would be wise to seek the advice of a professional financial adviser. The farmer considering this move could also apply the same basic rules of capital appraisal dealt with earlier in this chapter.

6 LIVESTOCK STUDIES: DAIRY ENTERPRISES

INTRODUCTION

Milk and dairy products constitute a major part of the output of British agriculture, the gross value of these products amounting in 1983 to a forecast figure of 21.4 per cent of the gross output in the United Kingdom (£2 486 million out of £11 595 million).

In common with other enterprises, dairying underwent a number of changes in the 1970s. Technological innovation apart the decade saw the dismantling of the UK system of guaranteed prices and their replacement with a target price for milk as part of a European dairy policy.

Inflation and high interest rates led to reduced margins which had the effect of slowing expansion and curtailing investment. Dairy cow numbers remained fairly constant throughout this period and the 1983 forecast figure of 3 331 000 head shows little change from the average figure of 1972–74 of 3 389 000 head. Milk production per cow and average dairy herd size increased over the period 1970–79.

Dairy farmers are now operating within the constraints of milk quotas, the declining level of liquid milk sales, and over-production within Europe which create a new set of business management parameters in which to work. Producing milk within a farm-based quota undoubtedly places the management emphasis in different areas to those which applied prior to 2 April 1984.

The need for care and sound husbandry will continue to apply as it has done before; the revised climate will perhaps produce less concern about: high yields; cow appearance; facilities and equipment – and more concern about: grass; monitoring; heifer rearing; alternative feeds.

The principles remain the same but the perspective should shift to cost reduction and increasing use of forage both grazed and conserved.

| | | Gross margin £/forage ha | | |
		Low	Average	High
Dairying:	Friesians	725	844	906
	Channel Island	582	687	783
	Other breeds	591	694	790
Fat lamb production		209	288	467
Rearing dairy replacements: Friesians		300	360	460
Beef:	Single suckling	—	235	297
	Multiple suckling	441	533	594
	Fattening store cattle	—	143	—
	18-month beef	—	569	—

Initial capital requirements for dairy farming are high, but milk production has the important advantage of being less dependent upon seasonal working capital than arable, stock-rearing or fattening enterprises, owing to the regular nature of its sales in the form of the monthly milk cheque.

When judged on the basis of gross margins produced per forage hectare, dairying would seem to be one of the most efficient ways of converting grass and forage crops into cash. Standard gross margins (Nix 1983) illustrate this point.

Great care is necessary in interpreting measures of profitability for the dairy herd. The gross margin comparisons quoted above must be used with caution since they only refer to one aspect of the enterprise and comparative gross margins are not necessarily an indication that the final profitability of the enterprise will be in the same proportions, since levels of fixed costs and capital investment will not be the same in all cases.

BASIC COST STRUCTURE OF MILK PRODUCTION

A wide range of factors are involved in determining the ultimate profitability of milk production. The significance of any one factor will vary from farm to farm and each case must be judged upon its own merits and special circumstances.

The most useful measure of profitability within an enterprise is the return on tenant's capital, since this single factor involves and is influenced by just about every other possible factor of production.

However, profitability is more frequently expressed for comparative purposes as gross or net margin per cow or gross or net margin per hectare.

Interpretation of profitability expressed in this way will depend largely upon the farm in question.

As already stated, a high overall return on capital is the aim. In order to achieve this, it will be necessary to obtain the maximum possible margin within the limits that are imposed. Thus, if physical factors, e.g. buildings, labour, etc. limit the number of cows to be kept, then it is necessary to achieve a high margin per cow in order to achieve a good return on capital for the enterprise.

However, if land is the only factor imposing a limit on the enterprise, then it may be possible to achieve the same or even better return on capital from a lower margin per cow, allied to a tighter stocking rate, provided that the stocking rate is increased sufficiently to result in an increased margin per hectare.

Final profitability or 'net margin' will be the difference between:
(a) gross margin;
(b) fixed costs,
whether expressed per cow or per hectare.

The factors affecting these two important aspects of profitability are therefore considered systematically according to the diagram of cost structure given in Fig. 6.1.

Factors affecting gross margin

Gross output per cow

1. Milk sales
   - (a) Quantity sold
     - Yield
     - Calving index
     - Quota
   - (b) Price obtained
     - Quality
     - Seasonality
     - Quota

The value of milk sold per cow per year is the result of a number of factors, which are now considered in turn.

(a) Quantity of milk sold

Quantity sold per cow per year is a function of (i) yield per cow per lactation, and (ii) calving index; although for the herd the sum total of milk sold is now constrained by the recent imposition of quotas.

Yield per cow per lactation.   This has increased steadily in recent years as Table 6.1 indicates.

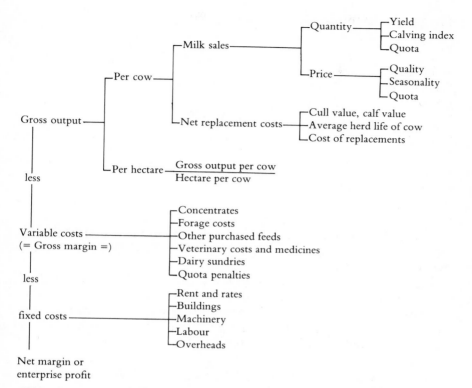

Figure 6.1   Factors affecting the profitability of milk production

Lactation yield is subject to the influence of many factors. The most important of these are health, management, level of feeding and environment, the technical implications of which would require

Table 6.1   *UK average annual milk yield per cow for all breeds*

Year	Litres
1974–75	4 050
1975–76	4 270
1976–77	4 275
1977–78	4 545
1978–79	4 650
1979–80	4 670
1980–81	4 760
1981–82	4 745
1982–83★	5 050

★ Provisional estimates.

Source: Dairy facts and figures 1983, Table 18, p. 22.

Table 6.2   Influence of breed of cow on milk yield and quality

Breed	Lactation yield (litres)	Average butterfat (%)	Average protein (%)
British Holstein	6 292	3.73 (235)*	3.20 (201)
Friesian	5 610	3.78 (212)	3.26 (183)
Ayrshire	4 988	3.90 (195)	3.38 (168)
Dairy Shorthorn	4 908	3.64 (179)	3.32 (163)
Guernsey	4 017	4.64 (186)	3.63 (146)
Jersey	3 876	5.19 (201)	3.85 (149)

* Figures in brackets are average weights in kilograms
Source: Dairy Facts and Figures 1983, Table 39, p. 44.

many volumes to cover adequately, and cannot be discussed here. Breed of cows has an important influence upon yield as the following summary, Table 6.2, from the MMB Official Milk Recording Scheme, illustrates.

Equally important is the strain within the breed and the level of genetic improvement within the herd.

Seasonality of calving will considerably affect yield, the optimum time of calving for maximum lactation yield being September to October for heifers and November to December for cows.

Calving index.   Calving index is the interval in days between calvings. Ideally this should be 365, i.e. one lactation per cow per year, and is made up as follows:

Cow calves
    4 days – interval between calving and commencement of milk recording
 305 days – recorded lactation
  56 days – dry period
Cow calves
 365 days

However, the ideal calving index of 365 days is seldom achieved in practice and the average calving index is about 395 days.

This means that the recorded 305-day lactation yield is not the same as the milk sold per cow per year, i.e. since the milk sales are spread over 395 days instead of 365 days the milk sold per cow per year will be:

$$\text{Lactation yield} \times \frac{365}{395}$$

Table 6.3 shows the effect of calving index upon actual milk output per cow per year.

Table 6.3   *Influence of calving index upon milk output*

| Lactation output (litres) | Output/cow/year (to the nearest £) | | |
| | Calving index | | |
	365	380	400
	£	£	£
3 500 at 14.5 p/litre	508	488	463
4 000 at 14.5 p/litre	580	557	529
4 500 at 14.5 p/litre	653	627	595
5 000 at 14.5 p/litre	<u>725</u>	696	662
5 500 at 14.5 p/litre	798	766	<u>728</u>
6 000 at 14.5 p/litre	870	836	794

In this way, the effective output of a 5 500-litre cow is reduced to that of a 5 000-litre cow if the calving index slips from 365 to 400 days, see figures underlined in Table 6.3.

An approximate relationship exists between the calving index, the percentage dry cows in a herd, the average lactation length and the average number of days in a year when a cow is dry. These can be expressed by the formulae:

I. Percentage dry cows in herd $= \dfrac{\text{Days dry in cycle} \times 100}{\text{Calving index}}$

  e.g. at the ideal calving index of 365:

  Percentage dry cows in herd $= \dfrac{56}{365} \times 100 =$ approx. 16

II. Lactation length = calving index – days dry

III. Lactation output = output per cow per year $\times \dfrac{\text{Calving index}}{365}$

A simpler way of calculating the calving index would be to relate the number of cows in the herd to the calves produced in a year. For example, if 100 cows produced 92 calves, the calving index is nearly 397 days, i.e.:

Calving index $= \dfrac{\text{Number of cows} \times 365}{\text{Number of calves produced in 12 months}}$

$= \dfrac{100 \times 365}{92} = 396.7$

Thus, if sufficient basic information is available for a dairy herd, it is possible to calculate a number of factors relating to breeding efficiency and frequency. This can be an extremely useful exercise in pinpointing management weaknesses within a dairy enterprise. For example, if recorded lactation output is greater than output per cow per year, then the calving index must be greater than 365.

If percentage dry cows is high, i.e. more than 16, then this will be due to either (i) poor calving index or (ii) short lactations.

In this way a process of elimination will reveal the basic weaknesses, the technical or managerial causes of which will then need investigation and rectifying.

(b) Price obtained

Government support, through guaranteed prices and standard quantities, ceased on 31 December 1977. Since then, support for the dairy industry has been provided by the Community's intervention buying of butter and skimmed milk powder. Government price control of milk intended for the liquid market has, however, continued, with maximum prices being set for wholesale and retail bottled milk prices only. At the start of every milk year (April–March) each Board publishes a provisional schedule of monthly prices which is updated and adjusted monthly. Monthly prices are higher in the winter than in the summer to encourage autumn calving and a more seasonal output of milk. At the end of the financial year, any shortfall owing to producers is paid out in a supplementary payment, payable on the year's milk supply from each producer to the relevant Board. Supplementary payments may also be made during the year. The imposition, on 2 April 1984, of milk quotas based a farm's milk production in 1983 (calendar year) less 9 per cent imposes a major constraint on the price a producer ultimately receives for each litre of milk if he is penalized for over-production on a farm basis.

Additions and deductions may be made according to whether the compositional quality of the milk is above or below that applicable to the basic price. Each Board operates its own milk quality scheme which in the case of England and Wales is paid for on the percentage of butter-fat, protein and lactose (see Table 6.4). Deductions will be made for hygiene failure, the presence of antibiotics, and the co-responsibility levy while additions may be made for Channel Island milk, brucellosis incentive or special service contracts.

Price received per litre depends upon four main factors:
(a) quality of milk produced;
(b) seasonality of production;
(c) bonuses for which the producer is eligible;
(d) deductions.

Quality

This affects price per litre and can be considered under two headings: (1) compositional quality; (2) hygienic quality.

Table 6.4 *Compositional quality – constituent value payments*

Constituent	Pence per 1%
Butterfat	1.832
Protein	1.792
Lactose	0.272

Source: Milk Producer, May 1984. Vol 31, No. 5, p. 25.

Compositional quality. All milk sold to the MMB is paid for according to analysis. Constituent values payments, which are subject to variation, are shown in Table 6.4. As from 1 April 1984 producers have been paid on a contemporary testing basis, the milk being tested in the month for which payment is to be made.

Hygienic quality. The centralized testing of farm milk for Quality Payment Scheme purposes was introduced in October 1982. This new hygiene scheme is based on total bacterial count (TBC) with each producer's supply being tested once a week. The average of these tests in a month being used to place the milk in one of four hygiene quality bands, each band receiving a different price as shown below:

Band A + 0.2 pence per litre
Band B NIL
Band C – 0.4 pence per litre
Band D – 1.2 pence per litre

For a 100-cow herd producing 5 500 litres per month dropping from Band A to Band B could mean the loss of over £90 month.

Seasonality of production

In line with previous observations regarding evenness of milk production, the returns to producers vary according to the month of the year. The seasonal adjustments for 1984/5 together with the old differentials are shown in Table 6.5.

Clearly, the proportion of winter milk produced will affect the average price per litre and subsequently the returns for the herd.

It is frequently claimed that summer milk production should be more profitable than winter milk production, since costs of producing milk off grass in the summer are very much lower than those of producing winter milk. An analysis, however, of Farm

Table 6.5   Seasonal adjustments to the monthly price of milk

Month of supply	Existing differentials (ppl)	New differentials (ppl)
April	−0.248	−0.5
May	−1.116	−2.5
June	−1.121	−2.5
July	−0.736	nil
August	−0.300	+1.2
September	+0.049	+1.2
October	+0.614	+0.8
November	+0.689	+0.8
December	+0.724	+0.8
January	+0.735	+0.8
February	+0.689	+0.8
March	+0.568	+0.5

Source: MMB, 'The new pricing package', Newsheet April 1984.

Management Services Costed farms 1978–79 (MMB, FMS Report 22) showed that this is not the case when assessed on a gross margin basis. The main reasons why it was not so were failure to feed less concentrates and achieve better stocking rates in relation to winter milk producers. There are, however, circumstances where specialized summer milk production could be more profitable than all-the-year-round or winter milk production. Since it is impossible to generalize, this can only be assessed by careful budgeting for the specific conditions existing on the individual farm.

Bonuses

Bulk milk premium.   Premiums apply only for the first 3 years after changing to bulk collection, after which a continuing premium of 0.10p/litre is paid regardless of vat size. The whole of the UK, except for Northern Ireland, went 'bulk' in July 1979 and the initial bulk addition ceased on 31 December 1983.

Brucellosis incentive scheme.   All milk from herds accredited under this scheme are eligible for a premium of 0.176p/litre.

Other premiums.   Channel Islands milk, level deliveries and special services are paid to individual producers within the terms of their contracts.

Deductions

Co-responsibility levy.   Since September 1977, contributions to the co-responsibility fund have been collected via levies on producers.

The fund is intended to provide aid for measures designed to expand the markets in milk and milk products. From 2 April 1984, the levy has been fixed at the general rate of 0.5244p/litre and at the reduced rate of 0.4370p/litre.

Antibiotics in milk.   Routine tests, at least once a week, are carried out to detect antibiotic residues. Price deductions currently start with the first failure at 5.00p/litre, 3.00p/litre for a second failure and for third and subsequent failures 1.00p/litre. Reversion to the normal sequence of the scheme occurs after six months without a test failure.

Capital contribution.   A contribution of 0.046p/litre will be deducted from producers' payments to pay for the Milk Marketing Board's capital requirements.

Net herd replacement cost

This is sometimes considered as an item of variable cost, but should strictly be deducted from sales at this stage in calculating the gross output per cow.

The net herd replacement cost is the difference between the cost of replacement animals brought into the herd and any livestock sales in the form of calves and culls from the dairy herd. This will depend on four main factors:
1. Rate of replacement;
2. Value of livestock sales from the herd;
3. Cost of replacement animals;
4. Difference in opening and closing valuations for the herd.

Since this is a large subject and involves a further enterprise, i.e. heifer rearing, the factors affecting herd replacement costs are dealt with more fully in the section on Dairy young stock enterprise (p. 168).

Enterprise gross output per forage hectare

This measure is simply a function of gross output per cow and stocking density. Gross output per hectare will increase as stocking density increases since it is not affected by extra feeds costs which usually accompany a heavier stocking density.

Enterprise net output per forage hectare

This is a far more valuable measure upon which to compare output per hectare, since it relates to the margin achieved per hectare after

000038
MMB use only
08 50165
Please quote when contacting the Board

PRINCIPAL   HAMPSHIRE
COLLEGE OF AGRICULTURE
SPARSHOLT   WINCHESTER
HA TS   SO21 2NF

MILK MARKETING BOARD
THAMES DITTON
SURREY KT7 OEL

TEST RESULTS FOR	APRIL 84						
Supply		Sample Date	ANTI BIOTICS	HYGIENE TBC BAND	B/FAT %	PROTEIN %	LACTOSE %	TOTAL
18		04		341	4.60	3.51	4.62	
		12		9	4.51	3.57	4.57	
		26		7	4.33	3.62	4.49	
	THIS MONTHS AVERAGE			119 A	4.48	3.57	4.56	
	PENCE PER 1.00%				1.832	1.792	0.272	
	YOUR PENCE PER LITRE				8.2074	6.3974	1.2403	15.8451
19		03		2	4.50	3.14	4.82	
		08			4.58	3.22	4.80	
		14		11				
		23		3	4.34	3.29	4.62	
	THIS MONTHS AVERAGE			5 A	4.47	3.22	4.75	
	PENCE PER 1.00%				1.832	1.792	0.272	
	YOUR PENCE PER LITRE				8.1890	5.7702	1.2920	15.2512
CI	NATIONAL MONTHLY AVERAGES				4.75	3.55	4.60	
	National Monthly Averages-For Information			13	3.82	3.12	4.61	

Please refer enquiries relating to the above advice to your Regional Office Tel.　READING (0734) 864242
THE NET RATE SHOWN AGAINST YOUR MILK SUPPLY LINE IS THE ADDITION OF YOUR
PENCE PER LITRE FOR BUTTERFAT,PROTEIN AND LACTOSE.
****
EEC QUOTA - INITIAL PROVISIONAL ALLOCATION

	SUPPLY LITRES	QUOTA LITRES	UNDER - OR OVER + QUOTA
* APR 84	60971	66559	- 5588

*EEC QUOTA APPLIES ON ALL MILK SUPPLIES FROM 2 APRIL. THE SUPPLY LITRES SHOWN
ABOVE EXCLUDE 1 APRIL MILK (CALCULATED AS 1/30 TH OF YOUR MONTHLY SUPPLIES).

QUOTAS - SOME QUESTIONS ANSWERED - PLEASE SEE PAGE 18 OF MILK PRODUCER.

MASTITIS CELL COUNT NOTIFICATION (thousands/ml)

Supply	Sample Date	Cell Count	Annual Average	Change Over past 12 months	
18	04 APR 84	267	327	+ 20	
19	03 APR 84	279	253	- 18	
Notes relating to this Notification are printed on the reverse.		PLOT THIS ON YOUR GRAPH ↑			Please refer any enquiries relating solely to cell count information to: Milk Marketing Board, Veterinary Laboratory, Cleeve House, Lower Wick, Worcester WR2 4NS Tel: Worcester (0905) 424940
NATIONAL AVERAGES - For Information		366	398	- 22	

Figure 6.2　An example of a sale invoice

deducting the cost of purchased and home-grown feeds from the
gross output. It is easy enough to increase gross output per hectare
simply by buying in large quantities of feeds and thereby increasing
stocking density. Any ultimate profit will come from the net
output, i.e. the difference between gross output and cost of
feedingstuffs.

TAX POINT FOR VAT (unless otherwise shown) 16 MAY 84	PRINCIPAL HAMPSHIRE COLLEGE OF AGRICULTURE SPARSHOLT WINCHESTER HANTS	SALE INVOICE 0874843 TO MILK MARKETING BOARD THAMES DITTON SURREY KT7 0EL
188 ⌐63 24 08 50165 YOUR VAT REG No. Please quote when contacting the Board	S021 2NF	

MMB Use Only	VAT Class	DESCRIPTION		LITRES (1 Litre=1.03 Kg.)	Rate p	Credit £	Debit £
6079	ZR	APR MILK SUPPLY	18	16007	15.8451	2536.33	
	ZR	HYGIENE TBC BAND A		16007	0.200	32.01	
	ZR	SEASONALITY ADJUSTMENT		16007	0.500		80.04
	ZR	NET PRICE @ 15.5451 P/L £2488.30					
	ZR	CI/OTHER PREMIUMS		16007	0.300	48.02	
102	ZR	C.I. PUBLICITY		16007	0.015		2.40
	**	CAPITAL CONTRIBUTION		16007	0.046		7.36
101	**	CO-RES LEVY .3394 P/KG 1 APR		534			1.87
101	**	CO-RES LEVY .5091 P/KG		15473			81.14
6716	ZR	APR MILK SUPPLY	19	47067	15.2512	7178.28	
	ZR	HYGIENE TBC BAND A		47067	0.200	94.13	
	ZR	SEASONALITY ADJUSTMENT		47067	0.500		235.34
		NET PRICE @ 14.9512 P/L £7037.07					
	**	CAPITAL CONTRIBUTION		47067	0.046		21.65
101	**	CO-RES LEVY .3394 P/KG 1 APR		1569			5.48
101	**	CO-RES LEVY .5091 P/KG		45498			238.58
						9888.77	673.86
	**	STATEMENT ITEMS £356.08DB					
	ZR	ZERO RATED ITEMS 9570.99					

BALANCE DEBITED FROM MMB INVOICE DATED 16 MAY 84	182.91

30-99-71 00025857 HANTS CNTY CNCL BANK ACCOUNT DETAILS	AMOUNT PAID TO BANK ACCOUNT	£9032.00

TAX POINT FOR VAT (unless otherwise shown) 16 MAY 84	PRINCIPAL HAMPSHIRE COLLEGE OF AGRICULTURE SPARSHOLT WINCHESTER HANTS	SALE INVOICE 0874843 FROM MILK MARKETING BOARD THAMES DITTON SURREY KT7 0EL
211 3035 34 MMB VAT REG. No. 08 50165 Please quote when contacting the Board	S021 2NF	

MMB Use Only	VAT Class	DESCRIPTION		Credit £	Debit £
175	01	APR F.M.R. & C FEES			85.00
189	01	RESULTS NOTIFICATION SERVICE	18		1.00
189	01	RESULTS NOTIFICATION SERVICE	19		1.00
160	01	MAY N.M.R.FEES	18		21.60
160	01	MAY N.M.R.FEES	19		33.65
170	01	GUERNSEY SOCIETY FEES	18		16.81
					159.06
	01	VAT @ 15.00% ON SALES OF £159.06			23.85

THIS AMOUNT DEBITED ON YOUR MILK INVOICE DATED 16 MAY 84	£182.91

For MILK MARKETING BOARD
D. C. BANKS, CHIEF ACCOUNTANT, MILK MARKETING

Please refer enquiries relating to the above Sale Invoices to
Producers Department, M.M.B., Thames Ditton, Surrey, KT7 0EL Tel. No. 01-398-4101

Variable costs

Concentrates and forage costs

As has already been mentioned, margins have narrowed for the dairy industry over recent years. It therefore behoves any producer to keep his costs of production as low as possible. To this end a great deal of importance must be placed upon the need by the farmer to exercise control over concentrate use, which whether purchased or home-grown, is usually the principal item of variable costs incurred in milk production, accounting for some 65–70 per cent or more of these costs. This approach should, however, be part of an overall feeding strategy involving forage use and stocking rate. Concentrates offer an alternative food source within a planned feeding programme and, provided that the nutritional criteria are satisfied, can be used to substitute for other foods. This substitution has not only nutritional but also financial implications for the producer who would be well advised to maximize the use of bulk foods

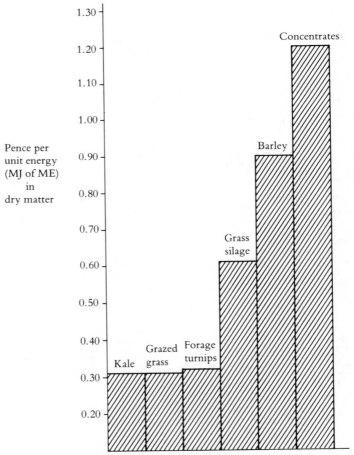

Figure 6.3   Costs of some example foods in pence per MJ of ME in the dry matter. (The relative costs of forage at Henley Manor – 1982–83. Information leaflet, p. 2)

which are cheaper per unit of energy than concentrates. Figure 6.3 illustrates the principle involved.

The relationship between forage and concentrates will, of course, vary according to the stage in the lactation of the dairy cow and the level of yield given. These varying requirements must be accommodated if only in the interests of good husbandry, but ultimately it is possible to review the relationship between forage and concentrate use and its effect on profitability. It is, of course, preferable to manage the relationship by planning for it before the event rather than after. If planning is carried out well in advance, the grazing and conservation requirements can be defined, and with techniques aimed at producing good-quality forage, concentrate use may be optimized with the consequent improving effect upon margin over feed costs per cow. Table 6.6 illustrates the effect of differing energy sources and milk yield upon the margin over feed costs per cow.

The message in Table 6.6 is clear. If a farmer can produce good-quality forage, then the chances are that if he utilizes it fully, reducing reliance on concentrates in the process, he will improve the profitability of the dairy herd. Circumstances may not allow him to feed as much forage as he would desire for various reasons, i.e. lack of land, lack of alternative bulk foods due to availability or price. In these situations he may have to use a higher level of concentrate feeding to maintain gross output up to quota level. Such concentrate feeding is economic up to the point when the cost of extra concentrates is equal to the value of extra milk produced. This is, however, an over-simplification since at certain stages in the feeding of a cow, whether it be by concentrates or not, is for longer-term reasons such as conception, foetal growth and subsequent lactations rather than the immediacy of current milk production. That care should be taken in feeding an expensive commodity such as concentrates is not at issue, since in practice by the time the autumn approaches with its calving and milk-producing activities the 'die', in terms of forage quality and quantity, will have

Table 6.6   Effect of differing energy sources and milk yield on margin over feed costs (per cow)

Milk yield (litres/cow)	Milk sales (£/cow) at 14.5 p/litre	Margin over total feed costs at different percentages of forage to concentrates			
		40/60	50/50	60/40	70/30
4 000	580.00	192.00	241.00	292.00	344.00
4 500	652.50	244.50	297.50	351.50	406.50
5 000	725.00	298.00	354.00	411.00	469.00
5 500	797.50	350.50	410.50	470.50	432.50
6 000	870.00	404.00	467.00	530.00	667.00
6 500	942.50	445.50	513.50	582.50	652.50

Table 6.7   *Margin over concentrates and concentrates per litre*

Performance level Milk yield per cow (litres)	Low 4 500		Average 5 250		High 5 750		Very high 6 250	
	(a)	(b)	(a)	(b)	(a)	(b)	(a)	(b)
	£	kg	£	kg	£	kg	£	kg
1.25 tonne (£194) concs. per cow	526	0.28	646	0.24	726	0.22	806	0.20
1.75 tonne (£271) concs. per cow	449	0.39	569	0.33	649	0.30	729	0.28
2.25 tonne (£349) concs. per cow	371	0.50	491	0.43	571	0.39	651	0.36
2.75 tonne (£426) concs. per cow	—	—	414	0.52	494	0.48	574	0.44

Source: Nix 1983 p. 24.

been cast and the farmer then seeks to monitor the main variable – namely concentrates. This perhaps explains the apparent popularity of the efficiency factor – margin over concentrates – as a guide to herd profitability. Table 6.7 illustrates the relationship between margin over concentrate, or concentrate use per litre of milk produced.

Again, the figures in Table 6.7 indicate that good use of concentrates is an important factor in profitability, but also that equal margins can be achieved at different levels of yield and concentrate feeding. Thus, a sound knowledge of nutrition allied to the production of good-quality forage and the full utilization of grazing is essential if good margins are to be maintained. In many farm situations there is a lot to be gained from reviewing nitrogen use and stocking rate.

During the period 1972–77 an analysis of 845 'herd years' was carried out on ICI Recorded Farms (Hawkins and Rose 1979: 203–8). The findings, which refer to Friesians only, were as follows. That 'the supply of an extra 1 kg N from fertilizer was associated with an average extra yield of 9.9 litres of milk. 4.9 litres of milk were associated with the extra N independently of any simultaneous changes in either stocking rate or concentrate feeding, and 4.5. litres were ascribable to a simultaneous increase in stocking rate.' There was, however, substantial variation in the 'milk yield per kg N' response from year to year.

It was found that the approximate response to an extra 1 kg of concentrate was 1 litre of milk. However, the survey does suggest that the herds surveyed had probably reached the optimum economic feeding level. The effect of quotas must therefore be to depress this level.

If a kilogram of nitrogen costs 35p then a response of 4.9 litres of milk at 12.2p litre is 59.8p. A margin of 24.8p, is obtained providing that no other additional capital inputs are required.

The relationship and break-even point between concentrates and

Table 6.8   The effect of different stocking rates on the gross margin per forage hectare

Forage hectare/cow	0.60	0.50	0.40
Performance level per cow	Gross margin per forage hectare (£)		
Low	651 (390)	770 (385)	938 (375)
Average	768 (460)	900 (450)	1100 (440)
High	835 (500)	960 (480)	1175 (470)
(GM/cow in brackets)			

milk response has already been considered. It should be pointed out that the above work showed a response ratio of 1 : 1. Where these circumstances pertain, then there is clearly a case for exploring the possibility of additional fertilizer nitrogen provided that the increased grass production is exploited through reduced concentrate use or increased stocking rate, or both.

In dairy herd costings there is a correlation between yield and profitability, and it is interesting to note that the highest contribution to milk output per hectare comes from nitrogen use, concentrates per cow and stocking rate. The relationship between stocking rate and gross margin per forage hectare is illustrated in Table 6.8.

Table 6.9 identifies the benefit to the producer of higher stocking rates. The effect that these higher stocking rates have upon individual cow performance is important to note. The trend shown is based upon work done on the effect of increasing stocking rate on milk yield. This information will be of the utmost value to producers wishing to reduce milk output and yet retain margins.

It is apparent from the foregoing remarks on stocking rate, concentrate and forage use that the number of possible combinations of circumstances is as numerous as there are dairy herds.

An attempt has been made to reduce the variables in this complex relationship by compiling a nutritional 'balance sheet'

Table 6.9   The effect of increasing stocking rate on milk yield (using a spring-calving head)

	Stocking rate (grazing)	
First year, stocking rate (cows/ha)	4.9	6.4
Milk yield at grazing (kg/ha)	14 064	16 502
Milk yield at grazing (kg/cow)	2 847	2 571
Second year stocking rate (cows/ha)	4.3	5.6
Milk yield at pasture (kg/ha)	13 893	16 985
Milk yield at pasture (kg/cow)	3 181	2 963

Source: F. J. Gordon, *Management of the spring calving herd*. Agricultural Research Institute of N. Ireland, Hillsborough, Co. Down, May 1979.

Table 6.10   *Energy production from forage (expressed in gigajoules)*

	Top 25%* of herds	Bottom 25% of herds
Energy requirements per cow		
Maintenance plus calf production	25.0	25.0
Milk	31.8	26.5
Total	56.8	51.5
Energy supply per cow		
Concentrates and purchased bulk feed	23.4	21.4
Forage (by difference)	33.4	30.1
Stocking rate (LSU/ha)	2.51	1.55
Forage energy utilized per hectare	84	47

* Selected by gross margin per hectare.
Source: A. H. Poole, J. A. Craven and S. J. Mabey, *An analysis of F.M.S. costed farms 1982–83*. Report No. 39, Dec. 1983, MMB.

aimed at establishing the efficiency of utilization of forage on the farm. The steps in this calculation are as follows:
(a) the herd's maintenance and production needs in energy terms are established;
(b) the energy contribution to these needs from concentrate sources is evaluated:
(c) the productive capacity of the farm's grassland is categorized;
(d) the relationship between the energy potential of the grassland and the cows' remaining energy requirements to be met from forage is established.

The answer, expressed in gigajoules per hectare and termed 'efficiency of utilization', will give a guide to grassland utilization.

That there is a relationship between forage utilization and profitability is further illustrated by the figures shown in Table 6.10.

Miscellaneous variable costs
It is always difficult to pinpoint any single factor in this group of costs and to isolate it for specific criticism. These costs are not very controllable and relative to the feeding aspects of the dairy cow are of minor importance only. However, they can erode profits and unduly high levels per cow should be investigated, particularly veterinary costs. Average figures per cow are approximately:

	£
Veterinary and medicines	16
Service and recording fees	14
Dairy stores, etc.	25

If these items when grouped are greatly in excess of £60/cow then further investigation may be of value. High veterinary charges may indicate some basic fault in stockmanship, herd management or policy.

Service and recording charges will vary slightly according to the proportion of AI and nominated AI services, system of recording and size of herd.

Dairy stores are very difficult to pinpoint accurately and a very efficient system of accounting and stocktaking is required if the trading account figure for these commodities is to be really reliable. Economies may be effected in this direction, particularly in the field of cleaning material and detergents, but their effect on the final gross margin will be small.

Forage costs (see concentrates and forage costs)
Only the annual variable costs of grassland and forage crops are included here and comprise:
(a) seeds;
(b) fertilizers;
(c) sprays;
(d) consumable materials used in fodder conservation and utilization;
(e) casual labour and contract (e.g. silage and haymaking).

Forage costs are difficult to standardize and vary enormously according to situation, soil, climate, etc. but as stocking rate increases, forage costs are bound to rise not only per hectare but also per cow. The figures in Table 6.11 provide a guide to average lowland conditions.

As stocking density increases, the main cost to rise will be that of fertilizers, particularly of nitrogenous fertilizers.

Forage costs per cow increase with increased stocking density, and yield per cow at grass declines (see Tables 6.8 and 6.9). Consequently gross margin per cow will decrease with increased stocking density, but gross margin per hectare will rise.

Table 6.11 Forage costs at various stocking rates

	Seeds and fertilizer costs	
Forage hectare/cow	(1) £/ha	(2) £/cow
0.570	94	52
0.475	128	60
0.400	160	63
0.350	208	72

Source: Nix 1983, p. 28.

Since forage costs can amount to £70/cow or even more, they account for a large proportion of the variable costs incurred by the dairy enterprise. However, in gross margin analysis, forage variable costs are usually calculated from the difference between total seeds, fertilizers, sprays and other crop costs, and those allocated directly to cash crops. They are thus subject to accumulative error and must be interpreted with reservation.

Because of the difficulty of obtaining sufficient information upon which to calculate forage costs, there is temptation to base results on 'standard costs' of forage production. Such results can seldom be accurate and should be treated circumspectly.

Fixed costs

The basic principles affecting fixed costs have already been discussed in Chapter 3.

Final profit for any business or enterprise will depend upon the difference between the gross margin obtained and the fixed costs incurred. The dangers of careless gross margin planning have already been discussed in Chapter 2. However, it is again emphasized that while it is convenient for some purposes to regard fixed costs as a separate unit they are by no means constant and will almost certainly change with changes in stocking density and changing proportions of farm enterprises.

Most of the dairy units have high fixed costs which, within reasonable parameters, will not be greatly affected by variations in the level of milk sales. However, there is a lesson to be learnt from the effect of yield upon fixed costs per litre. If fixed costs were, say, £280 a cow for a 6 500–litre yield, the fixed costs would be 4.3p/litre, whereas at 4 400 litres the fixed costs per litre would be 6.4p – an extra 2.1p a litre in favour of the higher-yielding herd which must constitute a worthwhile gain.

Labour costs per cow may vary from £130 to £140/cow. Again the level of production affects the unit cost per litre; i.e. at 5 000 litres the labour cost per litre is 2.6p and 2.8p respectively. At 6 500 litres, however, it is 2.0p and 2.2p respectively.

More cows per hectare will usually result in higher fixed costs per hectare, even though some items, e.g. rent, rates, overheads, etc. remain constant. The full extent to which fixed costs will be affected by changes in stocking density will depend on changes in the actual size of the herd. If, for example, an improved stocking rate enables the dairy herd to be concentrated on to a smaller area without altering its size, then total fixed costs will not change. If, on the other hand, an increase in stocking density is achieved by increasing the size of the herd, then extra capital buildings charges will be incurred and fixed costs will rise. The general trend towards an increase in the size of dairy herd has meant that this has been the case in the past but is almost certainly not going to occur in the foreseeable future.

The fixed-cost items which will be most affected by changes in the dairy enterprise are:

1. Labour;
2. Buildings costs;
3. Capital charges.

In planning farm policy involving the dairy enterprise, it is necessary to consider very carefully any changes that are likely to occur to the fixed costs, since these will represent a large proportion of the total cost changes and will have an important bearing upon the ultimate level of profit.

Do not under any circumstances plan changes involving the dairy enterprise solely upon the basis of changes in gross margins.

Ways in which profitability may be maintained or improved

The imposition of a milk quota on 2 April 1984 has added a new dimension to the many problems that milk producers face in trying to maintain or increase profits. The ways in which herds can be managed in order to stay within their quota are well documented but basically comprise the three following options or any combination:

(a) lower milk yield per cow;
(b) fewer dairy cows;
(c) alternative uses for surplus milk.

Although the alternatives may be easily reviewed on their own it would be unwise to consider them, or the dairy herd, in isolation from the farm business as a whole since the ramifications of such a policy as quota constraint are considerable. The quota restrictions add an additional constraint to be taken account of by management amongst all the other existing technical and financial constraints.

The scope for maintaining or improving profitability must lie within the twin fields of containing fixed costs and the improved utilization of forage (see Tables 6.6, 6.10 and Fig. 6.3). The differences between the top 25 per cent and the bottom 25 per cent of producers illustrate the scope for improvement (see Table 6.12).

Before we explore this area, it may be worth reviewing the differences between the most profitable and least profitable herds as depicted in Table 6.12.

Table 6.12   Comparison of the top and bottom 25% of March 1982 results selected by gross margin per hectare (excluding Channel Island herds)

Number of herds	Top 25% 262	Bottom 25% 262
Physical results		
Herd size	126	95
Yield per cow (litres)	5 888	4 867
Concentrate use per cow (kg)	1 929	1 805
Concentrate use per litre (kg)	0.33	0.37
Stocking rate (LSU/ha)	2.58	1.63
Nitrogen use per ha (kg)	326	212
Summer milk (%)	49	51
Dry cow (%)	14	16
Replacement rate (%)	21	21
Financial results		
Output per cow (£)		
Milk sales	862	700
Calf sales	69	62
Less herd depreciation	31	42
Gross output	900	720
Variable costs per cow (£)		
Concentrates	267	254
Purchased bulk feed	14	15
Forage	62	63
Sundries	50	51
Total variable costs	393	383
Gross margin per cow (£)	507	337
Gross margin per ha (£)	1 308	549
Margin over concentrates per cow (£)	595	446
Milk price received per litre (p)	14.63	14.37
Concentrate cost per tonne (£)	139	141

Source: A. H. Poole, J. A. Craven and S. J. Mabey, An analysis of FMS costed farms 1982–83. Report No. 39, Dec. 1983.

As Table 6.12 shows the better herds were larger, produced more milk per cow, stocked more heavily and used more nitrogen. They also fed slightly more concentrates per head, but the lower use per litre, 0.33 kg as against 0.37 kg, suggested more efficient utilization, and greater dependence on forage.

What scope, therefore, is there for the producer who wishes to make realistic improvements in order to increase profitability? The following suggestions are based on the information given in Table 6.12 given the current EEC policy.

Milk yield per cow.   Unless a producer reduces the size of his herd dramatically the scope for raising the volume of milk is, at the moment non-existent. However, there is scope for improving the quality of the milk output by concentrating on the yield of constituents (see Table 6.4). The potential contribution that quality can make to profitability should not be neglected. For example a difference of 0.2 per cent butter fat, at 5 500 litres yield for 120 cows would be worth £2 148. The aim must be to optimize the production of the constituent values of milk without excessive loss of volume within the quota.

Stocking rate.   Previous observations have clearly illustrated the value of higher nitrogen use allied to heavier stocking rates, and this pattern is reinforced by the differences between the top and bottom 25 per cent. Without doubt forage use must major in the maintenance or improvement of profit in British dairy herds whether it be by increased nitrogen use, increased stocking rates or the use of such techniques as buffer feeding (see Table 6.6).

Concentrate use.   Although the higher-performance herds fed more concentrates per cow, the concentrate use per litre was some 0.04 kg/litre lower. If the grassland utilization and forage quality had allowed a similar saving per litre in the lower-performance herds, then a saving of some £2 608 could have been made (0.04 kg × 4 867 litres × £141.00 tonne × 95 cows).

Calving index.   The dry cow (per cent) figure indicates room for improvement in the lower-performance group, since it stands at 16 per cent compared with 14 per cent. The scope for increased output, which would amount to some £1 329, is related to Table 6.12.

Finishing cull cows.   Recent MLC trial results indicate that there is a potential gross margin of £116/cow to be made over a period of approximately four months. Care in the selection of culls to be finished is needed and the possibility of incurring charges on as yet unsold culls must not be overlooked. In relation to Table 6.12 and by only finishing ten of the culls it is possible to generate an additional £1 160.

These observations are by no means exhaustive, and it is up to the reader to pursue them further, but it is unlikely that all these improvements would apply to any one farm at any one time, or that none of them apply to any farm. They do, however, represent realistic improvements which the best herds can and do surpass.

Very few farms can claim to have no scope for improvements which will lead to significantly increased margins.

THE DAIRY YOUNG STOCK ENTERPRISE

Statistics for the National Dairy Herd suggest that the average productive life of a dairy cow is only 4 years. Replacement heifers must therefore be available if the total number of dairy cows is to be maintained, and on the basis of future numbers 45 000 – 55 000 heifers will be required annually.

As this number of animals represents no small proportion of our total grazing livestock, it is necessary to look critically at replacement rearing as an enterprise.

The numbers of replacements required for a herd each year will depend on the size of the herd, whether the herd is constant or increasing in size and the rate of replacement.

The rate of replacement is closely linked with culling policy and will depend upon a wide range of factors.

The basic purpose of culling is to remove animals which are uneconomic in order to maintain or increase the productivity of the herd.

Principles of culling

Certain basic principles must be borne in mind when culling stock:
1. A rigorous system of culling will increase the depreciation rate of the herd and must be justified by increased productivity.
2. Removal of animals by culling will not result in a reduction of fixed costs. If culling leaves a smaller number of animals, then each must carry a larger share of fixed costs.

   Total herd output must therefore be maintained if the level of productivity is to be maintained or improved. This usually means that total numbers must be kept up.

   There is always a danger that while output per animal may be increased by culling, output for the herd or flock may be reduced.
3. When replacing an animal always replace with something better. Replacing an old cow with a heifer will result in an increase in costs, so unless the heifer's first lactation is better than the potential next lactation of the cow she replaces, then the old cow should be kept. For example, an old cow giving 4000 litres/year is a better financial proposition than a heifer giving the same

yield, providing that she remains healthy and that the variable costs remain the same.

Bearing these principles in mind, it is now necessary to consider the factors which affect the rate of replacement in practice. These can be broadly subdivided as husbandry factors and economic factors.

Husbandry factors affecting rate of replacement

In practice, the main causes for replacement of stock will come under this heading. There is usually less difficulty in deciding whether or not to keep an animal where such factors are involved since the answer is normally clear-cut.

Husbandry factors are as follows:
1. Disease, e.g. mastitis, brucellosis;
2. Infertility – cows persistently returning to service;
3. Incapacity, e.g. legs and feet;
4. Injury, e.g. cut teats etc;
5. Temperament;
6. Slow milker;
7. Genetic quality, e.g. an animal of exceptional past performance may be kept, in spite of other failings, in order to produce further stock.

Economic factors affecting rate of replacement

In any herd there will be a level of production below which it is not worth keeping an animal. It is necessary, therefore, to set a minimum tolerance level for both quality and yield below which an animal must be replaced.

The acceptable level of milk quality will depend on the type of herd. If compositional quality is a problem, then any individual animals which are particularly poor in this respect may have to go.

Yield is the main factor to consider since this has the greatest single effect upon output.

The problem now is to determine where to draw the line. What is an economic yield and what is not? Once again there is no universal answer to this question. The economic level can only be assessed in the light of the particular circumstances of the individual farm and will depend upon the following factors:
1. *The level of fixed and overhead costs incurred by the farm.* Where the fixed cost background is high then high yields are essential if a margin is to be obtained. If fixed costs are low then a lower

Table 6.13   *Net herd replacement gain/costs*

	Costs (£/cow/year)			
	Friesians			
	Example 1		Example 2	
	£	£	£	£
Cost of replacements ¼ herd/year	at 500	125	600	150
Less value of cull cows ¼ herd/year (allowing for casualties)	at 360	90	280	70
Herd depreciation		35		80
Less value of calves (allowing for deaths)		70		65
Net replacement gain/costs		35		15
(+) (−)		(+)		(−)

level of yield can be tolerated as it will still leave a margin.
2. *The amount of capital available.* Replacement stock will require working capital. If this is very limited, then it may be necessary to cull more lightly and to accept a lower level of yield.
3. *The cost of making a replacement.* Net herd replacement gain/costs are summarized in Table 6.13 and depend on three main factors:

Cull value of the animal replaced
This depends on:

Age and condition of animal.

Breed of animal. Heavier, fleshier animals, e.g. Friesians and Shorthorns, command a much better cull price than the lighter and more angular Ayrshire or Channel Island breeds.

Method of sale. This must be budgeted according to local preference, time of year and feed available. It is possible to sell bare as a 'chopper' or freshly calved with or without calf, or it may even pay to feed the cow up and sell her fat. (See p. 167).

Year and month sold. Fat and cull cow prices vary with season, but usually follow the general trend of the beef market, i.e. maximum price March to April, minimum price September to October. Exports of fat cows to the Continent can have a very significant effect on this general pattern which will be reflected in yearly variations.

Sale value of calves

This depends on:

Age and condition when sold.

Breed. Beef cross calves and those suitable for intensive rearing, e.g. Friesian, South Devon, command the best prices. Channel Island calves are worth little.

Sex. Bull calves are preferred to heifers for fattening.

Time of year. Calf prices are usually at their best in the spring.

The cost of the replacement heifer

If the replacement heifer is reared on the farm, then the costs of providing a down-calver can be subdivided between fixed costs and variable costs. The principles affecting fixed costs and forage costs have already been discussed in the dairy enterprise study. Of the remaining variable costs, by far the most important is that of foodstuffs. Rearing methods vary enormously and it is not the brief of this chapter to explore all the technical aspects of calf and heifer rearing, but a rough guide to the variable costs incurred in rearing a heifer on a conventional 5-week weaning system to calve down, in the autumn, at 2 years of age is given in Table 6.14. The costs illustrated in Table 6.14 are derived from recorded data, but it is possible, by using grazing livestock units, to assess the land required for rearing a heifer.

Table 6.14   Variable costs for rearing autumn-calving heifers at 2 years of age (per head)

	£	£
Calves		
Calf rearing – milk substitute 18 kg at 76 p/kg	13.68	
– concentrates 460 kg at 17 p/kg	78.20	
– hay 440 kg (see forage costs)		
Yearlings – concentrates 355 kg at £155 tonne	55.03	
– hay 152 kg included in		
– silage 4.75 tonnes the forage		
costs below		
Forage costs (stocking rate 0.8 ha per heifer		
reared)	88.60	
Straw – 1 tonne at £15 tonne	15.00	
Vet. and medicine and miscellaneous	25.09	
Cost to calving at 2 years of age		275.60

Grazing livestock units for young stock are as follows:

0–1 year old   0.4 grazing livestock unit
1–2 years old   0.6 grazing livestock unit
2+ years old   0.8 grazing livestock unit

For every heifer required to join the dairy herd each year it will be necessary to have on the farm at any one time a succession of 'followers' consisting of one heifer-in-calf backed up by younger animals coming forward to calve in subsequent years, i.e. heifer 1–2 years old, heifer under 1 year old.

The necessary young stock to provide one down-calving heifer each year is known as one replacement unit and contains the following number of grazing livestock units:

		g.l.u.'s
	1 heifer 2 years and over × 0.8 × ½ = 0.4	
1 Replacement unit =	1 heifer 1–2 years × 0.6 = 0.6	
	1 heifer 0–12 months × 0.4 = 0.4	
	Total = 1.4	

So for each heifer that calves down, it is necessary to carry 1.4 grazing livestock units of young stock. At a stocking rate of 0.57 forage ha per livestock unit this would represent a requirement of 0.8 ha to rear each heifer. The forage cost incurred on this area must therefore be included in the variable costs of producing a replacement heifer.

Gross margins from rearing dairy followers

Once the variable costs of heifer rearing have been calculated, it should be possible to credit this group of livestock with a gross margin, provided that a satisfactory figure can be assessed for their gross output.

Since no actual sale takes place when a heifer is brought into the herd, the gross output per heifer reared has to be based on an estimate of the market value of the down-calving heifer, less the value of the calf and an allowance for mortality and losses incurred during the rearing period.

An approximate gross margin account for rearing a heifer is as follows:

£

Market value of down-calver
(allowing for culls)   480

less value of calf + losses	70
Gross output/down-calving heifer	410
less food and miscellaneous costs	187
Gross margin/heifer reared	223
excluding forage costs	

From this figure it is possible to calculate the final gross margin and the gross margin per forage hectare from dairy replacements.

For example: if the stocking rate is 0.57 ha per livestock unit then 1 replacement unit requires 1.4 × 0.57 = 0.8 forage ha

$$\therefore \text{Gross margin per forage hectare} = \frac{£223}{0.8} \text{ less forage costs per hectare}$$

Assuming forage costs of £110.75/ha at this level of stocking density,

$$\text{Gross margin per forage hectare} = \frac{£223}{0.8} - 110.75$$

$$\therefore \text{Gross margin per forage hectare} = £168$$

Similarly, for a range of stocking densities at the levels of forage costs used in the dairy enterprise study, gross margins per forage hectare from dairy replacements are as shown in Table 6.15. These gross margins per forage hectare are obviously much lower than those obtained from dairy cows at the same stocking densities and at an average level of output.

Assuming that the rate of replacement is 25 per cent, then for every four cows in the herd one replacement unit must be carried. Therefore for every 4 livestock units as cows, 1.4 livestock units are required as followers.

Table 6.15   Gross margins from rearing dairy young stock

Ha/livestock unit	0.4	0.49	0.57	0.69
	£	£	£	£
Gross margin/replacement unit	223	223	223	223
Gross margin per ha = $\frac{223}{1.4 \times \text{ha per livestock unit}}$	398.21	325.07	279.45	230.85
less Forage cost/ha	200.00	145.00	110.75	65.20
Gross margin/forage ha	198.21	180.07	168.70	165.65

NB. It is interesting to note the gross margin per forage hectare at the highest level of stocking density (being the resultant of the level of gross margin per replacement unit, stocking rate and the level of forage costs per hectare) in relation to the second highest level of stocking density.

That is: for every 20 livestock units (cows)
7 livestock units (followers) are required.

Therefore at the same overall level of stocking density, for every 57 ha devoted to dairy cows, 20 ha will be required for heifer rearing. Therefore, 100 cows with their followers will require as much land as 135 cows with replacements bought in.

When replacement stock and dairy cows are competing for the same land, the advisability of rearing replacements compared with buying in replacements needs to be examined critically.

The following partial budget is based on the assumptions that the dairy herd, at Littledown Farm (see Ch. 1), is to be reduced as the result of quota constraints and that consideration is being given to the possibility of buying in all the dairy replacements needed for the diminished dairy herd whilst growing wheat on the 32 ha released. Labour savings on the livestock enterprises would be absorbed by the additional cereals and there is sufficient storage to cope with the extra wheat grain. The basic data is as given in Chapter 1.

Extra costs	£	*Costs saved*	£
Variable costs of growing an additional 32 ha of W. wheat:		*Variable costs of 9 dairy cows:*	
		Purchased feed at £277/cow × 9	2 493
Seed at £42/ha	1 344	Home grown feed at £32.30/cow × 9	290.70
Fertilizers at £85/ha	2 720		
Sprays at £70/ha	2 240	Vet. medicines at £15/cow × 9	135
Combining costs at £4/hour × 35 hours	140	AI and recording fees at £15.38/cow × 9	138.42
Drying costs for 240 tonne at £3/tonne	720	Sundries at £16.0 cow × 9	144
Replacement heifers for herd of 121 cows, 31 at £600 each	18 600	Forage costs at £88.53/cow × 9	796.77
		Variable costs of existing youngstock enterprise:	
		Purchased feed	6 125
		Vet. medicines	485
		AI and recording fees	225
Revenue foregone		*Extra revenue*	
Milk from 9 cows at £802.70 each	7 224.30	Sales of wheat at 7.5 tonnes/ha × £120/tonne × 32 ha.	28 800
Share of cull cows at £48.46/cow × 9	436.14	Sales extra of 29 heifer calves from 121 cows at £70 each	2 030
Share of calf sales at £55.38/cow × 9	498.42		
Increased income	7 740.03		
	41 662.89		41 662.89

Under these conditions, the farmer would be £7 740 a year better off if he were to give up rearing replacements and buy in all his down-calving heifers at £600 a head even with the dairy herd reduced to 121 cows. A considerable gain, bearing in mind that the wheat gross margin per hectare is lower than that of the dairy cows.

Many farmers, in spite of the cash benefits to be gained by alternative enterprise developments wish to rear their own replacements for many good reasons. If there are no opportunity costs related to the alternative use of the land occupied by the replacements then the question of land use becomes less critical. If, however, the circumstances, as shown by the budget, prevail, then a farmer who wishes to rear his own replacements must take steps to reduce the age at first calving and step up the stocking rate in order to avoid the profit generated by the dairy herd being diluted by an indifferent replacement unit performance.

Three possible alternatives that may be worth considering by the farmer faced with how to deal with the question of 'to rear or not to rear' are:

1. Buy in all replacements;
2. Reduce the cost of rearing replacements;
3. Have replacements reared away from the farm on a contract basis.

Buying in replacements

Although this appears the more profitable alternative in the budget, it would only be so if level of yield were maintained and the replacement rate were to remain at 25 per cent. In practice this may not be achieved as stock, whether bought in as down-calving heifers or at a later stage, tend to be of unknown quality and can never be expected to yield above breed average. It is difficult, in these circumstances, to carry on any programme of genetic improvement.

There is also always a danger of introducing disease when buying in stock, and a change to a policy of buying in all replacements is frequently accompanied by an increase in the herd replacement rate.

Prices of down-calving heifers vary enormously, it is impossible to rely upon stock being available when required and travelling round to markets and sales in the hope of finding suitable stock at a reasonable price can be costly, frustrating and a time-consuming occupation.

Reducing the cost of rearing replacements

This can be attempted in the following four ways:

1. *Reducing food costs.*
   (a) There are many and varied early weaning techniques that are available to the calf rearer and savings can be made in the

expensive area of whole milk and milk substitutes. However, although the development of different methods can result in savings in food costs and labour, the trend to calving down heifers at an earlier age has led to the need to feed at higher levels in order to achieve growth targets.

(b)   Early rumen development and greater reliance on high-quality grazing and forage can result in reduced concentrate costs, but unless this is matched with good grazing and conservation management together with the necessary level of fertilizer the savings can only be obtained at the expense of the stocking rate.

2. *Reducing land requirements.* The use of higher stocking rates and non-conservation foods, such as straw and a urea-based balancer ration in a cereal nut, can provide an alternative system for the farmer on a limited land area. However, although the dependence on land is reduced, there is a real risk of the cost per head increasing.

3. *Reducing time to calving.* Unless it is policy to calve a dairy herd all the year round most producers will aim to calve the herd in the autumn or the spring depending upon the inherent capabilities of the farm and the farmer's preferred production philosophy. In herds where the calving pattern slips it is possible to calve the heifers down at 2 and some at 2½ years of age. This flexibility does have its advantages even if the reason for its existence is undesirable and is indeed avoidable given the results of ADAS trials using progesterone where a calving index of 338 days has been achieved. The financial benefits of calving a heifer at 2 instead of 2½ or 3 years of age are well known, but carry the penalty of having to achieve a specific minimum target weight at calving if the growth and future lactations of the heifer are not to be permanently impaired.

4. *Reducing fixed costs.* The use of once-a-day feeding and disposable strawbale houses can considerably reduce fixed costs in calf rearing. Savings in labour can be substantial at all stages, as an examination of Table 6.16 will show.

Table 6.16   *Labour requirements for dairy followers*

(Per 'replacement unit', i.e. calf + yearling + heifer)	Labour hours per month	
	Average	*Premium*
During winter	3.7	2.1
During summer	1.4	0.9

Source: Nix 1983, p. 77.

Contract rearing

There are many benefits to be obtained from getting someone else to rear dairy replacements on a contract basis. This enables the breeder to follow a planned breeding programme of livestock improvement since his own calves will eventually return to the herd. With a well-organized contract scheme it is possible to plan the availability of replacement heifers at a reasonable cost, to avoid buying in diseases and to make the best possible use of all suitable land by stocking it with dairy cows and maximizing its output.

The system should also be of mutual benefit to both the breeder and the rearer. A farmer with limited capital may well find contract rearing of heifers to be a profitable way of using land and making a living without heavy investment in stock.

Many different contract-rearing systems are at present operating satisfactorily, and can be considered broadly in two categories:
1. where the breeder retains ownership of the heifer and pays the rearer to keep the animal until it is ready to return home;
2. where the rearer buys the heifer from the breeder but the breeder has the first option of buying her back.

An actual working example of each of these two systems is summarized below.

Example I

Breeder retains ownership of calf.
Calf is in the charge of the rearer from 10 days to at least 15 months.
Calves taken by rearer in autumn and returned to breeder in 15–18 months later.
Breeder pays rearer on following scale (Nix 1983, charges are approximate):

10–14 days to 6 months old	– £26 per month
6 months onwards	– £9 per month (in summer)
	– £26 per month (in winter)

As the rearer has no capital to bear, he supplies transport and pays veterinary and medicinal costs. Rearer refunds breeder for calf losses or replaces calf. Receipts for culls go to breeder, while he and rearer share the cost of the replacement calf equally.

The costs per heifer reared on the above system would be as follows:

		£
10–14 days to 6 months old	= 5.5 months × £26 =	143
6 months to near calving	= 18 months × £14.66 =	263.88 £406.88.

Allowances for culls and subsequent calf replacements would add to this cost.

An alternative arrangement would be as follows:

Calf 10 days to 3 months   – £80
3 months to near calving   – £ 9   month (summer)
                                – £26   month (winter)

The cost per heifer on the above arrangement would be, for an autumn–born calf, as follows:

Calf 10 days to 3 months   – £ 80
3 months (winter)   – £ 78
6 months (summer)   – £ 54
6 months (winter)   – £156
6 months (summer)   – £ 54   £422.

Although this is slightly dearer than the previous system, the rearer is bearing all costs and losses. The breeder is of course still retaining ownership.

Example II

The breeder sells the calf to the rearer at an agreed price. The rearer then gains ownership and consequently bears all costs and losses. When the heifers are reared the breeder has the first option on their purchase. Prices paid for the heifer vary, but may be £550 above the cost of the calf for Friesians and £330 for Jerseys. Transport arrangements are usually that the animals are collected and paid for by the purchasers in each case.

It is essential at the outset of such an undertaking to draw up a comprehensive contract agreement to be signed by both parties, i.e. the breeder and the rearer. Numbers of points need to be covered by this agreement and an example of a typical contract is reproduced below.

Suggested contract for heifer rearing

1. The breeder will retain ownership of the heifer.
2. An instalment system of payment will be undertaken, e.g. 3 months, 6 months or even 1 month.
3. The owner to have right of access to inspect the heifers at any time and the right to withdraw the animals if in his opinion the husbandry is not satisfactory. Any argument to be referred to an independent arbitrator, e.g. cattle valuer or auctioneer.
4. Any outstanding payments to be made before an animal is removed.

5.★　Reciprocal visits of veterinary surgeons to be made to establish suitability of rearing farm and risk of introduction of disease from the owner's farm.

6.　The rearer will be responsible for having all calves vaccinated against brucellosis under the Ministry of Agriculture, Fisheries and Food Scheme. Other precautions, e.g. against husk, warble fly, etc. could also be undertaken and presumably paid for by the owner.

7.　The rearer will be responsible in the case of sickness, for calling the vet and also notifying the owner. It should be decided who will pay the veterinary fees: normally it would be the rearer. Any outbreaks of disease should be reported promptly.

8.　The rearer will be responsible for getting the heifer in calf, but the owner will decide when the heifer will be served and with which bull.

9.　The owner may remove the heifer, when springing to calve, in order to acclimatize to the dairy herd environment and to allow for additional feeding.

10.　Should the heifer, at any age, prove to be unfit to rear further, it may be removed by the owner on payment of any outstanding charge.

11.　If for any reason the heifer dies on the rearer's farm, the rearer loses all his payment for that particular instalment period. A veterinary certificate could be obtained. If negligence is established, the rearer should reimburse the owner for all payments to date *and* the value of the calf when taken. If the heifer is injured or killed outside the rearer's farm (e.g. the New Forest) the full loss to the owner will be met by the rearer. (The rearer would normally insure against this risk.)

12.　Feeding will be left to the discretion of the rearer; but the system of feeding will, presumably, have been agreed by the owner before the calf is placed on the rearer's farm.

13.★　Every effort will be made to get the heifer in calf. If necessary the fertility of the bull should be checked before use. Pregnancy diagnosis could be made by the owner. The rearer will contact the owner as soon as possible if he has any reason to suspect infertility and/or abortion.

14.　Transport to and from the rearing farm will be met by the owner.

15.　The calf from the calved heifer will be the property of the owner of the heifer.

16.　The identification of the heifer will be made before placing on the rearing farm, e.g. by ear tags, cold branding or by the usual breed–identification sketch prepared by the owner, signed by the rearer, and retained by the owner.

17. The rearer has the right to refuse taking a particular animal for rearing.
18. The contract to run in the first instance for a minimum of 2 years, thereafter renewable annually.

Signed. . . . . (Owner)

. . . . (Rearer)

*Note. It is recommended that the veterinary surgeons for each party should in fact meet each other. It is impossible to eliminate all risks of disease, but providing one accepts that they are not going to be transmitted deliberately the matter should be covered in 5, 8 and 13, i.e. the owner deciding which bull is used (if AI is used the risk is negligible) together with the veterinary surgeons meeting to discuss the risk of the introduction of disease.

7 LIVESTOCK STUDIES: NON-DAIRY ENTERPRISES

BEEF PRODUCTION

In common with other livestock enterprises, the beef enterprise suffers from periodic ups and downs which, because of the long-term nature of the production cycle, tends to swing over decades rather than months and produces extremes of financial reward. In the 1970s prices rose until 1973, considered by many to be a boom period, to be followed by a slump in 1974 which heralded a prolonged period of poor profitability until 1978 and 1979 when the price in real terms for beef rose (adjusted by the Retail Price Index). Since then prices have dropped below the 1977 level. Breeding beef cow numbers have declined since 1978 whilst feeding cattle numbers have hovered between 8.7 and 8.6 thousand over the same period. In the UK affected as it is by the Common Agricultural Policy, it is expected that there will be a slight increase in beef production. This growth is expected to be in the order of less than 1 per cent per year and is not expected to change the current level of 98 per cent self-sufficiency in the EEC countries. Enlargement of the EEC in the 1980s could hold some promise since Greece (already in), Spain and Portugal are net importers of beef. However, the share of beef in the EEC meat market is declining and is expected to drop further as the effects of perceived price and the preference by young housewives for pigmeat and poultry are felt. This decline is expected to result in a drop from 30 per cent in 1980 to 26 per cent by the mid-1980s. This figure is supported by some economists who predict that household beef consumption, in the UK will, by the mid-1980s, be some 10 per cent below the 1972–75 period.

Altogether this and many other predictions paint a gloomy future for beef production, both in this country and world-wide. Even a rise in the world beef prices is not likely to affect prices within the EEC which maintains prices well above world levels. It is likely that the overriding dominant factor affecting beef production will be economic growth within and without the EEC. For those sceptics who have seen the theories of many economists dashed against the 'rocks' of the beef market there may be some basis in taking a hopeful view and being prepared for an upswing, but the odds against such optimism being fulfilled are high.

The economics of beef production are considered in two broad sections: beef breeding herds and beef fattening systems.

Beef breeding herds

Numbers of beef cows kept primarily for the production of beef calves have shown a steady decline since the early 1970s. This has been in response to the declining profitability of such enterprises.

Single suckling herds

The majority of beef breeding herds fall into this category and have followed a traditional system of spring calving to produce a weaned calf for sale as a store animal by the following autumn. This has been the practice with most hill and moorland breeding herds for generations and the store calves produced are usually taken on to arable units for fattening.

In recent years, however, there has been a greater tendency to adopt, wherever possible, an autumn calving policy for single suckling herds. The advantages of such a policy are:

1. A bigger and better calf is produced for the calf sales in the following autumn.
2. The calf, being older, is better able to utilize spring and early summer grazing.
3. Calves are usually stronger at birth due to a higher plane of nutrition in late pregnancy on summer and autumn pasture.
4. More milk is produced by the dam, and the spring grass gives a boost to the dam's milk production which can be fully utilized by the calf.
5. There is generally a lower mortality rate for both calves and cows, provided that shelter and supplementary feeding are available in mid-winter. Calving in the autumn does not coincide with the period of maximum risk of hypomagnesaemia.

The disadvantages of autumn calving are:

1. It is necessary to provide more shelter and more supplementary feed to calves and cows during winter. This involves additional

expense and may well eliminate the possibility of autumn calving on many true hill farms.

2. Cows must conceive at the most difficult time of the year, i.e. January and February for September and October calvings. Spring calving is more natural and allows bulling at a time when fertility is naturally at its highest.

The financial aspects of these two contrasting systems are clearly illustrated in Table 7.1 where the result of a higher calf sale and its effect on gross margin is demonstrated. It is interesting to note that the 'top third' herds (not shown) used similar amounts of fertilizer but achieved better stocking rates, obtained higher calf sale weights and were more economical on concentrate usage.

A third alternative which has been put forward has been the case for the summer calving herd. The advantages of such a policy are:

1. Cows calve when the weather is clement and less likely to lead to calf losses.

Table 7.1   Gross margin standards (average) for single suckling herds

	Lowland		
Autumn calving		*Spring calving*	
	Financial results (£ per cow put to bull)		
Calf sales	310	(0.92 calves, 232 kg, 98.7 p/kg)	229
(0.92 calves, 325 kg, 95.4 p/kg)			
Cow subsidy	11		11
Less			
Herd replacement	30		22
Gross output	291		218
Cow concentrates			
(222 kg at £120/tonne)	27	(117 kg at £120/tonne)	14
Calf concentrates	19		
(150 kg at £125/tonne)		(26 kg at £117/tonne)	3
Other purchased feed	16		8
Forage variable costs	44		38
Total feed and forage	106		63
Vet. and med. costs	9		8
Bedding	8		6
Miscellaneous costs	5		2
Total variable costs	128		79
Gross margin per cow	163		139
Gross margin per hectare	293		278
Stocking rates			
(cows per hectare)	1.8		2.0
N fertilizer (kg/ha)	154		132

Source: MLC. *Results for recorded suckler herds 1982.* Data Sheet 83/3

*Table 7.2   Gross margin standards (average) for summer calving single suckling lowland herds
Financial results (£ per cow put to bull)*

Calf sales	268
(0.93 calves, 226 kg, 100.8 p/kg)	11
Cow subsidy	
Less	
Herd replacement	15
Gross output	264
Cow concentrates (126 kg at £125/tonne)	16
Calf concentrates (266 kg at £120/tonne)	32
Other purchased feed	12
Forage variable costs	45
Total feed and forage	105
Vet. and med. costs	12
Bedding	9
Miscellaneous costs	4
Total variable costs	130
Gross margin per cow	134
Gross margin per hectare	241
Stocking rates (cows per hectare)	1.80
N fertilizer (kg/ha)	146

Source: MLC. *Results for recorded suckler herds 1982.* Data Sheet 83/3

2. Feed quality is still relatively high, being on grazed grass, but is low in cost.
3. During the winter period calves respond well to creep feeding.
4. At turnout in the spring the weaning of the calves allows for the different grazing requirements of the cow and calf.
5. Conception is likely to be higher.
   All of these factors are likely to lead to higher output.
   The disadvantage of summer calving is likely to be the higher calf wintering costs. Table 7.2 shows the financial potential of such a system.
   It is interesting to note the results from the upland and hill single suckler herds (Table 7.3) to see what can be achieved under these conditions albeit with an enhanced cow subsidy.

Factors affecting the profitability of the breeding herd
A systematic breakdown of the cost structure of single suckling is shown in Fig. 7.1 which, when related to Tables 7.1–7.3 will give a good illustration of the factors involved.

Table 7.3 Gross margin standard for upland and hill single suckler herds

Upland		Hill	
	£ p		£ p
Calf sales	296.00		248.00
(0.93 calves, 295 kg, 100.3 p/kg)		(0.90 calves, 256 kg, 96.9 p/kg)	
Cow subsidy	52.00		55.00
	348.00		303.00
Less			
Herd replacements	29.00		27.00
Gross output	319.00		276.00
(per cow put to bull)			
Cow concentrates			
(134 kg at £118/tonne)	16.00	(193 kg at £124/tonne)	24.00
Calf concentrates			
(109 kg at £121/tonne)	13.00	(106 kg at £115/tonne)	12.00
Other purchased feed	10.00		10.00
Forage variable costs	47.00		30.00
Total feed and forage	86.00		76.00
Vet. and med. costs	9.00		6.00
Bedding	6.00		5.00
Miscellaneous costs	5.00		3.00
Total variable costs	106.00		90.00
Gross margin per cow	213.00		186.00
Gross margin per hectare	270.00		149.00

Source: MLC. *Results for recorded suckler herds 1982.* Data Sheet 83/3

Multiple suckling

This is essentially a system for the better land and the milkier strain or breed of cow. Many variations of this technique have been practised, the idea being to make full use of the cow's milking abilities by allowing her to suckle more than one calf at a time.

While appearing on paper to be an admirable system, it is in practice fraught with difficulties. Firstly, there is the problem of obtaining the right type of calves at the right time to foster on to the cow; then there is the job of persuading the cow to take to the extra calves, and furthermore, there is always the danger of producing two or more light calves at the end of the season which will not be forward enough to fatten at the end of their first winter. These factors, together with the higher cost structure and increased complexity of management created by the system, means that in

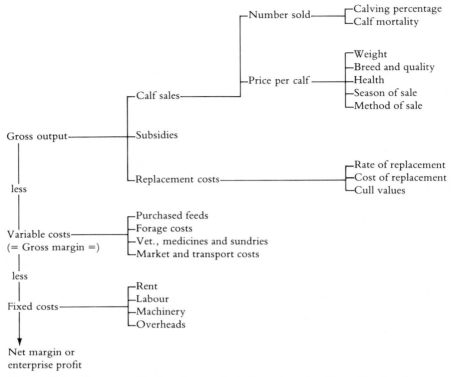

Figure 7.1   Factors affecting the profitability of the beef breeding herd

most cases it is not an attractive alternative to single suckling or one to be taken lightly.

Capital profiles

A single-suckling enterprise is considered in Fig. 7.2 and it is assumed, for simplicity, that all calves are sold off in the autumn.

With an autumn calving herd it is assumed that replacement heifers are bought in late autumn for bulling at around Christmas.

Cull cows sales are divided between two times of the year:
1. empty cows are sold after pregnancy testing (June for autumn calves);
2. old cows not bulled are sold off after weaning their calves.

A high proportion of the marginal capital for this enterprise is tied up in the breeding stock. The profile indicates that an average capital requirement of approximately £600–£650 per cow is required with a peak requirement of approximately £750 per cow occurring September to November in the case of the autumn calving herd used in the profile illustration. Since the peak capital requirement

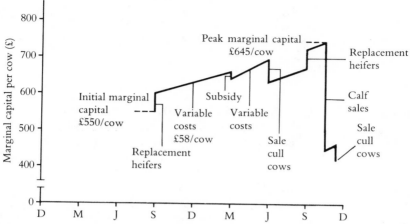

Figure 7.2   *Marginal capital profile for single suckling herds (autumn calving)*

is significant it is common practice when considering return on capital for a beef enterprise to calculate the return on peak capital (see Ch. 5 – Measuring return on capital in the farm business, p. 122). If this calculation were done in relation to Fig. 7.2 then the result would be entitled 'Percentage return on peak marginal capital'.

In view of the long build-up of capital before the sale of the calves occurs, it behoves any beef producer to consider the cost of the capital involved. High interest charges could soon change a reasonable margin into a deficit which, with the attendant risk of paying interest upon interest, could soon lead the enterprise into extreme difficulties.

Beef fattening systems

The economies of beef fattening are considered under two headings: immature cattle and mature cattle.

Immature cattle

This broad term is intended to include cattle which are sold fat before they have cut their permanent incisor teeth, i.e. before 20 months of age. This form of fattening has become more popular for reasons already discussed and is most commonly employed in the following circumstances:

1. Fattening single suckled beef calves in their first winter.

2. Finishing by-product calves from the dairy herd either on: (a) full intensive system, e.g. barley beef; or, (b) a semi-intensive system, e.g. grass and cereal beef (18-month beef) and grass silage beef.
3. Veal production.

Fattening single suckled calves in their first winter

The aim is to finish a single suckled calf, aged between 6 and 12 months at sale, in late winter or early spring when finished cattle prices are usually at their highest. This means that an autumn-born calf will finish at 15–18 months while the later-born and poorer animals will be carried through a store period, after sale at weaning, to be finished on grass at 18–24 months. Clearly, there will be a considerable range in the ages at slaughter and slaughter weights. This range – not only affected by time of calving but type of cattle used – is clearly shown in Fig. 7.3.

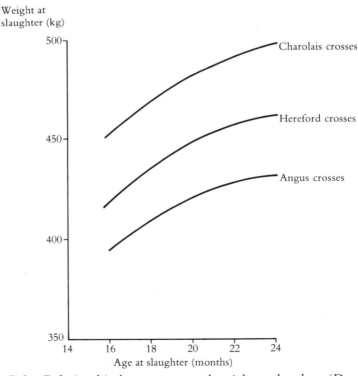

Figure 7.3   Relationship between age and weight at slaughter (D. Allen and B. Kilkenny, Planned beef production, Granada 1980, Fig. 4.1, p. 61)

The relationship between age and weight at slaughter. Not only is there a wide range in the age and type of cattle available for fattening during the winter, but there is also a large choice in the type of foods available for fattening. These types of food and food combinations can be broadly divided into three groups:

1. High-quality conserved grass forage supplemented with concentrates;
2. Arable products and arable by-products supplemented, usually at a higher level than (1), with concentrates;
3. Maize silage supplemented with a protein concentrate.

Whichever combination is adopted it is important to plan the feeding so that: (i) the daily liveweight gains enable the animal to reach slaughter weight at the right time; (ii) the requirement for

Table 7.4   *Winter finishing results for suckled calves and stores, 1981/82*

	Suckled calves	Stores	
	£		£
Sales (448 kg at 100.7 p/kg)	451	(488 kg at 97.3 p/kg)	475
Less			
Cost of suckled calf (318 kg at 98.1 p/kg) and mortality	312	(363 kg at 86.5)	314
Gross output	139		161
Concentrates (502 kg at £110/tonne)	55	(453 kg at £133/tonne)	51
Other feed	4		7
Forage	12		12
Total feed costs	71		70
Vet. and med.	2		3
Bedding	6		6
Miscellaneous	6		7
Total variable costs	85		86
Gross margin per head	54		75
Physical results			
Days feeding – average	165		144
Daily gain (kg)	0.8		0.9
Feed cost per kg gain (p)	54.6		56.0
Mortality (%)	0.4		0.1

Source: MLC. *Winter feeding and finishing suckled calves and dairy-bred stores.* Data Sheet 82/6

food matches the supply; and (iii) that the cost per kilogram of gain is economic.

Winter finishing results vary considerably from year to year depending upon the relationship between the buying price and the value of the finished product – known as the 'feeder's margin'. This term is the same as gross output, being the gross sales less the store or calf. Table 7.4 depicts some typical winter finishing results, and key performance factors, for the winter period 1981/82 and illustrates the level of gross margin performance to be obtained from using grass silage and concentrates during the winter finishing period for suckled calves. This is a short-term fattening enterprise and, for the purpose of calculating a cash flow, can be considered in the same way as a pig-fattening enterprise, providing that concentrates are bought in as required. If home-grown cereals are used, then the working capital requirements will be slightly less, but spread over a longer period.

Intensive fattening on a 'barley-beef' diet
This technique now has an established place in beef production, and can be used for calves born at any time of the year. The system has the advantage of being completely independent of forage area and as such is comparable in many respects with 'concrete' enterprises such as pigs and poultry.

Calves are reared on an early weaning system and are kept on a high level of concentrate feeding throughout their lives. Rolled barley and a small quantity of protein supplement is available *ad libitum* from about 4 months of age. Rapid rates of gain are experienced and the calves usually reach slaughter weights at 11–14 months.

Factors affecting profitability   These are illustrated diagrammatically (see Fig. 7.4).

Gross output or 'feeder's margin' is the difference between livestock receipts including subsidies, and calf purchases.

Sale price is a function of weight and price per kilogram, and since food conversion efficiency drops rapidly after the animal reaches about 320–350 kg, barley beef animals are usually marketed as soon as they reach certification weights. Provided that animals maintain the necessary rate of liveweight gain to finish at 12–14 months, then quality of carcass is fairly uniform. The main danger of the system is over-finishing, which often results from using early maturing breeds, and especially heifers.

Price per kilogram is usually at its highest in the spring, as indicated by the monthly target prices, and consequently most

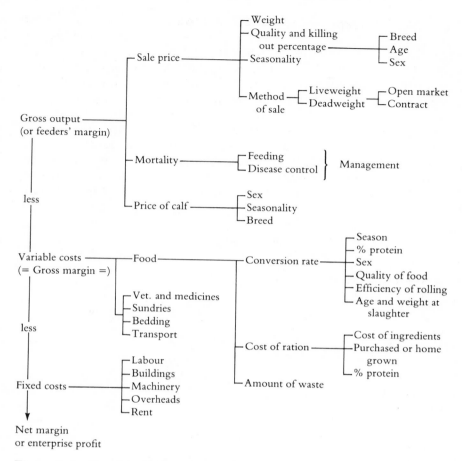

Figure 7.4 Factors affecting the profitability of barley beef

barley beef systems are geared to a spring sales programme using spring-born calves. If an all-the-year-round price can be negotiated on a contract basis, then the system may well be integrated with a dairy herd producing calves throughout the year. A fairly standard product is produced which is consequently well suited to contract marketing with all its adherent benefits. If a contract can be negotiated which will accept bull beef, then so much the better since the superior liveweight gains and leaner carcass are features that are well documented.

Barley beef is essentially a high-risk business and a mortality rate of about 6–7 per cent should be allowed for when budgeting. Profitability is sensitive to relationships between the prices of calves, barley and beef.

The price of calves and their suitability for barley beef fattening is important, and consequently bull calves of the larger, fast-growing breeds are preferred. Feedingstuffs are by far the greatest single item of expenditure, with the cost of early weaning foods being fairly predictable at about £40/head. After this, food costs are influenced by a number of factors. Total requirement depends upon the conversion rate which for the fattening period should average 5.5 to 1 from 106 kg to 440 kg. The heavier the animal at slaughter, then the poorer the overall conversion rate, since efficiency of food use falls steadily after 320–350 kg due to an increase in intake coupled with a decrease in liveweight gain. The sensitivity to the barley price is important since a rise in the cost of barley by £5/tonne will mean a rise in the feed cost of approximately £7/head.

Table 7.5   Gross margin and physical results for cereal-fed beef cattle

	£ p
Sales and beef premium (441 kg at 100.5 p/kg)	443.00
Less	
Calf and mortality	90.00
Gross output	353.00
Milk powder (18 kg at £670/tonne)	12.00
Early weaning concentrates (175 kg at £166/tonne)	29.00
Calf rearing costs	41.00
Finishing concentrates (1 705 kg at £114.5/tonne)	195.00
Other feeds (80 kg hay or equivalent)	5.00
Total feed	241.00
Veterinary and medicines	3.00
Bedding	10.00
Miscellaneous	3.00
Total variable costs	257.00
Gross margin per head	96.00
Physical results	
Average days to slaughter	345.00
Liveweight at start (kg)	54.00
Liveweight at slaughter (kg)	441.00
Daily gain (kg) – overall	1.12
– from 12 weeks	1.2
Feed cost per head per day (p)	69.9
Feed cost per kg gain (p)	62.3
Mortality (%)	3.0
Kg concs. per kg gain from 12 weeks	5.4

Source: MLC. *Beef plan results for calf rearing, cereal beef, grass silage and maize silage beef 1982.*
        Data Sheet 83/4

Table 7.5 gives some indication of the gross margins that may be attained by the barley beef system of fattening.

Capital profile (see Fig. 7.5) The peak marginal working capital profile shows a requirement of £347/head, before interest charges, with an average marginal working capital per head of:

	£ p
Calf (plus mortality)	90.00
Plus half the variable costs $\dfrac{£257}{2}$	128.50
Average marginal working capital	218.50

If this were to attract interest charges at 16 per cent then the gross margin of £96.00 would be reduced accordingly to £55.04/head. Given these circumstances either the enterprise cannot afford to

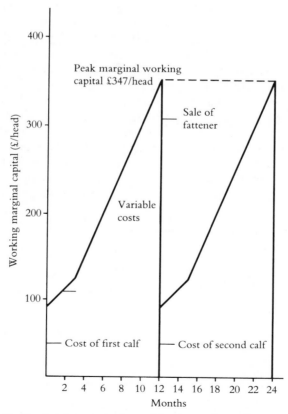

Figure 7.5   Barley beef: marginal working capital profile

borrow the working capital, or else the enterprise must raise its level of performance to a point where the interest levied may be justified.

Semi-intensive or 'grass and cereal' beef

This system, which is known as '18-month beef', involves one grazing season sandwiched between two winter periods using autumn-born calves out of dairy cattle crossed with a beef bull. In the main these beef-cross calves are likely to come from a Friesian herd, although in more recent years this dominance has been challenged by crosses from the Canadian Holstein. Data suggests however, that the Holsteins, specialized as they are for milk production, are inferior to the Friesians as a source of animals for the fattener (see Tables 7.6 and 7.7) although if managed well will produce gross margins only slightly lower than Friesians.

As can be seen from Table 7.8, the major beef bull used is the Hereford followed by the Charolais.

The reasons for the popularity of the Hereford are well known, but it is worth noting the relationship between breed, age and weight at slaughter as depicted earlier in Fig. 7.3 (p. 188).

Most producers use steers for fattening since heifers mature earlier and produce lighter carcasses. For the purposes of fattening, heifers are better suited to a grass system which allows the animal to be carried to greater weights without becoming overfat. The use of bulls up to 18 months of age is hedged about with legislation, particularly in relation to the grazing period, but set against this is the financial benefit of a potentially greater carcass weight and gross margin in spite of slightly higher concentrate use and longer period to slaughter. An alternative to bull beef is the use of growth promoters implanted in steers during the finishing winter period. Meat and

Table 7.6   *Comparison of Friesian and Holstein steers*

	Friesian	Holstein
No.	45	45
Daily gain (kg)	1.05	1.03
Feed (kg)		
3–12 months	2 346	2 769
12 months to slaughter	881	1 344
Kg feed per kg gain		
3–12 months	8.7	9.4
12 months to slaughter	9.6	11.5
Slaughter weight at equal fatness (kg)	443	507
Slaughter age (days)	404	468

Source: British Friesian Journal, March 1981, 63, 137.

Table 7.7 *Comparison of carcasses from Friesian and Holstein steers*

	Friesian	Holstein
Saleable beef (% of carcass)	70	68.5
% of saleable beef in high-priced cuts	45	43.5

Source: British Friesian Journal, March 1981 **63**, 136.

Livestock Commission (MLC) field trials have explored both these areas and some of their findings are documented in Data Sheet 22, 1980.

The 18-month beef system has probably increased in popularity for the following reasons:

(a) Satisfactory gross margins are obtainable from grazing livestock without heavy capital investment.

(b) Autumn-born calves can be finished in the spring when prices are at their highest.

(c) The system is sufficiently intensive to finish by-product calves from the dairy herd.

Autumn-born calves, weighing 40–43 kg, are early weaned and kept growing at about 0.75 kg/day until turnout the following spring, when they will weigh about 175 kg.

Intensive summer grazing for the next 6 months results in yearlings being rehoused in the following autumn at about 320 kg liveweight. If a steady rate of liveweight gain of 0.8 kg/day can be maintained, the beasts will finish by the following spring weighing 470–490 kg.

The factors affecting profitability are in essence the same as those for barley beef, but since forage is involved, efficiency of forage utilization in the form of stocking density, liveweight gain from grazing and conserved forage and costs of forage production must also be considered.

Table 7.8 *Beef inseminations*

Breed	1981/82 ('000)
Angus	68
Charolais	147
Devon	6
Hereford	384
Limousin	89
Simmental	21
Murray Grey	11
South Devon	5

Source: MLC. Extract from *Beef Yearbook 1983*, p 63.

Difficulties arise in apportioning a suitable forage area to such an enterprise, particularly where grazing and conservation is shared with other grazing livestock. Recordings show that overall stocking rates, including summer grazing and silage, of 3.6 cattle/ha are reasonably easily achieved.

Grazing requirements increase as the summer progresses and as the cattle grow, but this allows for a large proportion of spring and early summer grass to be conserved for fattening in the following winter. If summer grazing requirements are considered exclusively, these will amount to an average requirement of 0.2 ha/beast for the whole summer.

Table 7.9 indicates the level of costs and gross margin that may be achieved on a typical 18-month beef set-up.

As can be seen from Table 7.11 the effect of changes in stocking rate can quite substantially affect the gross margin results on a per hectare basis. The capacity that this system of beef fattening has in allowing the farmer to influence profitability, together with the reasons already listed, explain why this system has its followers.

Capital profile.   The peak marginal working capital on this enterprise (see Fig. 7.6) amounts to approximately £429 per head including forage, conservation and miscellaneous variables.

Table 7.9   Gross margin costings for 18 months grass/cereal beef, 1980/82 (per head)

	£ p
Sales (including variable premium (487 kg at 96.9 p/kg))	472.00
Less	
Calf (mortality 4%)	77.00
Gross output	395.00
Milk powder (12 kg at £670/tonne)	8.00
Concentrates in first winter (380 kg at £155/tonne)	59.00
Forage variable costs (£117.8 ha – at 217 kg N/ha)	38.00
Supplementary feed at grass (110 kg at £82/tonne)	9.00
Concentrates in second winter (520 kg at £112/tonne)	58.00
Silage in second winter 4.2 tonnes (see forage costs)	
Total feed and forage costs	
Veterinary and medicines	6.00
Miscellaneous	14.00
Bedding	7.00
Total variable cost	199.00
Gross margin per head	196.00
Gross margin per hectare	598.00

Source: MLC. *Results for grass/cereal system, 1982*

Table 7.10   *Grass silage beef*

	£
Sales (449 kg at 102.2 p/kg)	459
Less	
Cost of calf (100 kg)	160
Gross output	299
Concentrates (804 kg at £113/tonne)	91
Forage (Silage 5.3 tonnes)	17
Total feed and forage	108
Veterinary and medicines	5
Miscellaneous	7
Total variable costs	120
Gross margin per head	179
Gross margin per hectare	1430
PHYSICAL RESULTS	
Days feeding – average	442
Daily gain (kg)	0.96
Mortality (%)	1.6
Stocking rate	8.0

Source: MLC. Extract from *Beef Yearbook 1983* p 30

The average working capital for the 18-month cycle is thus:

$$\frac{429 + 77}{2} = £253.00$$

At the end of the cycle the marginal capital will be repaid by the sale of the first batch of cattle, leaving a margin to cover fixed costs and profit having secured the continuation of the cycle with the second calf ready to start on the grazing/supplementary feed stage.

Again, the observations referring to interest charges given at the end of the section of barley beef hold good for grass/cereal beef, although note must be made of the longer period involved.

Table 7.11   *Effect of stocking density on gross margin/forage hectare*

Ha/beast	0.32	0.3	0.28
	£ p	£ p	£ p
Gross margin/ha excluding forage	715.80	775.18	835.40
Less forage costs/ha	117.80	122.50	128.40
Gross margin/ha	598.00	656.68	707.00

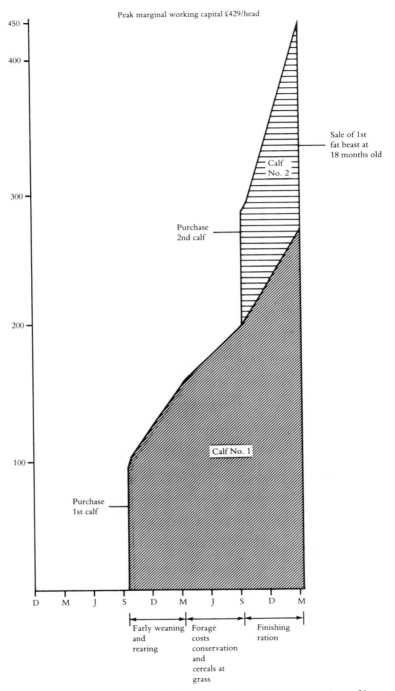

Figure 7.6   Eighteen-month beef: marginal working capital profile

Grass silage beef
This is an indoor system of fattening dairy-bred calves on grass silage and concentrates for sale at 14–17 months of age. It has some of the characteristics of traditional 18-month beef (but can achieve higher stocking rates) and cereal-fed beef, being housed indoors without incurring the high concentrate costs of the latter. Of course as intensity increases there will be a need for greater investment in buildings, livestock and possibly machinery.

The advantages of such a system are that:
(a) As an all-the-year-round system it provides a steady cash flow and may attract premiums from butchers for a product that is predictable both in supply and quality.
(b) It allows the maximum use to be made of grass not only on livestock farms but also on arable farms where fencing may be inadequate for utilization by grazing livestock.
(c) By-products may be introduced as and when available and economic.
(d) It simplifies the problem of matching grass supply to livestock requirements by providing 'buffer' silage stocks.
(e) High gross margins per hectare are possible, making land using beef a real alternative to other enterprises.

Table 7.10 gives some indication of the gross margins and physical data associated with this relatively new system of beef production.

Veal production
The practice of feeding calves on an all-milk diet for slaughter at about 15 weeks old has long been popular in the EEC countries, but has enjoyed only mixed success in the UK. Veal production in the UK has risen from 5 300 tonnes in 1980 to 6 100 tonnes in 1983. Production in 1984 is expected to reach 8 000 tonnes. However, throughout this period the consumption per head of population has remained steady at 0.2 kg/head per year, with deficits in production being made up by imports.

Calves are usually kept under conditions of controlled environment and are fed on milk or reconstituted milk with no dry feed. Rapid growth is possible and the conversion rates achieved are comparable with those obtained by fattening poultry, i.e. 1.5 kg dry matter/kg of liveweight gain.

Veal production is essentially a high-risk business because of the decimating effect of infectious disease, e.g. bacterial scour, under conditions of controlled environment, and a successful unit demands an extremely high level of stockmanship.

The example given in Table 7.12 relates to a dressed carcass of 102 kg killing out at 60 per cent, suitable for the restaurant or

Table 7.12   Gross margin for veal production

Sale value (£2.89/kg, 102 kg/d.c.w.)	295
Less calf (strong Friesian)	101
Gross output	194
Concentrates (192 kg milk powder)	146
Miscellaneous	8
Total variable costs	154
Gross margin per head	40

Source: Nix 1983, p. 41.

'Wiener schnitzel' trade and is based on an assumed 6 per cent mortality.

This type of calf would be slaughtered at 12–15 weeks of age having produced an average daily gain of 1.1 kg. Capital costs for controlled environment buildings are high per calf housed, but with a throughput of four batches of calves per house per year, and a writing-off period of 10 years, the individual cost can be reduced considerably.

Mature cattle

This loose definition is intended to cover all cattle of 18 months and over, which are fattened by less intensive methods than those so far mentioned: firstly, summer fattening off grass, secondly, winter fattening.

Summer fattening off grass. Grass fattening accounts for the majority of cattle sold at this stage, and in examining the profitability of this enterprise a large number of factors need to be considered as Fig. 7.7 will illustrate.

Variable costs are minimized, being only transport, a small veterinary and medicines charge and the forage costs incurred in providing grazing.

Output, usually termed 'feeder's margin', is affected by:
1. Mortality;
2. Increase in weight, i.e. speed of growth with time;
3. Difference in price per kilogram of the store animal and the finished beast.

Price differences are extremely important and, therefore, no satisfactory standards can be calculated for this type of enterprise since so much of the success of this type of business depends upon

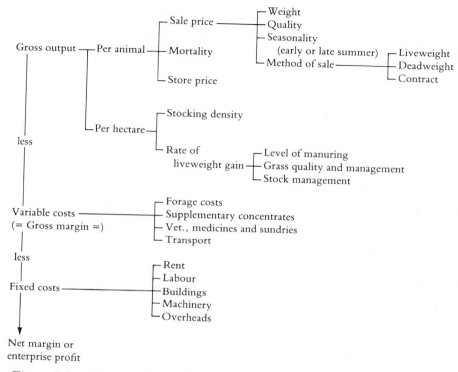

Figure 7.7   Factors affecting the profitability of grass-fed beef

marketing skill – mainly in buying suitable store cattle at the right prices.

The final feeder's margin must be sufficient to cover the following:

(a) forage and agistment costs;
(b) transport;
(c) any supplementary feeds costs;
(d) veterinary, medicines and sundries;
(e) fixed costs, e.g. rent if appropriate;
(f) interest on capital tied up in the cattle;
(g) profit margin.

Winter fattening.   The basic principles listed above will also apply to winter fattening.

Price per kilogram will tend to increase during the fattening period, but fattening variable costs will be higher since concentrates will be required to finish this type of beast.

Once again standards are of little value, since buying skill is the major factor determining the final feeder's margin and profit.

Table 7.13   Gross margin results for grass finishing and winter finishing stores

Grass finishing		Winter finishing	
	£		£
Sales			
(439 kg at 91.8 p/kg)	403	(488 kg at 97.3 p/kg)	475
Less			
Store cost			
(335 kg at 90.7 p/kg)	340	(363 kg at 86.5 p/kg)	314
Gross output	63		161
Variable costs			
Forage	12	(silage 2.8 tonnes)	12
Supplementary feed (at grass)	2	Supplementary feed	
(18 kg cereals at £118/tonne)		(453 kg cereals at £111/tonne)	51
Veterinary and medicines	2		3
Other feed			7
Miscellaneous	5		13
Total variable costs	21		86
Gross margin per head	42		75
Gross margin per ha	235		—
Physical results			
Daily gain (kg)	0.7		0.9
Mortality	—		0.1
Grazing stocking rate (cattle/ha)	5.6		—
Liveweight gain per ha (kg)	582		—

Source: MLC. Beef YearBook 1983, pp. 33, 35

If, however, a grower decides to take winter-born calves through on a 2-year grass/cereal system then justification becomes difficult since, not only is it possible to manage the cattle so that the majority will be slaughtered off grass in their second summer but the period of working capital is extended.

Unless one possesses the necessary skill at buying store cattle it is easy to tie up capital in stock without showing any return at all. It is therefore necessary to assess very carefully the maximum price that can be paid for store cattle, above which it will pay to invest

Table 7.14   Gross margin less interest on working capital (before labour and depreciation)

	Summer finishing	Winter finishing
Gross margin per head (£)	42	75
Average working capital per head (£)	180.50	200.00
Interest on working capital at 15% (£)	27.08	30.00
Gross margin less charge on working capital (£)	14.92	45

the money elsewhere see Table 7.13, where only if suitable cattle can be obtained at £382 a head for summer fattening or £389 for winter fattening, or less, will there be any point in going ahead with such a venture, since these prices represent the break-even point before fixed costs are considered.

As soon as one considers the interest on working capital (see Table 7.14) then the break-even price falls back to £355 head and £359/head respectively.

THE SHEEP ENTERPRISE

Sheep are to be found in every county of the British Isles, yet they only produce about 5 per cent of our national agricultural gross output. Fat sheep and lamb sales constitute the greater part of this, with wool sales amounting to about 9 per cent of the total sheep gross output.

Throughout the 1970s there has been a small but consistent upward trend in total sheep numbers, see Fig. 7.8.

Statistics on the distribution of flock size in the 1960s showed that approximately 30 per cent of sheep were in flocks of less than 300; 30 per cent in flocks of 300–700, and 30 per cent in flocks of 700 ewes or more. The 1970s have not only been characterized by an increase in total sheep numbers but by an alteration in the flock size distribution for England and Wales (see Table 7.15).

The trend into the 1980s towards large flock size is clearly shown,

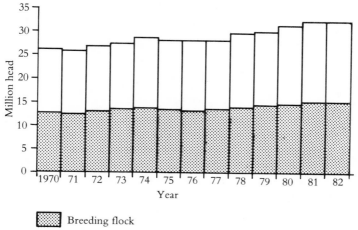

Breeding flock

Figure 7.8   United Kingdom sheep numbers (June) (MLC Commercial Sheep Production Yearbook 1979/80)

Table 7.15　Analysis of sheep numbers by size of flock – England and Wales

Size of flock (total sheep)	1970		1974		1978		1980		1981	
	Percentage of total sheep									
1–24	0.5		0.4		0.3		0.3		0.3	
25–49	1.3		1.0		0.8		0.7		0.7	
50–99	4.4	30.0	3.2	23.4	2.7	19.4	2.5	18.3	2.4	17.4
100–199	11.8		8.8		7.5		6.9		6.6	
200–299	12.0		10.0		8.4		7.9		7.4	
300–399	10.3		9.0		8.1		7.7		7.3	
400–499	8.7	32.2	7.9	30.1	7.5	28.3	6.9	27.7	6.8	26.9
500–699	13.2		13.2		12.7		13.1		12.8	
700–999	12.9		13.6		14.2		14.5		14.7	
1 000–1 499	11.6		13.9		15.1		15.7		16.3	
1 500–1 999	5.7	37.8	7.0	46.5	9.0	52.0	8.9	54.0	9.1	55.7
2 000 and over	7.6		12.0		13.7		14.9		15.6	
	100.0		100.0		100.0		100.0		100.0	

Source: MLC. *Commercial Sheep Production Yearbook 1979/80 and 1981/82.*

reflecting the lower average costs related to larger flocks and hence greater economy.

A superficial examination of gross margin figures obtained from sheep enterprises on lowland areas is likely to give the impression that sheep are something of a 'Cinderella' enterprise and have very little part to play in the economy of farms on better-quality land. At traditional stocking densities of 7–9 ewes/ha the gross margin from sheep is disappointing at £240/300/ha and compares unfavourably with the average level of gross margins obtainable from other grazing enterprises or from cereals.

Great care is required, however, in interpreting such information for the sheep enterprise, whose influence is reflected in the outputs of other enterprises on the same farm. On a mixed farm, for example, the sheep themselves may not show a very high gross margin per hectare, but their presence on the farm may well be reflected in increased crop yields resulting from better soil fertility and disease control when a grass break is introduced into the rotation.

Sheep on a general farm may also contribute indirectly to the economy of the farm by helping to establish leys and utilize by-products and by the technical advantages accruing from mixed grazing.

High-performance lowland flocks at high stocking rates can produce gross margins per hectare which equate well with spring barley performance and still contribute to the general fertility and rotational aspects.

Apart from making the farm economy more diversified and thereby spreading risk, the sheep enterprise has the added advantage of requiring very little fixed capital investment, and unless winter housing is contemplated, almost all the capital tied up in the sheep enterprise is that invested in the sheep themselves, i.e. working capital in every sense of the word and fully realizable.

Being lightfooted, sheep can often fit in well on a mixed farm, because of their ability to graze late into the winter without causing excessive poaching. They are frequently able to utilize outlying and inaccessible fields and those with an inadequate water supply for cattle.

It is often claimed that a small flock can be handled between the main jobs on a mixed farm and will contribute to the economy without requiring additional labour. On the other hand, fencing must be of a higher standard than that usually required for cattle, and some of the routine work involved in flock management does require certain very specialized skills.

Systems of sheep farming

Before the economics of the sheep enterprise can be discussed further, it is necessary to appreciate that sheep enterprises on farms in the UK exist in a wide variety of possible forms.

With a wide range of topographical and climatic conditions prevailing, over thirty recognized breeds and several possible products from the flock, sheep-farming systems are extremely diverse and cannot be easily classified.

One can generalize broadly, in order to avoid considering an unnecessary number of combinations and permutations and divide sheep-farming systems into three main groups.

Hill flocks
Breeding pure under true hill and moorland conditions and supplying their own replacements in a normal year.

Marginal and cross-breeding flocks
These are mainly 'flying flocks' relying upon bought-in, cast-for age ewes from the hill areas as replacements. They are still on marginal and upland grazing. Long-wool rams are used to produce hybrid females for sale to better-quality land and store wethers for finishing.

Lowland flocks

Producing mutton, lamb or store sheep from good-quality grassland or in conjunction with an arable rotation. These may breed
their own female replacements or they may rely on purchased
replacement stock. Increasingly the trend is to rely upon the purchase
of half-bred replacements.

Factors affecting the profitability of the sheep enterprise

The basic principles of costing the sheep enterprise remain the same,
however diversified the individual systems may be.

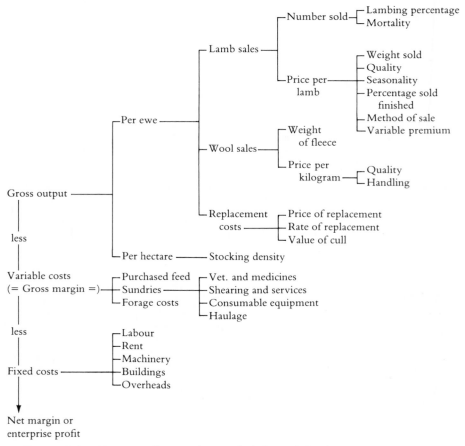

Figure 7.9   Factors affecting the profitability of the sheep enterprise

Factors affecting the ultimate profit are numerous and are expressed diagrammatically in Fig. 7.9. (The diagram relates to a breeding flock, but can be suitably modified to deal with enterprises which rely on purchasing and reselling sheep.)

Individual factors affecting profitability can now be discussed systematically.

Gross output per ewe

Lamb sales

Numbers sold per ewe. This combines two factors: lambing percentage; post-weaning lamb mortality.

Lambing percentage can be expressed in several ways and a very fair method of making this calculation is as follows:

$$\text{Lambing percentage} = \frac{\text{Number of lambs in flock at weaning} + \text{lambs sold before weaning} \times 100}{\text{Number of ewes tupped}}$$

Lambing percentage is itself affected by a wide range of factors, e.g. fertility of ewes and rams; level of environment (feeding, protection, attention at lambing); breeding (fertility is partly a genetic factor); management before tupping (flushing, etc.); ewe mortality; pre-weaning lamb mortality.

Under exposed hill conditions a lambing percentage of 80–100 is usually considered good, whereas in the lowland, with a higher level of nutrition, better protection against the elements and closer shepherding, the same breeds have been shown capable of up to 200 per cent.

Price obtained per lamb. *Weight of lamb sold.* The implications of the EEC Sheep Regime on lamb weights is to reduce the maximum carcass weight qualifying for support payment from 23 kg under the old regime, down to 21 kg in April 1981. For hoggets the maximum carcass weight is reduced from 27.5 to 24.5 kg.

A careful watch on developments within the EEC regime must be maintained in order for sound marketing practice to benefit farmers. Hasty decision-making based solely on lamb weight should be avoided.

Quality. The most important consideration here is that the carcass should meet the grading standards laid down under the EEC Sheep Regime. Lambs and hoggets are graded into the MLC Sheep Carcass Classification Scheme and the eligibility of carcasses for sheep variable premium is defined by classification.

Producing a product which meets the market requirements from a quality point of view is important. When marketing on a live-weight basis, evenness of quality throughout a group of lambs will increase the demand from the butcher, and careful penning and sorting is often well justified. Regular drawing of lambs at weekly intervals should obviate the presentation of overfat lambs.

Seasonality of production. Lamb production in the UK tends to be seasonal in nature, and with a relatively constant demand only partly satisfied by imports, lamb prices tend to follow a predictable seasonal pattern.

The bulk of the home-produced crop is marketed in the late summer and early autumn and consequently prices are at their lowest at this time of the year. As production falls off in the autumn, a steady rise in price is usually experienced until a maximum is reached at around Easter, after which a steady decline is once again apparent.

The producer has therefore to assess the market to which his system of production is best suited. He must decide whether it is more profitable to go for the high-priced product by lambing out of season and by the costly hand-feeding to produce a fat lamb for the Easter trade, or whether to lamb later and aim to produce a more cheaply fed lamb to be marketed at a lower price. Such a decision can only be made by careful budgeting in the light of all the circumstances affecting the individual farm business.

The best prices on a conventional grassland system of finished lamb production are obtained when a high proportion of lambs are finished and marketed before the end of June. This form of marketing is particularly well suited to intensive grassland management, since the first lamb sales coincide with the peak of grassland production and thus enables numbers of grazing stock to be better equated with falling grassland production as the season progresses.

Percentage of lambs sold finished. On many farms, lambs which are not finished by the autumn are sold as stores to be fattened elsewhere. The return of a finished animal will almost certainly be higher than that of a store animal sold at the same time of the year. Therefore, the higher the proportion of animals sold finished, the higher the overall price per lamb sold.

Method of sale. Lamb is a seasonal product and consequently organization of orderly marketing is more difficult than with all-year-round products such as pigmeat or poultry.

A properly organized contract system which allows suitable bonuses for quality will generally realize a better price than short-term haphazard selling on the open market. Long-term contracts are as yet only offered to the larger producer, and a great need exists for co-operative marketing organizations which allow the smaller producer to gain more benefit from planned and orderly marketing of his lambs.

Wool sales

Wool is essentially a by-product of the British sheep industry, whereas in some countries, e.g. Australia and South Africa, wool is the most important output of the flock.

British wools do not generally satisfy the requirements of the top-quality market, and although there are some notable exceptions for highly specialized users, e.g. tweed wools and mattress stuffing, most of our home-bred wool is sold on a low-grade market and commands a low price when compared with fine-quality worsted wool like that of the Merino.

Weight of fleece is the most important single factor affecting wool output per ewe, and while affected by feeding and management, this is primarily a function of breed and will range from about 0.9 to 1.1 kg for a Scottish Blackface ewe in her native habitat, to 5.5 to 6.5 kg for some of the long-wool and close-wool breeds on good-quality feed.

Handling and presentation of the fleece both affect price, and although presentation and final marketing of the wool is now the responsibility of the British Wool Marketing Board, much can be done on the farm to ensure that the fleece is kept free from contamination and is properly shorn, rolled and stored. Heavy penalties are deducted by the British Wool Marketing Board where careless handling or storage might result in a reduction in the market value of the clip.

Replacement costs

On the debit side of the gross output calculation must be considered the flock depreciation.

With an orthodox breeding flock, this simply entails the cost of new ewes and rams joining the flock, set against the cull value of those which are no longer suitable and are sold.

Replacement costs depend on rate of replacement, mortality, cost of replacement and value of culls.

Rate of replacement. Female replacements usually join the flock at about 18 months of age as 'gimmers' or 'two-tooths'. This is by no means a standard practice and the age at which ewes join the flock will vary according to system and area. On good lowland conditions and with early maturing breeds, it may be possible to tup ewe lambs in their first autumn and still get a fair crop, thereby saving the cost of a year's unproductive keep. Other systems rely entirely upon cast ewes to provide their replacements, and since these will have a shorter breeding life ahead of them, a much larger proportion of the flock will need to be replaced each year.

Under lowland conditions and with good management an average breeding life of 4–5 years should be possible for a ewe. Full-mouthed ewes which are cast for age from hill country will usually last for a further two to three seasons when brought down to better conditions. (The degree of culling practised in any livestock enterprise is governed by the principles discussed in the section on dairy replacements p. 168.)

Cost of replacement.   The price paid for replacement ewes is extremely variable, but basically will depend on the likely productive life of the animal and its suitability for immediate production. Gimmers from the north usually fetch £65 to £75 a head in the finished lamb producing areas.

Rams will usually have an active life of four or five seasons and their rate of inclusion in the flock varies from 2 per cent to 3 per cent depending upon their age, virility and the type of country in which they are running. (Smaller enclosed areas require less rams than when mating under open-range conditions.) Ram prices are again extremely variable, but sound commercial crossing rams for fat lamb production are available in the £150–£350 range.

Value of culls.   The price paid for a cull ewe will depend upon the possible alternative uses of the animal. A cast-for-age hill ewe will still have a value as a breeding animal, whereas a cull ewe from a lowland flock is usually only assessed on her carcass value, which will depend upon weight and degree of finish and will also vary according to the time of year.

Variable costs

The principal variable costs affecting the sheep enterprise are:
(a) concentrate costs;
(b) other purchased feed costs and agistment charges;
(c) forage costs;
(d) veterinary, medicines and sundries.
These are best illustrated by the MLC gross margin accounts in Tables 7.16–7.18.

Stress has already been given to the widely varying systems of sheep production that occur in this country and no single set of standards is universally applicable.

The MLC gross margin accounts in Tables 7.16–7.18 illustrate the likely levels of costs and outputs that will occur in average situations under three completely different systems of sheep farming in the British Isles.

A true hill flock (see Table 7.16)

A full rate of subsidy is payable on flocks of certain breeds in specified hill and moorland areas. This would be a pure breeding flock

Table 7.16   Physical and financial results for hill flocks, 1982

No. of flocks:	51	
Financial results (£ per ewe)	Average (£)	Top third (£)
Sale of lambs	19.54	23.66
Sale of draft ewes	5.56	7.01
Wool sales	1.42	1.53
Hill ewe subsidy and premium	7.62	7.41
Gross returns	34.14	39.61
Less		
Flock replacement (rams)	1.58	1.36
Output	32.56	38.25
Variable costs		
Concentrates	2.44	1.61
Purchased forage	0.43	0.24
Forage variable costs	1.44	1.34
	4.31	3.19
Total feed and forage		
Veterinary and medicines	1.52	1.30
Miscellaneous and transport	0.51	0.54
Total variable costs	6.34	5.03
Gross margin per ewe (output–variable costs)	26.22	33.22
Physical results		
No. of ewes to ram (Av. flock size)	708	681
Ewe to ram ratio	43	46
Per 100 ewes to ram:		
No. empty ewes	7	5
No. dead ewes	4	3
No. ewes lambed	91	93
No. of lambs reared	100	113
No. of lambs retained for breeding	28	37

Source: MLC. *Sheep Yearbook*, Nov. 1983, Table 4.6, p. 45.

lambing percentage of only 100 per cent is likely to be achieved, most of the females bred are needed for flock replacements.

The outputs from the flock consist of wool sales from the breeding flock and replacements, sales of cast ewes, cast rams, all wether lambs and occasionally a few surplus ewe lambs or gimmers.

Livestock replacement costs are minimal, consisting only of bought-in replacement rams. At a low stocking density, veterinary and medicine costs are kept fairly low and so also are concentrate costs, since only a very small amount of concentrates will be fed, 21–23 kg/ewe being given in the last few weeks before lambing. A little hay will probably have to be bought in for late winter feeding.

A major item of costs incurred is that of away wintering the replacements ewe lambs in their first winter. This is a recognized practice in the hills in order to give maximum attention to the ewe flock and to give the ewe lambs the chance of making better growth than would be possible at home.

Marginal upland flock (see Table 7.17)

This represents an intermediate situation between the true hill farm and the lowland unit producing finished lamb.

Typical lowland flock (see Table 7.18)

A typical lowland flock producing summer finished lamb. In this case replacements are bought in as gimmers.

The main output will be the sale of finished lambs. There will also be a few store lambs at the end of the season, along with cull ewes, rams and the wool cheque.

Expenditure on feedingstuffs will be higher as more concentrates are used in the period immediately before and after lambing.

Further systems of lowland sheep production

Lowland sheep farming is not restricted to the production of fat lamb, and other systems deserve consideration.

Keeper sheep

A valuable contribution to the income of many farmers with winter grazing to spare is the provision of agistment for 'keeper

Table 7.17   Physical and financial results for upland flocks selling finished and store lambs off grass in summer and autumn, 1982

No. of flocks:	105	
Financial results (£ per ewe)	Average (£)	Top third (£)
Lamb sales	44.83	49.74
Wool sales	2.08	2.18
Ewe subsidy and premium	5.21	5.01
Gross returns	52.12	56.93
Less		
Flock replacements	6.84	5.31
Output	45.28	51.62
Variable costs		
Ewe concentrates	5.02	4.41
Lamb concentrates	0.27	0.18
Purchased forage	0.54	0.21
Fertilizer	3.45	3.46
Other forage costs	0.64	0.54
Total feed and forage	9.92	8.80
Veterinary and medicines	1.79	1.47
Miscellaneous and transport	0.94	0.92
Total variable costs	12.65	11.19
Gross margin per ewe	32.63	40.43
Gross margin per hectare	388	615
Gross margin per grass hectare	392	619
Physical results		
No. of ewes to ram (Av. flock size)	541	443
Ewe to ram ratio	42	42
Percentage ewe lambs in the breeding flock	12	17
Per 100 ewes to ram:		
No. of empty ewes	6	5
No. of dead ewes	4	3
No. of ewes lambed	92	93
No. of lambs born alive	134	141
No. of lambs born dead	6	6
No. of lambs dead after birth	4	3
No. of lambs reared	130	138
No. of lambs retained for breeding	11	11
No. of lambs sold or retained for feeding	40	25
No. of lambs sold finished	74	97
Stocking rate (ewes/hectare):		
Summer grazing	13.2	16.6
Overall grass	12.0	15.3
Overall grass and forage	11.9	15.2
N fertilizer kg. per hectare	87	121
N fertilizer kg. per ewe	7	8

Source. MLC. *Sheep Yearbook* Nov 1983, Table 4.3, p. 40.

Table 7.18   Physical and financial results for lowland flocks selling most of their lambs off grass in summer and autumn 1982

No. of flocks:	349	
	Average	Top third
Financial results (£ per ewe)	(£)	(£)
Lamb sales	52.70	57.56
Wool	2.82	2.93
Ewe premium	1.31	1.22
Gross returns	56.83	61.71
Less		
Flock replacements	8.68	6.82
Output	48.15	54.89
Variable costs		
Ewe concentrates	6.20	5.87
Lamb concentrates	1.19	1.21
Forage variable costs:		
Fertilizer	5.03	4.59
Other forage costs	1.18	0.81
Purchased forage	0.61	0.51
Total feed and forage	14.21	12.99
Vet. and Medicines	2.47	2.30
Miscellaneous and transport	1.06	1.05
Total variable costs	17.74	16.34
Gross margin per ewe	30.41	38.55
Gross margin per hectare of grass	417	626
Gross margin per hectare	386	599
Physical results		
No. of ewes to ram (Av. flock size)	492	434
Ewe to ram ratio	39	38
Percentage ewe lambs in the breeding flock	8	10
Per 100 ewes to tup:		
No. of empty ewes	6	5
No. of dead ewes	4	4
No. of ewes lambed	93	93
No. of lambs born alive	155	163
No. of lambs born dead	9	9
No. of lambs dead after birth	8	7
No. of lambs reared	148	156
No. of lambs retained for breeding	7	9
No. of lambs sold finished	91	106
Stocking rate (ewes/hectare):		
Summer grazing	15.0	17.8
Overall grass	13.7	16.2
Overall grass & forage	12.7	15.5
Kg N/ha	159	176
Kg N/ewe	12	11

sheep'. These are usually ewe lambs or store sheep benefiting pasture by removing surplus growth.

The remaining sheep enterprises all depend very heavily upon skill at buying and selling and consequently no reliable standards can be calculated for them.

Store finishing

Winter store finishing involves the purchase of store lambs in late summer and early autumn and then taking them on to finish during the winter, usually on roots or green crop with some hay and concentrates.

Couples

Draft ewes purchased in the autumn are mated and then 'sold in the wool' with their lambs early in the following summer.

The ewe is shorn and then sold after weaning the lamb which is fattened. This system is well suited to farms with surplus winter grazing, but where sheep would compete with more valuable stock if kept all the year.

Comparisons on the basis of gross margins alone can be extremely misleading. In all the cases demonstrated, the gross margins fail to illustrate one of the great advantages of the sheep enterprise, namely its extremely low fixed capital requirement.

Return on capital invested in the sheep enterprise must always be given due consideration in assessing its contribution to the farm business.

THE PIGS ENTERPRISE

Pigmeat in its various forms accounts for approximately 10 per cent of the UK national agricultural output. Home consumption of pigmeat is rising to the level of the early 1970s and home production accounts for about 68 per cent of our total requirements. Consumption of pigmeat has, over the last 14 years, remained fairly static at around 27 kg/head with a temporary drop to 23 kg/head in the mid-1970s. Hidden within these figures is the increase in freshmeat consumption, i.e. pork, from 10.4 kg/head to 12.9 kg/head, and a slight decline in bacon and ham consumption, linked perhaps to consumer preference and changing breakfast habits in the UK.

The relative stability in pigmeat consumption is reflected in the total numbers of pigs in the UK which have hovered around the 7.7–8.0 million mark since 1976. However, as is typical of an enterprise sensitive to concentrate food costs and carcass values, the number of pigs has recently shown a downward trend in response to reduced profitability and it is expected that slaughterings for 1984 will fall below the 1983 figure. In an attempt to benefit from the advantages of scale, pig herds are still increasing in size with over 90 per cent of the pig population in the hands of 36 per cent of the holdings. Of the total pig population shown above, 943 000 of these comprise the breeding herd of which it is estimated that some 75 per cent are planned crosses or hybrids – a figure which gives some indication of the breeding improvement that has been made in the last decade.

The margin from pig production is extremely finely balanced and a high standard of managerial efficiency is absolutely essential if a satisfactory return on capital is to be achieved. In examining costings, there is always a very noticeable difference between the results of the 'average' and 'premium' farms – probably more so than with any other enterprise. This is because a large number of factors are involved and attention to detail is extremely important since the effect of small improvements in efficiency tends to be cumulative. In the examples which follow, the sensitivity of profitability to small changes in production efficiency is amply illustrated.

In the past, pig prices have been notorious for their instability and pigs have had the reputation of being either 'copper' or 'gold' – never 'silver'. Prices have tended to follow a cyclic pattern with increased output leading to over-production – low prices – falling numbers – increased prices – increased output – over-production, etc.

Production economics and profitability

When dealing with crops and with grazing livestock, land use has always been a major factor to consider, since land is usually the most limiting factor of production. Efficiency of such enterprises has always been assessed primarily on the basis of land use (gross margin per hectare, etc.), while always bearing in mind the importance of an adequate overall return on capital. In these cases return on capital was often closely linked with efficiency of land use, and except in cases of excessive capital investment the two factors were more or less synonymous.

In assessing the profitability and viability of the 'concrete' enterprises, i.e. pigs and poultry, a completely different approach is called for. Land is not a serious limiting factor of production where these enterprises are concerned, consequently output and margins per hectare are virtually useless in assessing profitability.

Efficiency of production is more suitably assessed according to the use made of the remaining resources, i.e. labour and capital.

Capital is the major limiting factor of production in the case of the pigs enterprise and return on capital must be given top priority in assessing and comparing the efficiency of pig production.

Outline efficiency factors

While the importance of assessing efficiency in relation to capital is acceptable in theory, it may not always be possible to evaluate the capital involved, particularly when sorting out a farm trading account which includes pigs along with other farm enterprises.

If capital cannot be assessed, how then can one attempt to evaluate the productivity of the pigs enterprise?

The following simple measures can be calculated from a basic trading account and will give outline pointers to efficiency when compared with figures for other farms or with standards:

Output factors.   Gross output from pigs – per pig sold or per sow.

Feed economy factors.   Feedingstuffs are the major cost item in pig production, therefore feed economy and profitability are closely related.

Net output from pigs – total – per pig sold or per sow. Net output (i.e. gross output less purchased feed costs) is an extremely useful factor in assessing the efficiency of the enterprise since it represents the actual output generated by the pigs themselves. It could otherwise be called 'margin over purchased feed costs'.

Feeds costs per £100 gross output. The standards in Table 7.19 based on the calculation of average ratios of feed costs to output for 1983

Table 7.19   Output: feed cost ratios for pig production

	Feed cost/£100 gross output	Gross output/£100 feeds costs
Weaner production	71.5	140
Bacon	82.3	122
Pork	93.6	107
Cutters	82.6	121

Table 7.20   Efficiency factors for breeding and feeding herds

Breeding – weaning at 5 to 6 weeks, weaning at 3 to 4 weeks in parentheses	Poor	Average	Good	Best
Live pigs born per litter	9.8	10.5	11.1	12.0
Weaners per litter	8.2	9.0	9.8	10.5
Creep feed/weaner to 8 weeks (kg)	17	15	13	12
Litters per sow a year	1.75	1.9	2.05	2.1
	(2.05)	(2.25)	(2.45)	(2.5)
Weaners per sow a year	16	18	20	21
	(18.5)	(21.0)	(23.5)	(24.0)
Feed used per weaner (kg)★	76	68	60	60
	(66)	(58)	(50)	(45)
Feed used per weaner to 25 kg liveweight (kg)	113	100	87	83
	(107)	(94)	(81)	(73)
Feeding (from 25 kg lwt.)				
Mortality rate (%)	2.7	1.7	0.7	0
Feed conversion rate				
Porkers (69 kg lwt.)	3.2	2.9	2.6	2.3
Cutters (88 kg lwt.)	3.4	3.15	2.8	2.6
Baconers (93 kg lwt.)	3.5	3.25	2.9	2.7
Quantity of feed per pig (kg)				
Porkers	136	123	110	100
Cutters	206	188	180	155
Baconers	238	218	198	180

★ Includes creep feed for young pigs.
Source: Ridgeon 1983

give a quick measure of feed efficiency for any form of pig production. A combined standard can easily be constructed where both breeding and fattening occur simultaneously.

Sophisticated efficiency factors
Detailed records of feedingstuffs used, together with information on births, deaths, sales, purchases, transfers and miscellaneous costs will enable a wide range of sophisticated efficiency factors to be calculated. These can then be compared with standards such as those in Table 7.20.

Comparative profitability of alternative outputs
Systems of pig production can be broadly classified under: breeding, meat production (pork, cutters, bacon) and a combination of both.

    In order to assess and compare profitability the following factors must be considered: gross margin per pig; net margin per pig; gross margin per unit house space per year; net margin per unit house space per year; net margin per unit of capital per year, i.e. percentage return on capital.

Return on capital is the most important single factor and, since much of the capital invested will be tied up in housing and equipment, the margin per unit of house space is a closely related factor. This involves another dimension, namely time or rate of throughput and this must be given full consideration when judging the relative importance of margin per pig and margin per unit. The following examples illustrate this point:

Example

	Pork	Bacon
Net margin per (£)	4.09	7.69
Fattening time	12 weeks	19 weeks
Batches per year	4.3	2.7
Net margin per pig space per year	£17.59	£20.76

Clearly, the relationship between net margin per pig and per pig space is a close one, but in order to make the comparison valid the unit used must be common. It is necessary, therefore, to relate the net margin to area of usable floor space. In the following example the above net margins all related to throughput and floor area (the standard used is 0.8 m² per 100 kg pig).

Example

	Pork	Bacon
Net margin per m² per year	£33.24	£27.67

In this example the pork pig comes out best, but the calculation is very sensitive to returns, weaner and food costs. These examples are, of course, simplistic since other factors such as pen size and pen shape have a bearing on the possible alternatives that are open to the farmer.

Calculation of return on capital

This is basically net margin per £100 capital invested.

Capital invested in the pig enterprise will be in the following forms:

A = Fixed capital in housing and equipment and breeding stock

plus B = Trading capital in the growing pigs

plus C = Working capital to cover running expenses, i.e.:
   Food costs
   Labour
   Miscellaneous costs and overheads

Evaluation of A and B is straightforward and can be taken as the average of valuations. The averaging of opening and closing valuations is perfectly satisfactory where the breeding stock numbers are stable, but an average of twelve monthly figures is preferable where fluctuations occur through the year.

Working capital C is more difficult to evaluate since this form of expenditure is a continuous process. One needs to assess the average amount of capital tied up during a production cycle, e.g. fattening a batch of pigs.

Example

To find the working capital employed in food for a batch of fattening pigs:

Average capital in food = half total food cost

This calculation is adequate if foods are paid for as they are consumed, but if merchants' credit is given, and the producer is allowed a month's grace in which to pay for his foodstuffs, then correspondingly less working capital will be tied up on this item.

Thus the formula for calculating the amount of capital invested in food becomes:

$$\text{Average capital in food} = \text{half cost} \times \frac{\text{fattening time} - \text{credit time}}{\text{fattening time}}$$

Miscellaneous costs and all other costs for which credit time is available can be treated in the same way. The above procedure has been adopted in assessing percentage return on capital in all the examples quoted in this enterprise study.

Weaner production

The factors affecting profitability are set out in Fig. 7.10.

Variable costs per sow are partly constant and partly proportional to the number of pigs produced per year. The constant portion of these costs, however, is by far the greater, and the extra cost incurred by creep feeding additional piglets represents a very small fraction of the cost of keeping a sow for a year.

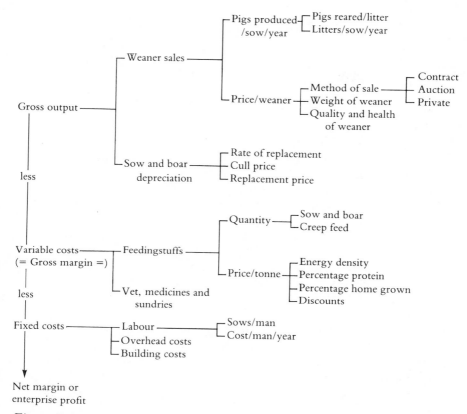

Figure 7.10 Factors affecting the profitability of weaner pig production

An increase in output per sow per year then represents a disproportionate increase in gross margin as Table 7.21 illustrates. Output per sow is a function of pigs produced per sow per year and price obtained per weaner.

Table 7.21 Relationship between numbers weaned and gross margin per sow

Pigs weaned/per annum	Output at £24/pig (allowing for stock depreciation) (£)	Variable costs (£)	Gross margin (£)	Cumulative increase in gross margin (£)
18	432	370	62	—
19	456	375	81	19
20	480	380	100	38
21	504	385	119	57
22	528	390	138	76

At a constant price per weaner, gross output will depend on numbers of weaners sold per sow per year and this in turn upon numbers of weaners sold per litter and farrowing index or litters per sow per year. Ability to produce and rear large litters is partly genetic and partly controlled by nutrition and management. Both these characteristics are of low heritability and – apart from exploiting heterosis by cross-breeding – most progress in increasing piglets per sow per year has been made by improving the farrowing index and by raising numbers weaned per litter. Increasing the number of litters per sow per year has been made possible by early weaning techniques. Table 7.22 illustrates the relationship between age at weaning and the breeding performance.

The increase in output suggested by Table 7.22 has a price which is exacted in terms of not only labour and management skills but also capital. A marginally higher capital investment per sow will be required on earlier weaning systems, since the sow will spend most of her time in the breeding quarters, and the young piglets will require specialized feeding and housing in the early stages.

However, it should be borne in mind that although Table 7.22 supports evidence coming through that early weaning is having an effect upon performance, it should be noted that some producers weaning at five weeks of age still outperform the 'average' for three-week weaning. Clearly, there is a potential difference between these extremes, but so far the shortfall, between expected and actual, increases the earlier the piglet is weaned. In spite of this the producer starting from new, because of high building costs, will have to commit himself to an early weaning system with its inherent potential for greater output. However, within the above weaning dates there is normally considerable scope for improved performance without reducing the weaning age, and those constructing budgets should avoid the pitfall of apparently solving all their difficulties by merely reducing the age at weaning.

Price obtained per weaner will depend on the type of pig and its

Table 7.22   Breeding results related to age at weaning

Age at weaning (weeks)	Less than 3	3 and 4	5 and 6	7 and 8
Average age at weaning (days)	17	25	37	52
Litters per sow	2.29	2.20	2.00	1.82
Live pigs born per litter	10.2	10.3	10.4	10.2
Weaners per litter	8.9	8.9	8.8	8.8
Weaners per sow	20.4	19.4	17.6	16.1
Weight of weaners at 8 weeks (kg)	18.5	17.9	17.6	17.9

Source: Extract from *Pig Farming*, Mar. 1981, p. 37. Cambridge Costings, Vol. no. 29.

suitability for a given market when finished. It will also depend on the way in which the weaner is sold.

Auction markets are considered unreliable for this class of stock and the advantages of producing under contract are well worth considering. This gives a guaranteed outlet either direct to a fattener or through an agency or weaner pool.

Points to be agreed in drawing up such a contract are:
(a) forward scale of prices per kg liveweight;
(b) health standards – approved farms, disinfected vehicles, etc.;
(c) numbers supplied per month or quarter with acceptable degree of variation, e.g. 10 per cent;
(d) period of agreement (usually 6 months);
(e) period of credit (usually very short, agents will not give credit);
(f) transport and delivery charges;
(g) agent's commission;
(h) arbitration in case of dispute.

Sow and boar depreciation can be calculated as follows:

Average herd life of sow	2 years
Average herd life of boar	2 years
Average number sows per boar	20
Average price gilt	£130
Average price young boar	£300
Average cull price sow	£ 90
Average cull price boar	£ 50

$$\text{Annual depreciation sow} = \frac{130-90}{2} = \text{£20.00}$$

$$\text{Annual depreciation boar} = \frac{300-50}{2} = \text{£125}$$

$$\text{Sow's annual share of boar depreciation} = \frac{\text{£125}}{20} = \text{£6.25}$$

$\therefore$ Total annual depreciation expressed per sow $= $ £26.25

Food costs per sow and boar are controllable within limits. This control can only be exercised by the stockman observing body condition, since until more is known about nutrition and reproductive performance, standards can, at best, only act as guides. However, economy is possible and savings can be made as indicated in Table 7.23.

Cost of food per tonne may also be reduced by bulk buying or by such agreements as paying merchants by direct debit.

Sensitivity to changes in output costs

Profitability is finely balanced in this enterprise, and small changes

Table 7.23   Effect of level of feeding during pregnancy on annual food cost of sow

Level of feeding (kg/day)	Food/year* (kg)	Cost/year	Food cost saved
3.5	838	£150.84† (£159.22)‡	—† (—)‡
3.0	718	£129.24† (£136.42)‡	£21.60† (£22.80)‡
2.5	599	£107.82† (£113.81)‡	£43.02† (£45.41)‡
2.0	479	£ 86.22† (£ 91.01)‡	£64.62† (£68.21)‡

* At 2.1 litters/sow/year.
† Food at £180 tonne.
‡ Food at £190 tonne – representing food of equal energy density.

in basic input-output ratios can have very considerable effects upon net returns and return on capital, as is illustrated in Table 7.24.

Meat production

This term is chosen in preference to 'fattening', since lean meat is at a premium and the production of fat is an expensive exercise. The main outlets for finished pigs are pork, cutter, bacon and heavy hogs.

Readers should note that these rather arbitrary terms have been given precision under the revised MLC price-reporting system. In the interests of clarity this section will use the more familiar terms with due regard to the weight ranges implied by the classification. While various intermediate stages, e.g. heavy and light cutters, all find a market, the meat production enterprises are best illustrated by these four products. Each of these products requires a different carcass weight. The pigs are, therefore, slaughtered at appropriately different ages, involving a different rate of turnover for each enterprise and also different building space requirements. It must also be remembered that food conversion efficiency tends to decrease with increasing weight of carcass, while this is to some extent compensated for by a different energy density requirement and the consequent possibility of a cheaper ration.

The essential physical differences between these products are in Table 7.25.

Apparent advantages in one direction are usually offset by disadvantages in another, consequently there is no 'best' system for all circumstances, one can only aim to select the system best suited to an individual set of farm conditions.

Table 7.24 Example of costs and outputs for a sow producing weaners for sale

	Example A (£)		Example B (£)	
Sales				
Weaners	18.5 at £27	499.50	22.5 at £27	607.50
$\frac{1}{3}$ cull sow at £90		30.00		30.00
$\frac{1}{40}$ cull boar at £50		1.25		1.25
		530.75		638.75
Total sales				
Less purchases				
$\frac{1}{3}$ in-pig gilt at £130		43.33		43.33
$\frac{1}{40}$ boar at £300		7.50		7.50
Gross output		479.92		587.92
Variable costs				
Foods: Sow and weaners				
1.6 tonne at £214/tonne		342.40	1.7 tonne at 363.80	
Boar – 1 tonne at £190		9.50	£214/tonne	
				9.50
Total food		351.19		373.30
Veterinary and medicines		12.50		12.50
Other miscellaneous		25.00		25.00
Total variable costs		388.69		410.80
Gross margin		91.23		177.12
Fixed costs				
Labour £7 800/90 sows		86.67	£7 800/90 sows 86.67	
Depreciation on buildings 10% of £380		38.00	£380 at 10% 38.00	
Overheads		22.00		22.00
Total fixed costs		146.67		146.67
Net margin/deficit		−55.44		+ 30.45
Average capital investment/sow				
Sow		105.00		105.00
$\frac{1}{20}$ boar		15.00		15.00
Buildings $\frac{1}{2}$ (£380)		190.00		190.00
Food $\frac{1}{2} \times \frac{5}{6} \times 175.60$		73.17	$\frac{1}{2} \times \frac{4}{5} \times 186.65$ 74.66	
Misc. $\frac{1}{2} \times \frac{5}{6} \times 37.5 \times \frac{1}{2}$		7.81		7.81
Labour $\frac{1}{2} \times 86.67 \times \frac{1}{2}$		21.66		21.66
Overheads $\frac{1}{2} \times \frac{1}{2} \times 22$		5.50		5.50
		418.14		419.63
Return on average capital		—		7.26
Feed costs/£100 gross output		73.2		63.5
Time to complete production cycle	< 6 months		5 months	

The factors affecting profitability of pigmeat production are basically the same whichever product is chosen. These are summarized diagrammatically in Fig. 7.11.

The examples in Table 7.26 are an attempt to show the likely margins, capital investment and yield in a prescribed set of circum-

Table 7.25   Basic data for pigmeat production enterprises

	Pork	Cutter	Bacon	Heavy hog
Space requirements	0.6–1.0 m²/100 kg of pig, total area for pigs in groups (fully slatted or mesh floors, 0.5–0.8 m²/100 kg of pig)			
Space requirements relative to pigs/unit/space	100	87	77	69
Ventilation	0.3 m³–2.0 m³/hour per kg of pig weight Average of 1 m³/hour per kg of pig weight			
Fattening time (weeks)	14	15	18	19.5
Batches/pig space/year	3.7	3.5	2.9	2.7
Pigs/year/100 pork pig spaces	370	305	223	186
Average conversion rate kg food/kg				
Liveweight gain	2.8	3.00	3.05	3.17
Liveweight at slaughter (kg) –circa	60	73	85	94

Source: Extracted in part from C. T. Whittemore, *Pig production*, Table 8.2, p. 117.

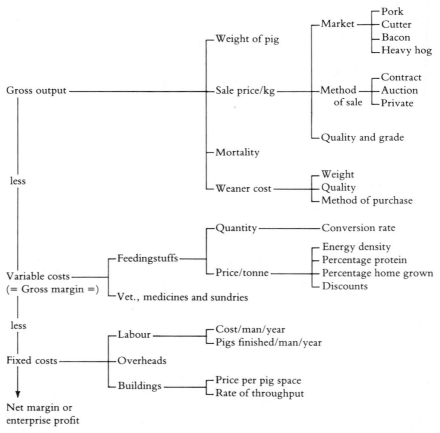

Figure 7.11   Factors affecting the profitability of pigmeat production

Table 7.26   *Example of outputs and costs for pigmeat production*

	Pork	Cutter	Bacon	Heavy hog
Gross output				
Deadweight per pig (kg)	48	63	68	82
Net price per kg dead-weight (p)	108	101	106	99
Sale price per pig (£)	51.84	63.63	72.08	81.18
Less				
Mortality – percentage	2.2	1.9	2.3	1.8
– cost (£)	1.14	1.20	1.66	1.46
Weaner cost (£)	26.80	26.80	26.80	26.80
Gross output or feeders margin	23.90	35.63	43.62	52.92
Variable costs				
Feed – quantity per pig (kg)	114	178	195	270
– cost per tonne (£)	180	160	160	157
– cost per pig (£)	20.52	28.48	31.20	42.39
Miscellaneous variables (£)	0.95	1.25	1.36	1.48
Total variable costs (£)	21.47	29.73	32.56	43.87
Gross margin per pig (£)	2.43	5.90	11.06	9.05
Fixed costs				
Labour (£)				
$\dfrac{\text{Cost of labour/year}}{\text{No. of pigs} \times \text{batches year}}$	1.76	2.70	2.89	3.21
Buildings (£)				
$\dfrac{\text{Housing cost/pig}}{10 \text{ years} \times \text{batches year}}$	1.48	2.16	2.81	4.06
Miscellaneous fixed costs (£)	0.59	0.62	0.98	1.07
Total fixed costs	3.83	5.48	6.68	8.34
Net margin/pig	−1.40	0.42	4.38	0.71
Average capital investment/pig space (£)				
Buildings				
$\dfrac{\text{Housing cost/pig}}{2}$	31.82	38.00	43.00	48.50
Weaner	26.80	26.80	26.80	26.80
Food				
$\dfrac{\frac{1}{2} \times \text{fat'ng tm-cred.tm} \times \text{food cost}}{\text{fattening time}}$	6.84	10.44	11.93	17.34
Labour				
($\frac{1}{2} \times$ labour cost)	0.88	1.35	1.45	1.61
Miscellaneous				
($\frac{1}{2} \times$ cost)	0.77	0.94	1.17	2.55
	67.11	77.53	84.35	96.80

stances. Small changes in basic input–output relationships can have very significant effects upon the final net margin and, consequently, upon return on capital. Because of this 'sensitivity' factors have been calculated (see Table 7.26) to show the effect of changing any one item of output or cost, while others remain constant.

The term 'pork' can be applied loosely to pigmeat from a wide range of carcass weights, when sold in a fresh uncured state. The lighter carcass, usually 50–57 kg liveweight invariably commands the higher price, but many producers favour a slightly heavier animal (57–65 kg) since this will realize a higher gross price and will gain the additional weight at an economic conversion rate. Carcass grading, at one time restricted to bacon pigs, is now applied to pork, quality premiums being paid on carcasses with a high proportion of lean and minimum fat.

Slaughter at these light weights allows for rapid turnover of working capital, and a favourable output/feed costs ratio. At lower weights, however, gross output is reduced along with margin per pig. More recently the rapid turnover has not compensated for the advantages of the higher gross output to be gained from, say, the bacon pig.

The cutter pig ranges across the familiar divisions between pork, bacon and heavy hog since it is possible to obtain cutters in all of the weight ranges that embrace the requirements traditionally filled by these categories – cutters being jointed by the factories and different parts going for curing and fresh pigmeat sales. Producers can and do take out specific contracts for all these four forms of pigmeat production, and in so doing tend to specialize or major in one particular type. The old idea of the heavy hog being a large fat carcass is now outmoded. Fat is no longer desired although the larger size which goes with the higher slaughter weight is. Many specialist heavy hog producers do, however, take advantage of local sources of cheap food, such as swill or biscuit waste. It is often these producers who have survived the cost and quality squeeze to which this particular type of production has been subjected. All the above forms of pigmeat production have their merits and disadvantages, but in all cases it is worth each category of producers working to ensure that, within any contractual constraints, the carcasses are marketed at the optimum weight. To achieve a top weight average near the limit may be penalized by too many overweight pigs, unless the unit is large enough to market pigs twice weekly. The optimal average weight is something that each producer must determine for himself, although there are commercial programs that have been developed to do this calculation on programmable calculators and microcomputers.

The examples shown in Table 7.26 depict a situation that few producers could tolerate for very long, particularly in view of the fact that interest charges have not been levied against any of the enterprises shown. For some producers the picture may not be as bad as shown in Table 7.26 since the examples used show average gross outputs and variable costs which reflect the current position for the average producer. Note should be taken that the fixed costs in respect of housing are current costs, and therefore the producer who has 'written off' most of his pig housing will be carrying far lower fixed costs – a factor which will be reflected in an enhanced net margin per pig. There are, however, two other factors to be taken into account in relation to Table 7.26. Firstly, these figures relate to feeding herds which only account for about 15 per cent of herds which fatten to slaughter. Where a breeding and feeding herd is combined, for costing purposes, then the weaner would appear at cost, currently *circa* £25. This would add, to each type of production, a benefit of around £6.50, a considerable contribution to output. Secondly, pig production has been suffering over the last 8 years, and more severely of late, from feed prices rising faster than pig prices (see Fig. 7.12).

It is clear from these observations that within any system of pigmeat production there are many input and output variables

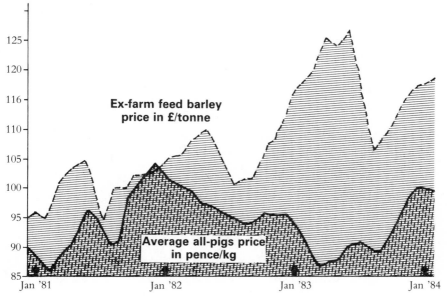

Figure 7.12   Feed and pig price indices: A comparison of fluctuations in the ex-farm price of feed barley and the average all-pigs price over the past three years. (British Farmer and Stockbreeder, No. 31, Vol. 2, 1984, p. 38)

Table 7.27   Sensitivity of pigmeat production to changes in input/output data

Factor	Net margin per pig (£)			
	Pork	Cutter	Bacon	Heavy hog
± 10% GO per pig	± 2.39	± 3.56	± 4.36	± 5.29
± 10% food costs/tonne	± 2.05	± 2.85	± 3.12	± 4.24
± 10% building costs/pig space	± 0.15	± 0.22	± 0.28	± 0.41
± 10% weaner cost	± 2.68	± 2.68	± 2.68	± 2.68
± 5% food conversion rate★	± 1.03	± 1.42	± 1.56	± 2.10

★ Using a high energy density ration would increase sensitivity to changes in conversion ratio.

operating at any one time and that the financial situation for any one producer is going to be unique to each according to circumstances and level of management. The enterprises vary in their sensitivity to changes in each variable, as is illustrated in Table 7.27.

Apart from an improvement in the feed and pig price indices (which if restored to the relative level of some 8 or 9 years ago would lift the net margins in Table 7.26 to break-even and above) which is, broadly speaking, outside the control of the individual producer, it is clear from the data in Table 7.27 that it is possible to raise the level of profitability by marginal improvements in a number of areas within the control of the pig producers. Where a deficit net margin has been identified, or is anticipated, then those variables which are within the control of the operator must be re-examined. In the cases presented in Table 7.26, features such as food conversion ratio, efficient labour use, carcass quality and food cost economy (by home mixing or better buying techniques) are all possible avenues of improvement within the scope of a pig producer. A simple partial budget evaluating improvements within the capabilities of the staff and the units resources could be drawn up and simple targets set for the next production period. An even simpler initial approach would be to take, say, the porker deficit net margin, and establish the food saving needed to bring the margin to a break-even point. This could be done as follows:

$$\text{Net margin (deficit)} \qquad \qquad \text{£1.40}$$
$$\text{Cost of food per tonne} \quad = \text{£180}$$
$$\therefore \text{ kg food to be saved} \quad = \frac{\text{Deficit net margin}}{\text{Price per kg food}} \quad = \frac{140}{18} = 7.78$$
$$\text{Food originally consumed per porker} \qquad \qquad = 114.00 \text{ kg}$$
$$\text{Less estimated saving needed} \qquad \qquad = \quad 7.78 \text{ kg}$$
$$\qquad \qquad \qquad \qquad \qquad \qquad \qquad \qquad 106.22 \text{ kg}$$
$$\text{Cost of food at £180 p/tonne} \qquad \qquad = \quad 19.12$$

Original cost of food $= £20.52$
∴ Saving $= £1.40$

The feed level of 135 kg of food represents a food conversion ratio of 2.94 : 1. The break-even feed level of 106.22 kg represents a food conversion ratio of 2.73 : 1, an improvement of 7.6 per cent (see Table 7.27).

Other calculations could be done looking at carcass quality or even the possibility of increasing the average weight of each pig sold up to the limit imposed by the contract, a simple and yet often overlooked point.

It is important to note that in all these calculations the basic data should come from the pig unit under scrutiny. When comparing units ensure that they are operating under similar conditions and on the same feed energy density ratios. Many pig units are now getting help from commercial and government agencies who, using the 'model pig' (computer matrix) concept, will recommend level of energy density and scale of feeding in order to maximize net returns.

It is this approach which has resulted in the comment: 'It seems that once again the plight facing pig producers has been partly alleviated by their own efforts in improving efficiency.' (Ridgeon, 1980). This comment is as true today as it was four years ago.

THE POULTRY ENTERPRISE (EGG PRODUCTION)

Poultry enterprises are often referred to as 'concrete' enterprises, since they require only a very small land area. Therefore, as with the pigs enterprise, efficiency measures calculated on a per hectare basis provide no useful guide to efficiency. There are, however, certain specific efficiency measures applicable to this enterprise which is well known for its finely balanced profit margins. Margins per bird are often calculated and these do provide useful efficiency measures when compared alongside appropriate standards, but probably the most significant efficiency measure for poultry enterprises is that of return on capital invested in the enterprise.

Post-war developments in the poultry industry have almost certainly been more rapid than those in any other branch of livestock farming. The days of the 'farmyard' hen have gone; even a poultry unit of 500–1 000 birds as a farm enterprise is made to look small nowadays when units of 10 000 birds are commonplace, and several units of 100 000+ birds exist. In addition to the establishment of larger and larger egg production units since the Second World War, very specialized units, usually on a large scale, have been developed for meat production (broilers), hatching eggs and for rearing stock which have been carefully bred, and often such units have been programmed by computer.

The formation of larger units in the poultry field undoubtedly results from the impact of economic pressures which have left poultry enterprises with smaller and smaller profit margins. Poultry producers have, therefore, moved towards larger units in order to gain advantages of scale.

The poultry industry today has many facets, most of which are highly specialized, ranging from commercial egg production on general farms, to highly specialized units producing table meat or hatching-eggs. Since a high degree of specialization is inevitably involved in the latter, it is unlikely that more than a few general farmers will carry any other poultry enterprise than an egg production unit and, therefore, this chapter will be confined to this subject.

Nowadays, it is generally agreed that the most profitable systems of egg production can be classified under three headings: deep litter, battery and wire or slatted floor systems – all in a controlled environment.

Capital costs for different egg production systems

Capital costs of housing and equipment, assuming a reasonably level site, road access and electricity and water supply, for units of between 10 000 and 20 000 birds, are likely to be as follows:

Deep litter (50 per cent litter, 50 per cent raised slatted or wire floor: stocking density on overall area 0.14 m² per bird)

£9.00 per bird

Battery cages (5 birds to 500 mm wide cage)   £7.50 per bird

The amount of capital invested in laying houses and equipment will vary and depends largely on the following factors – size of unit, standards of ventilation, the amount of automatic equipment, stocking density and any extra equipment needed.

A summary of the factors influencing the profitability of the poultry enterprise is given in Fig. 7.13.

Factors influencing gross output from egg production units

Assuming a high standard of housing, feeding and general manage-

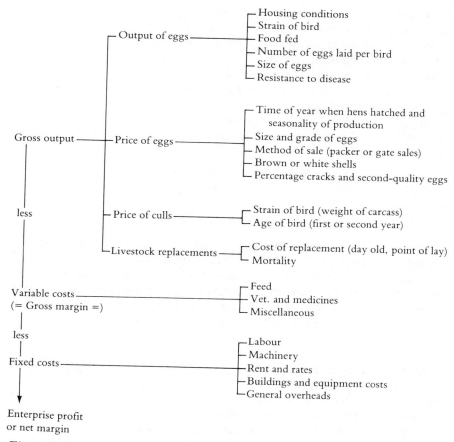

Figure 7.13   Factors affecting the profitability of egg production

ment, the following factors will influence levels of gross output in egg production units.

Strain of bird

The effect of strain of bird is probably the greatest of all the factors influencing gross output. Therefore, probably the biggest decision the poultry farmer has to make is choosing the right strain of bird. Since feed costs account for about 70 per cent of the cost of egg production, food conversion rate or the number of eggs produced for the food consumed is a most important ratio. This varies with strain of bird and, generally speaking, high-yielding birds usually show good returns for food consumed, and the high-yielding bird generally turns out to be more profitable in the end.

Light strains of birds produce more eggs than heavy strains, but the price realized per dozen is generally lower. Light strains consume less food, which is usually of a higher price than that fed to heavy-strain birds. The light-strain bird commands a lower cull price than the heavy-strain bird. The net effect of this is that a poultry farmer must select the strain that will give him the best output under his particular circumstances.

In a 52-week laying period the following levels of egg output provide a guide to average levels of performance that may be expected:

Strain	Egg output – 52-week laying period
Light	22 dozen (264)
Medium	20.5 dozen (246)
Heavy	19 dozen (228)

In addition to strain of bird, light patterns may influence the number of eggs laid per bird. Also, stresses that may occur could depress the number of eggs produced, as could a low house temperature and a poor level of nutrition. The number of eggs laid varies with the season of the year, and also fewer eggs are laid in the second year if birds are kept through a moult.

The size of eggs laid
Since there is a premium for larger eggs, egg size will have an influence on gross output. Heavy strains tend to produce larger, but fewer, eggs than do lighter strains, and also the older the hen the larger the egg that will be laid. Hens kept through a moult into their second year will generally produce larger eggs, but unfortunately production in the second year will be lower.

Incidence of disease
Obviously incidence of disease will influence egg output, and all precautions including medication of a preventative nature should be taken wherever possible.

Factors influencing price of eggs

Time of year when birds are hatched
Egg prices follow a definite pattern through the year. In winter, spring and early summer the price differential between eggs is lower than during the late summer and early autumn. It will be beneficial,

therefore, to have flocks hatched in the late summer/early autumn, so that birds come into lay between December and February, i.e. when they are approximately 18–20 weeks old, so that the maximum number of eggs will be laid when the price for those grades is greatest. As the bird gets older more large eggs are produced which command the highest price per dozen.

Size and grade of egg
The proportion of large and standard eggs produced will influence the overall price realized since seconds, cracks, etc. receive a much lower price.

Method of sale
Considerably higher prices can be obtained by selling eggs at the farm gate than by selling to packing stations. Eggs sold privately tend to attract a premium, especially if they can be acclaimed to be 'free range' eggs. In recent years the return of the traditional free-range unit has taken place with the important difference that its outlets are the more lucrative health food shops and up-market department stores.

Shell colour
Brown-shelled eggs always command a better price than white ones, although, in fact, the egg inside the shell is exactly the same.

External and internal egg quality
The price obtained for 'seconds' is much lower than that obtained for other eggs and so the proportion of seconds will obviously have a considerable influence on final profit margins. Different strains of hybrid layers vary considerably in respect of the internal quality of eggs produced by them, although much emphasis is placed on this aspect in the selection of breeding stock. Egg quality can also be influenced considerably by the way in which eggs are handled, cleaned, collected and stored. Quality in eggs is likely to be a more important factor in the future than it has been in the past.

Livestock replacement costs

When considering the gross output of a laying flock it must be remembered that livestock depreciation must be included as well as output and prices of eggs. Livestock depreciation covers the cull prices obtained for hens at the end of their production period as well as the cost of replacements brought in to replace them in the flock. Cull prices will be greatest for the heavier strains of bird and lowest for the lighter strains. Carcass value will also vary somewhat with the age of the bird when culled and also the time of the year when sold.

When it comes to replacing stock the poultry farmer must consider whether to buy his stock as day-old chicks, 3–4-week-old chicks, 8-week-old stock or birds at point of lay (18–20 weeks of age). If rearing facilities and labour are available the day-old chick may be the best proposition since purchase price is low and this, together with the cost of its rearing to point of lay, will come to less than the cost of a point of lay bird. An advantage of buying in 3–4-week-old birds is that mortality will be lower than for day-old chicks but, of course, brooder equipment will still be needed. Eight-week-old birds are quite popular; risks of mortality are mostly over, and brooder equipment is no longer necessary. Buying point-of-lay pullets means that the capital invested begins to produce almost immediately and the problems associated with rearing do not arise.

There are various arguments for, and against, keeping laying stock for a second year. In summary, the advantages are that larger eggs will be produced and little extra livestock depreciation costs will be incurred. However, fewer eggs (about 20 per cent) will be produced and a lower percentage of these comes in the winter months, and of course feed costs will be incurred during the moult period.

At the present time most poultry farmers do, in fact, cull their laying stock completely at the end of one year's production.

Variable costs

Feed costs
Feed accounts for approximately 70 per cent of the costs of egg production. The actual amount of food consumed will depend on the strain of bird, type of ration fed and the temperature of the environment. Since food is a major cost item in egg production, poultrymen should pay particular attention to wastage. Common causes of wastage are badly designed troughs, incorrect adjustment and overfilling of feeders.

The actual cost of the feed itself is more important. Purchases of bulk quantities may lower price, but, of course, the installation of a bulk bin will be necessary and the feasibility of purchasing feed in bulk quantities will depend on the size of the egg production unit and the distance from the supplying mill.

Veterinary, medicines and other miscellaneous variable costs

These will not be very great per bird, but nevertheless are very important despite the fact that these are often applied as a preventative measure, since the consequence of disease outbreak in a poultry unit can be devastating.

Fixed costs

Labour represents about 5–10 per cent of costs of production. It comprises only a small proportion of the total, but it can prove to be false economy to reduce it too much. Stockmanship is most important especially where large numbers of birds are being looked after by one man. An extra 5p per bird spent on labour is covered by a few eggs per bird per year. While it may be difficult actually to obtain these extra eggs per bird, it is very easy to lose them if the poultryman neglects certain aspects of his work.

It may be possible to reduce labour costs by mechanizing certain jobs. Of course, any labour saved must be profitably employed in some other way otherwise there is no financial gain to the business. At the same time, the extra costs (both capital and operational) relating to the extra machinery installed must not be forgotten. Furthermore, certain fixed costs can be easily overlooked with intensive enterprises like pigs and poultry, for example fixed cost items like electricity can be quite high for such enterprises and therefore should be watched carefully.

Measures of efficiency in egg production

The main efficiency measures are:

1. Egg returns per bird
   - (a) price per egg
   - (b) yield of eggs per bird
2. Food cost per bird
   - (c) quantity fed per bird
   - (d) price per tonne of feed
3. Flock depreciation
   - (e) replacement cost at point of lay less cull price

4. Food cost per dozen eggs   – encompassing (a), (b), (c), and (d) overleaf

5. Food cost per £100 output   – encompassing (a), (b), (c), (d) and (e) overleaf

6. Profit margin per bird   – either gross margin or net margin per bird.

When dealing with an enterprise like poultry it is most important

Table 7.28   *Egg production: gross margin and net margin per 100 birds*

	Flock A (buying in point of lay pullets)	Flock B (rearing own replacement stock from day-old chicks)
Period:	12 months in lay	5 months' rearing 12 months' laying
Gross output	£	£
Egg returns:		
21 dozen at 50 p/dozen	1 050.00	1 050.00
Livestock depreciation★	169.90	126.90
Gross output/100 birds	880.10	923.10
Variable costs		
Feed: 45 kg/bird at £148/tonne	666.00	666.00
Miscellaneous, inc. medicines at 57 p/bird	57.00	57.00
Total variable costs/100 birds	723.00	723.00
Gross margin/100 birds	157.10	200.10
Fixed costs		
Labour at 55 p/bird	55.00	55.00
Overhead costs:		
Depreciation on house and equipment, electricity and running costs at £0.95 per bird	95.00	95.00
Total fixed costs	150.00	150.00
∴ Net margin/100 birds	7.10	50.1

★ Livestock depreciation

Flock A		Flock B	
Cost of point of lay 100 pullets (£2.18/bird)	£218.00	Cost of 100 chicks and rearing to point of lay (£1.75 bird inc. mortality)	£175.00
Mortality in laying year	12½%	Mortality in laying year	12½%
Cull value at end of year (£0.55/bird)	£ 55.00	Cull value at end of year (£0.55/bird)	£55.00
Depreciation = £218 − £48.10 = £169.90		Depreciation = £175 − £48.10 = £126.90	

to look beyond the profit margin per bird and to consider the capital invested per bird and the return obtained on that capital.
7. Return on capital
   This may be either gross margin or net margin expressed as a percentage over the average capital invested in the hen, hen housing space, equipment and working capital – see Table 7.28 where gross margin and net margin per bird are given for two flocks, one buying in point of lay pullets and the other rearing replacements from day-old chicks.

The figures in Table 7.28 show that the flock B, rearing its own replacements, finishes up with the better net margin per 100 birds.

Scale of enterprise in egg production

There are a number of arguments for smaller units and various reasons that support large ones.

In favour of small farm units
1. Certain facilities and services are already on the farm and can be used, e.g. roads, concrete, cottages, buildings, machinery (e.g. tractors) and milling, mixing and possibly bulk storage equipment for feedingstuffs.
2. Family or supplementary labour may be available, and labour peaks created by the poultry enterprise can be integrated with other farm work.
3. The fact that the poultry enterprise is based on a farm may facilitate manure disposal.
4. The rest period after depopulation can be more easily borne since some income will probably be coming in from other enterprises.
5. Risks generally are lower – disease risk is less serious if it occurs.
6. There may be scope for farm gate sales because of location and limited production.
7. Egg production may be higher per bird from the smaller unit.

In favour of large, specialized units
1. Because of scale of enterprise, the capital cost per bird for housing and equipment may be lower.
2. Feed can be purchased in large quantities and will therefore be cheaper per tonne.
3. Specialist labour can be employed and the cost per bird can be minimized. Also, specialist management can be engaged.

4. Mechanization, on a large scale, can be justified.
5. In a large unit certain costs may be saved by rearing replacements and even hatching day-old chicks for replacements.

Conclusions

Post-war developments in the poultry industry have brought about decreases in egg producers' profit margins and this has led to the setting up of larger units with the inevitable demands on capital to try to maintain profits. This increase in specialization has meant that greater skills and attention to detail has been required of poultrymen and a more astute business approach and degree of expertise has been necessary at managerial levels. Whatever is the future of the poultry industry, it is certain that considerably more emphasis will be placed on quality rather than quantity in egg production, and so this high degree of operational and managerial skill is likely to continue to be necessary if poultry enterprises are to be profitable and survive the economic pressures and the growing social pressures from the animal welfare lobby.

8 | CROPS ENTERPRISE STUDIES

THE CEREALS ENTERPRISE

Since the mid-1970s dramatic changes in the methods of producing cereals has taken place on most farms. The basic understanding of the applied husbandry, the revolution in the agricultural chemical industry and the ability to drill large areas at the optimum time with direct drilling and minimal cultivation techniques have all contributed towards the significant changes in cereal production.

The resultant trends have been an increase in the area of winter wheat and winter barley grown and a subsequent decrease in the spring barley area. Against a background of increasing fixed cost items on most farms, improved yields have been sought after and achieved. There is a close correlation between cereal yield and final profit margin, but attention to detail and skill in using increasingly expensive variable cost items has become a feature of any business where cereals form a significant part of the output.

Cereal growing continues to change with reference to the degree of specialization accorded to the main types grown. This specialization is already moving towards a recognition of the need to manage individual varieties according to their characteristics. In the 1970s farmers ceased to grow cereals and began to grow winter wheat, winter barley, etc. The basic techniques are unchanged; the farmers' ability to manipulate them is a result of greater understanding, improved plant breeding and the associated research and development which has taken place on all fronts.

The total area for each of the three main cereals is shown in Table 8.1. The trend towards increasing land area devoted to growing wheat is clearly highlighted. During the 1960s with allowance for seasonal variations, the area of wheat remained around 800 000–900 000 hectares. Since the early 1970s this figure has increased at the expense of spring barley and also reflects the trend to grow more cereals.

Table 8.1   Wheat, barley, oats: estimated production area, yield per hectare and total production

| Harvest year | Wheat | | | Barley | | | Oats | | |
	Production area ('000 ha)	Yield per hectare (tonnes)	Production ('000 tonnes)	Production area ('000 ha)	Yield per hectare (tonnes)	Production ('000 tonnes)	Production area ('000 ha)	Yield per hectare (tonnes)	Production ('000 tonnes)
United Kingdom									
1978	1 258	5.25	6 613	2 352	4.19	9 848	180	3.92	706
1979	1 372	5.22	7 169	2 348	4.10	9 623	136	3.99	542
1980	1 441	5.88	8 466	2 330	4.43	10 323	148	4.08	602
1981	1 491	5.84	8 707	2 329	4.39	10 227	144	4.30	619
1982*	1 663	6.17	10 266	2 223	4.91	10 906	130	4.50	583

* Provisional data.
Note. From 1981 barley and oats figures include estimates of the area, yield and production on minor holdings.
Source: Agricultural Statistics United Kingdom 1982, Table 2.1, p. 8.

Factors affecting the profitability of the cereal enterprise

A summary of the main factors affecting the profitability of cereal enterprises is presented in Fig. 8.1. Gross output is mainly influenced by yield and price, and the costs have been grouped as variable and fixed costs which, when deducted from the gross output, leave the final enterprise profit or net margin.

Factors affecting cereal yields

A number of factors will influence cereal yields, and these will be considered in turn.

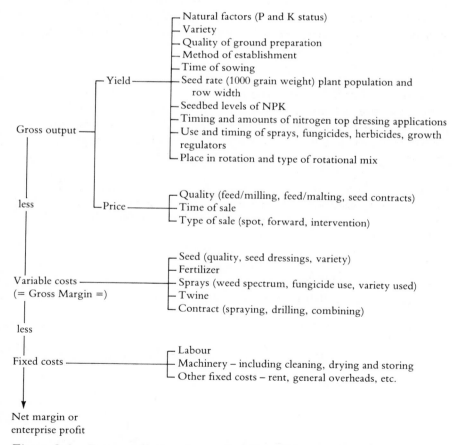

Figure 8.1   Factors affecting the profitability of the cereals enterprise

Natural factors

Cereals, like all farm crops, are influenced by a number of natural factors, e.g. rainfall, soil type, aspect, etc. These factors cause variations in cereal yields from year to year and area to area in any one year, and the farmer has no control over them.

Variety

Variety of cereal grown will influence yields obtained since each variety differs in its yield potential. Information on the performance of cereal varieties in different parts of the country is available in the *Recommended list of cereal varieties* published annually by the NIAB (National Institute of Agricultural Botany, Cambridge). Information should be sought by the cereal grower from the latest list available since varieties do vary from year to year – older ones become outclassed in terms of yield as new ones are introduced, and also some new varieties may break down in resistance to a particular disease and therefore produce lower yields after being 'on the market' for a few years.

Quality of ground preparation

The condition of the seedbed at the time of planting is one of the most critical areas relating to eventual yield. Evaluating soil and weather conditions for drilling operations will have a marked effect on winter-sown crop survival and the all important plant numbers per square metre in the spring.

Spring-sown crops show equal tendency to yield well when good-quality seedbeds are provided. Table 8.2 highlights the effect of seedbed conditions on eventual yield of winter wheat crops in 1980.

Method of establishment

For autumn establishment of cereals three main methods are used

Table 8.2   Effect of seedbed conditions on yield

Seedbed	Spring plant numbers as % of seeds sown	Yield (tonnes/ha)	Gross margin (£/ha)
Very good	69	7.4	544
Good	67	7.4	521
Average	65	7.1	508
Poor	58	6.1	413

Source: J. D. Hollies. 'Pointers to profitable wheat', *ICI 1980 Survey*, Table 13, p. 9.

Table 8.3 *Method of establishment*

Method	Number of fields	Sowing date	Date of first top dressing	Yield (tonnes/ha)
Plough	550	13 Oct.	11 Mar.	7.3
Minimal cultivation	255	8 Oct.	10 Mar.	7.4
Direct drill	71	4 Oct.	3 Mar.	7.2

Source: J. D. Hollies. 'Pointers to profitable wheat', *ICI 1980 Survey*, Table 12, p. 9.

(these are each capable of producing good yields and hence potential profit) – traditional plough and cultivate, minimal cultivation and direct drilling. The system chosen must suit the farm and the farmer. Economic aspects must, however, be considered, the important ones being timeliness, fuel use and labour/machinery requirements per hectare of established cereals.

In strict yield terms recent work on winter wheat crops suggest that there is little difference between the three systems of establishment (see Table 8.3). Selecting the right circumstances in which to use a technique is the real key to success.

Time of sowing

Sowing time of autumn cereals has been significantly brought forward in the farming calendar. Recognition that seeds establish more quickly and retain their vigour in seedbeds which are not wet and cold have led to better post-winter plant populations and potential yield.

The most important management aspect is not how early or how late the crop is sown, but in being organized in such a way so as to pick the optimum time. Labour and machinery planning plus skill in managing the soil are the key features of success. Tables 8.4

Table 8.4 *Effect of seedbed conditions, weather at drilling and soil moisture at drilling on yield.*

Seedbed conditions		Weather at drilling		Soil moisture at drilling	
Sowing date	Yield (tonnes/ha)	Sowing date	Yield (tonnes/ha)	Sowing date	Yield (tonnes/ha)
Good 2 Oct. 6.3		Mild, dry 2 Oct. 6.3		Dry 30 Sept. 6.2	
Poor 8 Oct. 6.0		Mild, wet 7 Oct. 5.7		Moist 5 Oct. 6.2	
		Cold, dry 8 Oct. 6.0		Wet 12 Nov. 4.9	
		Cold, wet 9 Nov. 5.1			

Source: J. D. Hollies and G. J. Perkin. 'Pointers to profitable winter barley', *ICI 1980 Survey*, Table 10, p. 7.

Table 8.5   Effect of sowing date on yield

	Sowing date average	Seed sown /m²	Plants/m² at 1st top dressing	Ears/m² at harvest	Yield (tonnes/ha)
Earliest sown 25%	17 Sept.	336	262	862	6.3
Next 25%	28 Sept.	336	263	832	6.3
Next 25%	5 Oct.	355	253	817	6.3
Latest sown 25%	22 Oct.	360	234	760	5.9

Source: J. D. Hollies and G. J. Perkin. 'Pointers to profitable winter barley', *ICI 1980 Survey*, Table 9, p. 7.

and 8.5 show the combined effect of sowing time, seedbed and weather conditions at drilling on winter barley crops in the *ICI 1980 Survey*.

Seed rate and row width

The basic principle to bear in mind when considering seed rates and row widths for cereals is that the overall objective should be an optimum plant population per unit area. Too high a seed rate will produce too many plants which will compete with each other for light, space and nutrients, while too low a seed rate will produce fewer plants, and although each plant may produce a larger number of ears of grain than usual the total yield per hectare will be lower due to fewer total ears per hectare.

Table 8.6

1 000 grain weight (g)	Grains/kg
37	27 027
38	26 315
39	25 641
40	25 000
41	24 390
42	23 809
43	23 255
44	22 727
45	22 222
46	21 739
47	21 276
48	20 833
49	20 408
50	20 000
51	19 607
52	19 230
53	18 867

The plant population per unit area can be manipulated by the farmer. An awareness of the 1 000 grain weight of the seed to be sown can be a useful guide when establishing seed rates (see Table 8.6).

Recent trials continue to support earlier work carried out in 1965 at High Mowthorpe EHF showing a small yield advantage where narrow (11 cm) drill spacings are used.

Fertilizer application

Nitrogen fertilizer applied in the autumn to winter cereals is important to encourage tillering of the cereal plants. Nitrogen fertilizer applied in the spring to either winter or spring cereals does lead to increased yields, but the extent depends on the time of the application of the nitrogen fertilizer (see Fig. 8.2).

The basic principles of economics underlying nitrogen application to cereals were covered in Chapter 4, where the law of diminishing returns was explained and also the technique of marginal analysis was used to locate the point of optimum level of input of a resource so as to maximize profits.

The effect of date of nitrogen fertilizer application upon final yield of cereals is in general terms as follows. Nitrogen fertilizer applied

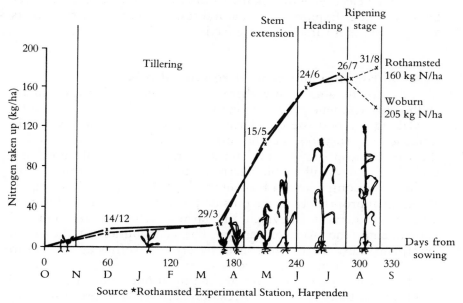

Source *Rothamsted Experimental Station, Harpenden

Figure 8.2   *Timing of nitrogen fertilizer application and cereal growth (Rothamsted Experimental Station, Harpenden)*

early in the spring will cause leaf and straw growth and consequently higher grain yields, whereas that applied later will not only increase yield of grain but will also cause the nitrogen content of the grain to be higher – which may be desirable for feeding grain or for wheat to be used in bread-making, but is most undesirable for malting barley, since a high protein content causes poor fermentation in the brewing process.

Use and timing of spray chemicals

Considerable variations can occur in cereal gross margins as a result of the selection and subsequent use of spray chemicals. The costs incurred on an individual farm will, in many cases, be a reflection of past farming activities and the sequence of cropping practised. Managing a business where cereals contribute a high proportion of the output will mean that considerable expertise is required if full benefit is to be achieved from the chemical being used.

Evaluating the many alternatives available to achieve the same end is a key business management area. Computerized systems can be used to aid with this task (see Fig. 8.3).

On farm evaluation will take a little more effort, but will enable the farmer to build in his own criteria with regard to the timing and cultural requirements of any combination of products.

Varietal selection with regard to disease resistance should never be overlooked. Exploiting the natural resistance of a variety to pests and diseases is invariably cost effective.

Place in rotation and type of rotational mix

Cereals can fit almost anywhere in a sequence of crops and by skilful management prove successful.

Making the best use of a farm's comparative advantages should influence the rotation and the mix of cereals and livestock where they are appropriate. Careful business management planning and good husbandry will enable a farm to do both of these things, e.g. evaluate the comparative advantage and get the rotational mix right. Reacting appropriately to the outside pressures on the farm business will direct the way in which any farm develops its rotation and subsequently the place of cereals. The contribution of the cereal enterprise must in the final analysis provide sufficient total farm gross margin to meet the fixed costs and leave a profit.

The factors discussed above are the main ones influencing cereal yields. Since there is a close correlation between final profit margins and yields, the impact of these factors must be considered carefully. If these factors are within the farmer's control then he should try

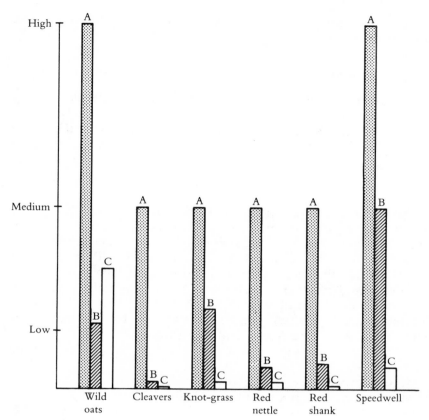

Chemical treatment

(A) None

(B) Hytane + Avenge 630   Autumn post – emergent
    Mecoprop   Autumn post – emergence

(C) Avadex BW   Pre-emergent
    Mecoprop   Autumn post-emergent
    Malet   Early spring

Result

(A) Yield 4.6 tonnes/ha, 56.9% of target.
    Net return £464.2/ha

(B) Yield 7.5 tonnes/ha, 94.1% of target.
    Net return £699.6/ha

(C) Yield 7.6 tonnes/ha, 94.8% of target.
    Net return £726.7/ha

Figure 8.3   *Weed infestation level (target yield 8 tonnes/ha) (Ciba-Geigy Agrochemicals 1980 Sprayplan)*

to organize them in such a way as to achieve the greatest possible profit margins from cereals.

Factors influencing price obtained for cereals

The factors influencing price obtained for cereals will fall under three headings, i.e. the purpose for which the grain is sold, the time of the year when it is sold and the method of sale.

The purpose for which grain is sold

Cereals may be grown for seed, and depending on the quality of the seed sample and the husbandry and hygiene standards under which the seed was produced, a premium of £15–20 or more per tonne may be obtained, especially if grown under contract.

Barley samples that are suitable may be sold for malting purposes and command a premium over feeding barley prices. The chief requirements of a malting sample are a low protein content of the grain which should be plump and thin skinned.

Payment for milling quality in wheat is related to certain standards:
1. Gluten content;
2. Alpha-amylase enzyme activity (Hagberg Test);
3. Protein test (normal 10 per cent); UK tests rarely above 13 per cent.

In addition, moisture content, admixtures, moulds etc. will all influence milling quality. Having selected a variety suitable for milling, the resultant price will be a function of husbandry skill during growth and harvest, coupled with sound storage policy where appropriate. Local, national, European and world cereal supply and demand have the final influence on price received.

Time of year when sold

The market price of cereals normally increases throughout the cereal year (1 July–30 June). Although the increase in actual market price that occurs may vary somewhat from year to year, the trend is generally upwards during the period.

Method of sale

Selling grain through merchants, farmers co-operative groups, etc. can influence the final price received. For minimum size grain, selling into intervention can improve the price received in an over-supplied market situation. Timing and method of sale can combine to produce significant price variations for the farmer. Where cereals form a significant part of a farm's output, care in marketing is vital.

Table 8.7 Cereal crop gross margins

	Winter wheat	Spring wheat
Yield (tonnes/ha)	Average 5.9	Average 4.25
Output	£	£
Feed wheat	735	530
Milling wheat	765	550
Variable costs:		
Seed	40	50
Fertilizer	85	70
Sprays	70	40
Total variable costs/ha	195	160
Gross margin/ha	£	£
Feed wheat	540	370
Milling wheat	570	390
	Winter barley	Spring barley
Yield (tonnes /ha)	Average 5.0	Average 4.25
Output	£	
Feed barley	585	500
Malting barley	625	530
Variable costs:	£	£
Seed	35	40
Fertilizer	80	60
Sprays	55	30
Total variable costs	170	130
Gross margin/ha	£	£
Feed barley	415	370
Malting barley	455	400
	Winter oats	Spring oats
Yield (tonnes/ha)	Average 4.9	Average 4.25
Output	£	£
Feed oats	550	480
Milling oats	590	510
Variable costs:	£	£
Seed	45	45
Fertilizer	65	60
Sprays	25	20
Total variable costs	135	125
Gross margin/ha	£	£
Feed oats	415	355
Milling oats	455	385

Source: Nix 1984 pp. 3–6.

Levels of costs in cereal production

The main variable cost items are seed, fertilizer, sprays, contract work – e.g. drilling, spraying, combining and casual labour if employed – as well as certain miscellaneous costs, e.g. twine.

Figures of average levels of outputs, variable costs and gross margins for cereals are given in Table 8.7.

Table 8.8   Economics of grain storage

---

1. Cost of storage/tonne for 8 months (Sept.–May)

Interest on grain at £100/tonne at 14% = £100 at 14% = £14 ÷ $\frac{8}{12}$	£9.33
Loss in weight = 30 kg/tonne (3% loss*) at £100/tonne	£3.00
Extra drying and handling, say £3/tonne	£3.00

Storage cost	£15.33

at 2% loss storage cost*	£14.33
5% loss storage cost	£17.33

2. Annual buildings cost/tonne

Capital cost/tonne ⎱ Storage space ⎰	10 years Life	15 years Life	20 years Life
£45/tonne	7.65	6.15	5.40
£85/tonne	14.45	11.61*	10.20
£105/tonne	17.85	14.35	12.60

* Example of above calculation:

£85/tonne capital cost spread over 15 years
= £5.66/tonne capital cost spread over 1 year (straight-line depreciation calculation)

Plus 14% on half capital invested, i.e. $\frac{£85}{2}$ at 14% = £5.95

Therefore, the total buildings cost = annual capital cost	£5.66
Interest on half capital	£5.95

	£11.61

---

3. Annual costs/tonne stored

	10-year life			15-year life			20-year life		
Capital cost/tonne storage space	£45	£85	£105	£45	£85	£105	£45	£85	£105
Annual buildings cost	7.65	14.45	17.85	6.15	11.61	14.35	5.40	10.20	12.60
Storage cost (8 months)	15.33	15.33	15.33	15.33	15.33	15.33	15.33	15.33	15.33
Total annual cost	22.98	29.78	33.18	21.48	26.94	29.68	20.73	25.53	27.93

Source: Calculated after Norman and Coote, Table 7.8, p. 240, *The Farm Business*

Economics of grain storage

When trying to evaluate the worthwhileness of storing grain, it must be remembered that in addition to the annual costs of the grain store itself, other factors must be costed. If the grain itself had been sold rather than stored, it would have realized capital that could have (a) brought in some return in the form of interest, or (b) reduced a bank overdraft position in the business cash flow and hence reduced charges against the business – particularly important when interest rates on borrowed money are high.

Therefore, interest on the value of grain in store over the period should be considered and also the benefit/requirement of reducing bank overdraft. During the storage period, grain losses of between 3 and 5 per cent can be expected, drying and handling charges will be incurred and over long periods a requirement to condition the grain may arise. (See Table 8.8).

Conclusions

The 1970s saw many changes take place in cereal production. The area of winter cereals being grown has increased and winter barley is now an accepted crop in many rotations.

Attention to detail has always been practised in livestock husbandry. Recent developments in cereal husbandry have demanded the same degree of careful supervision, e.g. regular walking of crops, identifying growth stages, if profitable cereal production is to be achieved.

In the final analysis, success from the individual farmer's point of view in cereal production results largely from marginal efficiency. The result of attention to detail all long the line is cumulative and the outcome is quite enormous in terms of effect on final profitability.

BREAK CROP ENTERPRISES

Break crops grown within a mainly cereal crop sequence must invariably meet certain basic requirements. These will relate to husbandry considerations – disease breaks, soil fertility and timing of main operations, e.g. planting, spraying, harvesting etc. – and financial considerations – possible effects on fixed cost structure

Table 8.9   Average levels of yields, prices and variable costs for some arable break crops

Arable break crop	Winter beans	Spring beans	Dried peas	Vining peas	Winter oilseed rape	Spring oilseed rape
Yield (tonnes/ha)	3.1	2.9	3.2		2.8	2.1
Price/tonne (£)	170	175	190		290	285
Output (£/ha)	525	505	610	740	810	600
Variable costs:						
Seed (£/ha)	55	55	95	80	25	25
Fertilizer (£/ha)	10	15	20	20	130	130
Sprays (£/ha)	40	30	55	45	60	60
Miscellaneous (£/ha)						
Total variable costs (£/ha)	105	100	170	145	215	215
Gross margin/ha (£)	420	405	440	595	595	385

Source: Nix, 1984, pp. 10–12, 14.

specialist machines – the gross margin or potential of a proposed break and the benefit to the following cereal crop.

For the cereal farmer the selection of a break crop becomes much narrower when applied to an individual farm situation. Break crops which can be grown, harvested, conditioned and stored using the same machinery and equipment as that used for cereals, clearly have advantages.

Deciding on and growing a particular break crop is an important business-management decision for the cereal farmer, thorough researching of the field-based practical problems right through to marketing must be done.

In spite of the farmer's ability to control chemically many of the aspects hitherto controlled by rotational breaks, the selection and use of break crops is still an important business management decision; since the 1960s various crops have been grown and a few brief comments on a number of them will now be made.

Beans

Beans are a legume crop and therefore supply nitrogen to the soil which can be utilized by the following crop. Beans also provide a break against soil-borne fungus diseases of cereals. While some weeds are controlled by using herbicides on the bean crop, grass weeds may continue to increase if proper control measures are not practised.

Winter beans
Varieties are susceptible to chocolate spot, but because of their forward growth in the summer may avoid aphid attack. The protein content of different varieties is fairly consistent.

Spring beans
Spring beans are not so susceptible to chocolate spot, but are very likely to be attacked by aphids, and in a bad season insecticide costs can be considerably more than those quoted in Table 8.9. Varieties do vary somewhat in protein content.

Peas

Like beans, peas are also legumes, and therefore improve soil fertility by fixing nitrogen in the soil. Peas provide a good break crop against soil-borne cereal diseases, but grass weeds and wild oats may continue to build up in the pea crop if proper control measures are not practised.

Dried peas (marrowfat peas for processing)
Harvesting of the dried pea crop can be quite a problem, especially in a poor summer when the peas may be shed from the pods before being harvested. Conditions at the point of harvesting will have a marked effect on the eventual quality of the sample, e.g. human consumption or stock feed, and hence price.

Vining peas (for freezing and dehydration)
Vining peas are usually grown on contract, and therefore the farmer wishing to grow this crop will need to be fairly near a processing factory or chilling plant. The capital involved in growing and harvesting vining peas can be high since either a mobile viner or access to a static vining machine is necessary. Labour costs are also high. Although the crop-produces a good gross margin per hectare associated fixed costs are high.

Oilseed rape

Since the mid 1960s the area of land devoted to winter oilseed rape has grown steadily and apart from 1968 when the area dropped it has developed from around 6 500 ha to over 200 000 ha in 1983. As with all crops attention to detail and regular crop walking linked to the appropriate cultural action is vital. In spite of new varieties and sound technical knowledge the success of the crop is still closely linked to something as basic as the control of wood pigeons. Heavy damage causes yield losses and subsequent sequential flowering is accentuated.

Herbage seeds

For those farmers who can produce good crops of herbage seeds, this is a very good break crop. Soil conditions and fertility are improved; some soil-borne fungus diseases tend to break down while land is down to grass (although certain grasses do act as host to take-all), and wild oats may be overcome to some extent. A range of average levels of gross margins that can be obtained is given in Table 8.10.

Broadly speaking, herbage seed production is a very specialized job and those who can do it well can obtain very good financial results. Crops grown for herbage seed can often be utilized by live-

Table 8.10   Average and high levels of gross margin per hectare from herbage seed crops

	Gross margin		Yield of seed (100 kg)	
	Average (£/ha)	High (£/ha)	Average	High
RVP Italian ryegrass	560	930	9.8	14.7
S24 Early perennial ryegrass	540	890	9.9	14.8
S23 Late perennial ryegrass	560	925	8.6	12.9
S352 timothy	345	585	3.5	5.2
S215 meadow fescue	460	760	6.2	9.3
S26 cocksfoot	505	825	6.5	9.7
Essex broad red clover	255	420	3.0	4.5
*Kent wild white clover and			0.8 (WWC)	1.2 (WWC)
*Kent indigenous perennial ryegrass	710	1 105	+4.0 (PR)	6.0 (PR)

* These are usually taken in the same cut
Source: Nix 1984 pp. 15–16.

stock, e.g. sheep, so the total gross margin for the crop will be greater than that of just the seeds harvested.

Other seed crops

Various other crops can be grown for seed production as a break in the cropping sequence where cereals predominate. Such crops are sugar-beet seed, mustard seed, coriander seed. Production of crop seed is usually done on contract and the financial results are very variable; technically these seed crops may help to overcome some of the husbandry problems that arise from 'continuous' cereal growing.

Field scale vegetables

On the right type of soil, field scale vegetables make a good break crop and yield a good gross margin per hectare. Since supply can easily exceed demand, growers should seek a contract to ensure a satisfactory price. A guide to likely average levels of gross margin per hectare is given in Table 8.11.

Root crops

Where root crops such as potatoes and sugar-beet can be incorporated into a rotation, these provide an excellent break against cereal

Table 8.11   Field scale vegetables: likely gross margins (£/ha)

Crop	Likely gross margin/ha
Brussels sprouts	£1 035
Winter cabbage	£1 380
Spring greens	£1 840
Dwarf beans (for processing) – sliced	£ 675
– whole	£ 695
Autumn cauliflower	£1 010
Winter cauliflower	£1 355
Carrots	£ 925
Onions (Dry bulb)	£1 250

Source: Nix 1984 pp. 19–20.

disease; the residual value of fertilizers left for the following crop is quite high. In addition, the gross margin per hectare is likely to be fairly high. Further details of these root crops are given in the potato and sugar-beet enterprise studies.

Leys

Short leys are often used as a break crop in cereal production. Unfortunately, however, certain soil-borne fungus diseases, e.g. take-all, can live on the roots of certain grasses, e.g. perennial ryegrass, and then attack cereals when the grass is ploughed up. Soil condition and fertility is improved under a ley and wild oats may be decreased by putting land down to grass. The gross margin which finally results depends upon the method of utilization of the grass, and if this involves grazing livestock the density of stocking will be a most important factor. One- or two-year leys may be cut for hay and sold as a cash crop. Lucerne may be grown; it does especially well on light dry soils where it can be grazed or conserved, but is usually left down for several years owing to the high cost of establishment.

Fallows

Some cereal growers may feel that where husbandry problems are particularly bad a field should be completely rested from cropping for a season – this is called fallowing. Fallowing a field should provide a farmer with opportunities to kill off grass weeds by cultivations and/or chemicals. Since no crop is grown there are no host plants for soil-borne fungus disease, and therefore their life cycle is broken. Soil conditions may also be improved by fallowing.

Fallowing offers many advantages, but unfortunately there is no direct output from it apart from the increased yield in subsequent crops. The cost involved in fallowing a field can be quite considerable. If an amount of fallowing is done on a farm in a year the overall farm gross margin will be tremendously 'diluted' by the fallowed hectares that make no contribution.

General conclusions on break crops

When trying to decide whether or not to grow a break crop and when choosing the type of break crop, the following points should be considered:

1. The effect that the break crop may have on the labour on the farm. Will the present labour force cope with the break crop; can there be a reduction in the present number of workers or will more labour be needed to cope with the break crop?
2. What effect will the break crop have on machinery? Will extra specialist machinery be needed, or will the machinery already available on a farm be better used, e.g. peak demands for machinery might be spread?
3. Will the break crop have any effect on the variable costs of the following cereal crop (i.e. it may be possible to use less expensive sprays if certain weeds have been eradicated in the break crop year; fertilizer costs for the cereal following the break crop may be lower, e.g. where a cereal follows a legume break crop)?
4. Will a cereal crop grown after a break crop produce higher yields as a result of the break crop?
5. What effect will the break crop have on the rotation of the farm, i.e. will the break crop fit into the present farm system or will a new cropping sequence have to be planned?
6. What effect will the introduction of a break crop have on the fixed costs of the farm business? While a break crop may produce a good gross margin per hectare, e.g. vining peas, any subsequent increase in fixed costs must be carefully considered and the likely effect on the net farm income of the farm budgeted.
7. The eventual choice of break crop should also acknowledge the need for agriculture to co-exist with urban and residential pressures. Siting of a break crop close to habitation, where pigeon control is likely to be a major requirement may need careful thought. Certain break crops need locating with care in relation to habitation and the opportunity for supervision; crop loss from theft can be a significant factor. The need to consider these items impose additional rotational and economic constraints and they should be borne in mind when evaluating break crops.

One of the problems of trying to evaluate the usefulness of a break crop is that beneficial effects may result over a number of years. A useful guide can be obtained by calculating a rotation or cropping sequence gross margin and comparing this with the gross margin that would result from a cropping sequence which did not contain a break crop over the same period of time. This has been done in Table 8.12.

Assuming that the level of fixed costs is not altered on the farm in Table 8.12, since the same machinery can be used for both barley and beans, then the better net margin over the 5 years came from the cropping sequence which included the beans break crop.

Table 8.12   Rotation or cropping sequence gross margin

1. Cropping sequence gross margin (no break crop)

Year	Crop	Gross margin (£/ha)
1	Spring barley	400
2	Spring barley	330
3	Spring barley	280
4	Spring barley	250
5	Spring barley	250
	Total	1 510
	Average/year =	302

2. Cropping sequence gross margin (break crop – spring beans)

Year	Crop	Gross margin (£/ha)
1	Beans	350
2	Spring barley	420
3	Spring barley	400
4	Spring barley	330
5	Spring barley	280
	Total	1 780
	Average/year =	356

3. Cropping sequence gross margin (break 'crop' – fallow)

Year	Crop	Gross margin (£/ha)
1	Fallow	0
2	Spring barley	420
3	Spring barley	400
4	Spring barley	330
5	Spring barley	280
	Total	1 430
	Average/year =	286

THE POTATO ENTERPRISE

Most households regard potatoes as a daily necessity and therefore national demand remains fairly constant irrespective of price – i.e. there is an inelastic demand for potatoes. Although demand is fairly consistent, yields of potatoes are affected considerably by natural factors, e.g. rainfall, blight, etc. so supplies fluctuate, and therefore the price the producer receives varies considerably from year to year. In the earlier years of this century, fluctuation in price gave rise to the 'potato cycle' where the area planted was influenced by prices obtained in the preceding year or two. In more recent years there has come between the producer, on the one hand, and the

Table 8.13   Human consumption of potatoes

Year	Potatoes consumed (kg)
1970–71	95
1971–72	97
1972–73	99
1973–74	102
1974–75	101
1975–76	87★
1976–77	84★
1977–78	91
1978–79	98
1979–80	100
1980–81	103

Average consumption 1959–60 to 1968–69 = 89 kg

★ Drought years.
Source: Potato Marketing Board.

consumer, on the other, the Potato Marketing Board which attempts to ensure an adequate supply of potatoes each year by regulating the hectares planted and absorbing, if necessary, excess potatoes in years of over-production.

Human consumption of potatoes per person has altered very little in recent years – as shown by the figures in Table 8.13. Annual demand for potatoes is, therefore, fairly predictable, but supplies are variable from one season to another. The data in Table 8.14 indicate the variations in national average yields over recent years, and it can be seen that these have been considerable. Even a small variation in yield per hectare can have a substantial effect nationally.

Table 8.14   Potato producer and production statistics

Crop year	1976	1977	1978	1979	1980	1981	1982
No. of PMB registered producers	34 938	35 286	33 387	32 149	30 225	28 760	27 498
Registered producer plantings ('000 ha)	195	199	184	171	174	162	161
Total GB Plantings ('000 ha)	208	214	200	189	191	179	179
Yield (tonnes/ha)	21.4	28.8	34.9	32.4	35.1	32.9	36.5
GB production ('000 tonnes)	4 458	6 163	6 980	6 138	6 707		6 539
UK guaranteed price per tonne	£39.37	£45.77	£43.94	£43.94	£43.94	£43.94	£43.94
UK average market price per tonne	£131.58	£42.81	£44.08	£58.81	£44.45	£83.62	£53.06 (prov)

Source: Potato Marketing Board annual report and accounts 1983. pp. 8, 9.

The influence of seasonal factors on yields obviously creates an almost insurmountable obstacle to any attempt at the regulation of national output. However, the Potato Marketing Board set up in 1955 (under the 1931 and 1933 Agricultural Marketing Acts) tries to regulate the national output of potatoes, and makes this one of its main objectives.

The main functions of the Potato Marketing Board

Area control
In an attempt to prevent over-production of potatoes in one year and scarcity in another, every potato grower who grows more than 0.4 ha of potatoes must register with the Board. Each grower is allocated a basic area. New growers can apply to the Board for a basic area allowance. The Board charges a levy, currently £36.0 ha (in 1984), for each hectare grown by a registered producer; hectares grown in excess of a producer's basic area are levied at a higher rate, currently £180.00/ha (in 1984).

In certain years, the Board may reduce or increase each registered producer's area – and this is called his quota. Basic areas have been reduced by certain percentages in the following years.

1979 – quota was 90 per cent of basic area
1980 – quota was 92½ per cent of basic area
1983 – quota was 97 per cent of basic area
1984 – prescribed at 95 per cent of basic area

Control of the ware size
The Potato Marketing Board can also regulate the amount of ware potatoes coming on to the market by regulating riddle size. Usually only bottom riddle sizes are stipulated, but top riddle size can also be set so that very large misshapen potatoes are removed, thereby further reducing the amount of potatoes coming on to the market.

Market control and support
In years when there is a surplus of potatoes, the Potato Marketing Board can enter the market and buy excess potatoes through a contract-buying programme. An assured market scheme is operated by the board and for 1984 the first stage of the scheme is set at 500 000 tonnes. A guaranteed price is still set by the Government (1984 = £43.94/tonne).

Future support arrangements are still being discussed, with a prospect of an agreement on a European Community regime for potatoes some time in the future.

Research

The Potato Marketing Board conducts research into certain aspects of the potato crop. An experimental station at Sutton Bridge is currently investigating storage management problems, humidity control in potato stores, and control of sprouting and disease during storage. Funding of research at Universities and postgraduate studentship awards also benefit the producer.

Publicity

The Potato Marketing Board also undertakes certain publicity campaigns and general advertising of potatoes to promote various ways in which potatoes can be used by the consumer.

Factors affecting the profitability of the potato enterprise

Potato producers should be concerned with more than just the husbandry of potato growing; they should make it their business to be aware of factors which influence the net margin (or enterprise

Table 8.15 Range of gross output, variable costs and gross margins for potatoes

Maincrop potatoes			
Yield (tonnes/ha)	Low 23	Average 34	High 45
	£	£	£
Output	1 410	2 080	2 755
Variable costs:			
Seed		350	
Fertilizer		215	
Sprays		125	
Casual labour for picking		235	
Sundries (PMB levy, bags, etc.)	155	190	225
Total variable costs	1 080	1 115	1 150
Gross margin/ha	330	965	1 605

Source: Nix 1984 p. 7.

profit) of the crop. Of course, many factors do influence this final net margin. Some of these are outside the control of the farmer, but there are several others which are clearly within the farmer's control so he can influence considerably final profit margins derived from his potato crop. Surveys of potato production clearly show a wide range in final net margins from the potato crop – a range of figures of gross output and variable costs for potatoes with the resulting gross margin is given in Table 8.15.

A summary of the most important factors affecting the net margin of the potato enterprise is given in Fig. 8.4.

Factors affecting gross output of potatoes

The two chief factors influencing gross output are yield and price

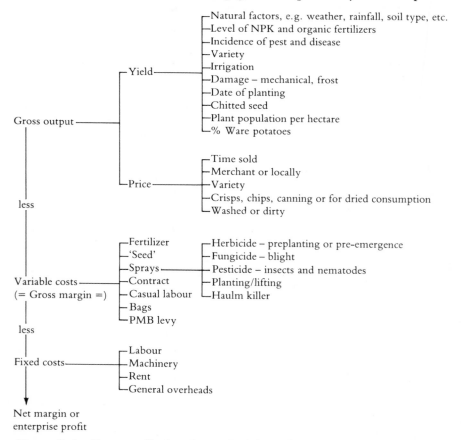

Figure 8.4   Factors affecting the profitability of the potato enterprise

obtained for the potato crop. The influence of certain natural factors such as rainfall, soil type, etc. will cause variations in yields from year to year, but this must be accepted by the farmer. Many other factors that influence yields are, nowadays, within the control of the farmer. For example, incidence of pest and disease attack can be controlled to a large extent by the judicial application of fungicides and insecticides. Many other factors such as levels of nitrogen, phosphate and potash fertilizer applied to the crop, the variety planted, use of irrigation, date of planting and the seed rate (or seed weight planted per hectare), sprouting of seed before planting and also any crop damage, will influence final yields and are all controllable by the farmer.

Having produced the crop and even having got the sample of potatoes ready to sell, the farmer should remember that price as well as actual yield go together in the calculation of gross output. The actual price that will be obtained for potatoes in a particular year depends to a large extent upon a number of factors, including the variety grown. The size and the shape of the potatoes as well as flesh colour and the proportion of misshapen, cracked and damaged tubers in the sample will also influence price received, as will the selling of potatoes loose or pre-packed. In addition, the farmer's own bargaining ability should not be overlooked together with the natural variations in potato prices that occur in most seasons. A further important factor is the purpose for which the potatoes are sold – whether for 'seed' or human consumption, or perhaps in a glut year to the Potato Marketing Board finally to finish up as stock feed. The price actually realized for potatoes can also vary considerably, depending on whether they are sold to a merchant, direct to a retailer, at the farm gate direct to the consumer or forward sold to the Board as part of a registered producer's entitlement.

Levels of costs in potato production

Variable costs
From Table 8.15 it can be seen that the variable costs per hectare incurred in the growing of potatoes is high. Seed planted at 2½ tonnes/ha may well cost £140/tonne or even more. Fertilizer may cost between £180 and £230/ha, with spray chemical charges ranging around £100–£150/ha.

Each grower growing more than 0.4 ha of potatoes must pay the Potato Marketing Board levy of £36.00/ha (1984). Further variable costs are casual labour and contract work if used, as well as sacks or paper bags.

Fixed costs

The potato crop is an expensive crop to produce; in addition to the high level of variable costs, high fixed costs can be incurred when the crop is fully mechanized for planting and harvesting. Furthermore, this crop creates a substantial demand for labour even where a high degree of mechanization is employed.

In conclusion, it must be reiterated that potatoes can be a very profitable crop, but a fairy large amount of capital is involved in its production. Despite the far-ranging effects of certain natural factors in some years on crop yields, the potato grower is, nevertheless, himself responsible to a large extent for the final financial success or failures of his crop. The fact that survey data shows a wide range in final profit margins suggests that many producers could achieve better financial results if they paid greater attention to the factors influencing potato production that are within their control.

THE SUGAR BEET ENTERPRISE

After the First World War, the government encouraged the introduction of sugar beet growing into England by the payment of a subsidy. Therefore, during the 1920s and 1930s sugar beet factories were built, mainly in the eastern part of the country, and sugar beet growing became established in those areas.

Today there are thirteen sugar beet factories under the control of British Sugar plc and the annual area of beet grown is about 212 000 ha. Each sugar beet grower must have a contract with a British Sugar plc factory which covers his area. This contract contains a number of stipulations covering the price that will be paid for the beet, which is reviewed annually, crop rotation so as to limit the spread of sugar beet root eelworm and arrangements for the delivery of beet to the factory.

Undoubtedly the beet crop is a useful root crop in a rotation and provides an opportunity for the control of certain weeds, deeper ploughing, etc. When first introduced in the 1920s it was very demanding on labour for chopping out and singling, as well as keeping the crop clean and harvesting by hand. Nowadays, with precision drilling, the use of herbicides and the mechanical harvesting of the crop, the demand for labour is much less, but the cost of production is, nevertheless, still high. However, on soils where a good yield and a reasonable percentage sugar content can be achieved a good profit margin can result.

British Sugar plc is allocated the whole of the UK sugar quota within the European Community. Sugar production in the UK produced within the quota is supported by an intervention price and growers receive a guaranteed minimum price for beet of standard quality (16 per cent sugar). Production levies are charged to fund disposal of over-quota sugar outside of the Community.

There is little that a sugar beet producer can do to influence the sugar content of his beet. Broadly speaking, soil type and weather conditions, especially hours of sunshine, are the main influencing factors, all of which are outside the control of the farmer.

Harvesting date will have an effect on final gross margin of the sugar beet crop. The later the crop is harvested the higher will be the yield of beet in most years. The percentage sugar content also increases as the autumn progresses, especially if the days are sunny, but falls somewhat in December and January.

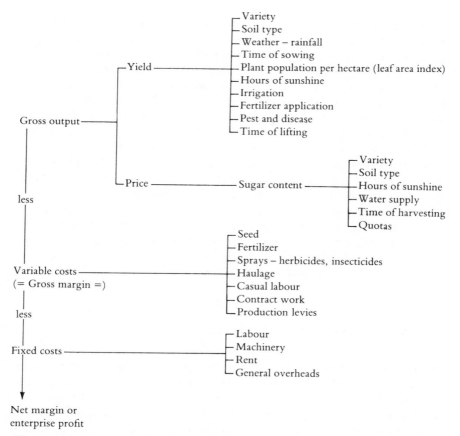

Figure 8.5 Factors affecting the profitability of the sugar beet enterprise

Table 8.16   Levels of output, variable costs and gross margins for sugar beet

Production level Yield: (tonnes/ha)	Low 28	Average 36	High 45
	£	£	£
Output	895	1 150	1 440
Variable costs:			
Seed		45	
Fertilizer		150	
Sprays		115	
Transport (contract)	95	120	150
Total variable costs	405	430	460
Gross margin/ha	490	720	980

Source: Nix 1984 p. 9.

A systematic presentation of the factors influencing the profitability of the sugar beet crop is given in Fig. 8.5. It has already been pointed out for other farm enterprises that comparison of gross margins must be done carefully, making sure that the same range of variable cost items is being compared. In the case of sugar beet casual labour and contract work may be involved in some cases and the inclusion of these costs will considerably influence the final gross margin figure. (see Table 8.16).

For those farmers near a beet factory with suitable soil, the sugar beet crop can be quite profitable in most years. But for those farmers who have to pay high transport costs because of distance to a factory, their profit margins will be that much smaller. From the husbandry point of view beet provides a good root break and also affords opportunities for cleaning ground. The capital involved in mechanizing the crop can be quite considerable, so the relevant fixed costs will therefore be correspondingly high. The result of this, of course, is a lower net margin.

THE FORAGE CROP ENTERPRISE

Many farmers have changed their outlook on grass in more recent years, but the potential of the nation's grassland remains unexploited in many areas. At first this may seem to be a sad state of affairs since the total area of leys and permanent pasture (excluding rough grazing) is greater than that of arable crops, but on reflection the potential in terms of national production from grass is enormous. Indeed, those grass farmers who wish to maximize profits from their farm business must come to regard grass as a crop in the same way as they do wheat or potatoes, rather than natural vegetation which just grows. The importance of a right outlook or philosophy on grass and forage crops cannot be over emphasized and the reasons for this will now be discussed.

United Kingdom hectares of grass

The area of leys, permanent pasture and rough grazings in the UK in 1982 are given in Table 8.17, where leys and permanent pasture (excluding rough grazings) accounted for 42.0 per cent of the total area of farmed land in the United Kingdom. The area covered by rough grazings was a further 30.1 per cent, leaving 27.8 per cent of the total farm land in arable crops.

Grass production and the level of sward management

Perhaps one of the reasons why grass has been a 'neglected' crop in the past is that certain species will grow under almost any conditions found in the British Isles, whether managed intensively, extensively or given no attention at all. Obviously, low yields result where little or no attention is given; if high levels of production are required, then very careful management will be necessary, and furthermore this will need to be coupled with a high degree of managerial skill so as to ensure good utilization of the grass produced.

Table 8.17   Hectares of arable crops and grass in the United Kingdom 1982

	Hectares	%
Arable crops*	4 606 000	27.8
Grass under 5 years old including lucerne	1 859 000	11.2
Grass 5 years old and over	5 097 000	30.8
Rough grazings (sole right excluding common land)	4 984 000	30.1
Total arable crops,* grass and rough grazings	16 546 000	100.0

* Cereals, potatoes, sugar-beet, oilseed rape and hops.

Source: Agricultural Statistics United Kingdom 1982, extracts.

Forage crops: efficiency of utilization

Forage production techniques are fairly straightforward and technically relatively simple. What is perhaps more important than its actual production is the efficiency of its utilization. By the simple application of high levels of fertilizers, especially nitrogen, to any reasonable grass sward, high yields of forage output will result. Unless the utilization of this is carefully planned – by using a high stocking rate per hectare and an appropriate grazing system, or a carefully planned conservation scheme, a lot of grass produced can go unused – either soiled by dung or urine, trampled underfoot or just left as stemmy grass which animals refuse to eat. Utilization by means of conservation is, of course, likely to be less efficient than by grazing animals, but the importance of defoliation of grass at the optimum stage of growth must be borne in mind, i.e. when the digestibility (or *D*-value) has not fallen lower than about 65 (see Fig. 8.6)

It is essential, then, that those concerned with forage production are quite clear in their minds on these two aspects of forage cropping, i.e. production of the crop and its utilization, and that they

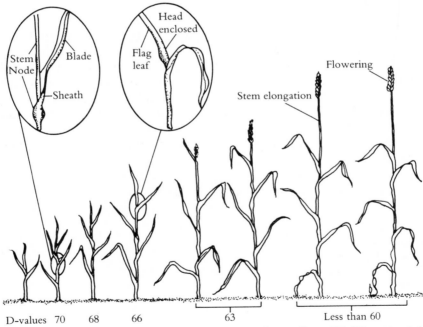

Figure 8.6   Stages of growth and D-values of one tiller of S.23 perennial ryegrass (H. Sandford, Farmers' Guide to Grassland, *UKF* Fertilizers, *Fig. 5, p. 12)*

plan utilization of forage as thoughtfully and thoroughly as they do the production and harvesting techniques for their other farm crops.

The economics of forage production

In considering the economics of forage production, it is necessary to survey the various factors that will influence yields of forage crops. These will now be considered.

Type of forage crop

Grass swards containing vigorous strains of grasses and clovers will respond well to high levels of nitrogen fertilizer and will produce high yields per hectare of dry matter. Certain crops, other than grasses and clovers, are also grown specifically for forage. Kale provides a useful 'green feed' in the autumn/early winter. Marrow stem kale usually produces the highest total yield per hectare, thousand–head kale produces a good yield of leaf per hectare and hungry-gap kale (curled leaf kale), although producing a lower total yield, can be grazed later in the winter since it is fairly frost resistant. Rape, which is a quick-growing brassica crop, is often grown for sheep grazing in the autumn. Because it grows quickly it rapidly covers the ground and is often sown on a field that has grown winter or spring barley. Certain legume crops, e.g. lucerne, produce high yields of forage and grow very well on dry soils, e.g. chalk, and are useful crops for conservation.

Level of fertilizer application

Fertilizer applications, especially nitrogen, can boost yields of forage crops and also influence the natural growth patterns of grasses, depending on the time applied (Fig. 8.7). Obviously, as the level of nitrogen fertilizer applied to a sward is increased, diminishing returns set in, but the limited amount of experimental results available indicate that, with efficient livestock utilization, up to at least 400 kg N/ha can be applied over a season and marginal return still exceeds the marginal cost.

Natural factors

Many natural factors will influence forage production and the extent of their influence will vary from place to place and from year to year. Such factors as soil type, aspect of fields, rainfall, sunshine and

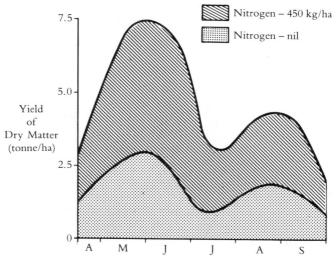

Figure 8.7   The response of grass to nitrogen (Rowsham 1970–73) (H. Sandford, Farmers' Guide to Grassland, UKF Fertilizers, Fig. 1, p. 7)

degree of exposure to cold winds are all relevant factors here. There is little that a farmer can do to alter the influence of these factors on crop growth, but their combined effect many mean the difference between being able to begin grazing pastures in March as opposed to the end of April, to have an intensive rather than an extensive stocking density and to be able to produce late season bite 'foggage' and thereby delay the beginning of inwintering.

The use of clovers in grass swards

The inclusion of some clover in a grass sward is traditional; even nowadays very few farmers grow swards of grass which contain no clover at all. Undoubtedly clover can be useful in a sward in that it 'fixes' nitrogen in the soil and the companion plants in the sward benefit. Furthermore, the forage produced is higher in protein content because of the clover. However, when high levels of nitrogen fertilizer are applied the clover is crowded out of the sward. It is important, therefore, that farmers really ought to consider, when selecting a seeds mixture, the function of the sward that is to be established. If it is to be grazed extensively at a low stocking density, then clovers will be very useful and should be included in the seeds mixture. If, on the other hand, the sward is to be grazed intensively or conservation cuts taken several times during the year, high levels of fertilizer – especially nitrogen – will

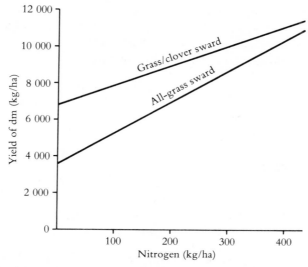

Figure 8.8 *Typical response of grassland to nitrogen (H. Sandford,*
Farmers' Guide to Grassland, *UKF Fertilizers, Fig. 10,*
p. 35)

be applied, and any clover included in the seeds mixture will be
simply a waste of money since very soon after establishment it will
be killed out (see Fig. 8.8).

Utilization of grass by grazing

Likely forage variable costs at different levels of stocking density
for grazing livestock were given in the appropriate enterprise
studies. When considering the intensification of stocking rates for
any class of livestock it is essential to consider the financial effect
of the proposed changes and their final effect on net farm
income.

The economics of forage conservation

Nutrient losses are inevitable whatever method of conservation is
employed. Even the most efficient systems will incur a loss of about
5 per cent of the digestible nutrients in the material when cut. The
actual loss of nutrients will depend on the system of conservation
employed and on the efficiency with which the work is carried out.
Systems of fodder conservation which claim minimum losses of
nutrients are generally those involving a very high investment of
capital in buildings and equipment.

Any budgeting on forage conservation systems must consider the real cost (after allowing for charges on capital invested together with operational costs) of retaining these nutrients, in relation to the cost of providing the nutrients in another form, e.g. purchased feedingstuffs.

Sophisticated conservation systems are, in the final analysis, only justified if the material conserved is efficiently utilized by livestock.

Conclusions

Forage crops, especially grass, probably present the greatest challenge of all farm crops to farmers and managers, since different species are involved, together with many other factors that influence production levels. Within the broad compass of forage cropping, planning of the utilization of forage crops is also involved and this is complex in that it needs to be geared to production which varies seasonally and from year to year. Utilization of grass by livestock means the employment of capital, and shortage of capital may well be one of the reasons why there is under-employment and poor utilization of grass both nationally and on many farms.

9
QUESTIONS AND WORKED ANSWERS

A selection of past questions set in the City and Guilds of London Institute Farm Business Examinations is given below. The questions have been selected as representative of the types of questions set in past years together with worked examples. In presenting this selection of past questions, permission is acknowledged for their publication from the City and Guilds of London Institute, but the worked answers remain our own work and so responsibility for the accuracy, or otherwise, of these cannot be attributed to the Institute.

When answering written questions such as these, candidates are advised to prepare a plan (a rough outline answer on spare paper) before commencing to answer the question proper. (Note the questions below marked★ indicate that they are questions from the short answer section of an examination paper where approximately fifteen such questions must be answered in about one hour.)

1.★ Show how the percentage return on tenant's capital can be calculated from the following information (per hectare).

Net farm income	£100.00
Regular labour (unpaid)	£55.00
Tenant's capital	£500.00

Answer:
The percentage on tenant's capital is a measure of the profitability of the business in relation to the tenant's capital invested.

$$\begin{array}{ll} \text{NFI} & £100.00 \\ \text{less UPL} & £55.00 \\ \text{MII} & £45.00 \end{array} \quad \text{\% return on TC} = \frac{45}{500} \times 100 = 9\%$$

(*Ref. 1981 City and Guilds Institute Phase IV, Question no. 3*)

2.★ Illustrate how you would calculate the total enterprise output for a *named* enterprise for the year ending 31 December 1980.

Answer:

Total enterprise output for a named enterprise must embrace: total sales, adjusted for opening and closing valuation changes, plus produce consumed, less any livestock purchases. Livestock enterprises transfers of livestock should not be forgotten.

Opening valuation 1.1.80		*Closing valuation 31.12.80*	
Ewes		Ewes	
Rams		Rams	
Livestock replacements		*Sales* during 1980	
acquired during 1980		Lambs	
– Gimmers		Culls – ewes	
– Rams		– rams	
		Produce consumed	
Total enterprise output	£		
	£X 000		£X 000

(Ref. 1981 City and Guilds Institute Phase IV, Question no. 4)

3.★ Show the layout including all appropriate items, without any figures, for a partial budget to expand an existing and correspondingly reduce another enterprise.

Answer:

The partial budget 'heading' should indicate clearly what comparison is being made in the partial budgets, e.g.

10 extra dairy cows v. spring barley on 5 ha

Layout of the partial budget:

Extra costs		*Costs saved*	
	£		£
Replacement heifers per year		Barley variable costs:	
Concentrate feed		fertilizer	
Vet., medicines and sundries		seed	
Fertilizer on grassland		sprays	
Grass seeds for leys		twine	
Revenue foregone		*Extra revenue*	
Barley straw		Milk	
Barley grain		Calves	
		Cull cows(s)	
(?) Extra income		(?) Loss incurred	
	£X 000		£X 000

(Ref. 1981 City and Guilds Institute Phase IV, Question no. 8)

4.★   List the assets that could be found on a balance sheet.

Answer:
Liquid assets:
Cash in hand, cash at bank, sundry debtors, valuation of crops and saleable stores, livestock for sale, shares and other realisable investments.
Fixed assets:
Valuation of farm buildings, fixed equipment, machinery and livestock (not for sale), land and houses.
(*Ref. 1981 City and Guilds Institute Phase IV, Question no. 14*)

5.★   Define a gross margin and illustrate your answer with a simple example.

Answer:
A gross margin is the total enterprise output (or gross output) of an enterprise less its variable costs, e.g.

   Potatoes

		£
Total enterprise output – Ware sold		
Chats sold		_____
		_____
less Variable costs:		
Fertilizer		
Seed		
Sprays		
?Casual labour		
Sundries (e.g. PMB levy, bags, etc.)		_____
		_____

   GM = Total enterprise output less variable costs
(*Ref. 1980 City and Guilds Institute Phase IV, Question no. 4*)

6.★   List the principal sources of credit available to farmers or growers.

Answers:
The principal sources of credit are:
   The Agricultural Mortgage Corporation
   The Lands Improvement Company
   Private mortgages
   Insurance companies
   Banks
   Hire-purchase companies
   Syndicates
   Co-operatives

'Lease-back' arrangements
Merchants
Creditors
(*Ref. 1980 City and Guilds Institute Phase IV, Question no. 11*)

The following questions require longer answers: normally approximately 30 minutes would be available for each answer.

7.   Explain, with an example, how you would justify an enterprise from which the gross margin per hectare does not cover the fixed cost per hectare of the whole farm or holding.
(*Ref. 1980 City and Guilds Institute Phase IV, Question no. 17*)

Answer:
Named enterprise: sheep (lowland fat lamb production).
Using 1980 average figures, a gross margin per forage hectare of £167 could be achieved from a sheep enterprise producing lowland fat lambs. This enterprise could be situated on a dairying/arable farm where the average level of fixed costs per hectare were £247/ha. The average level of fixed costs being £80 higher than the gross margin per hectare for the sheep.
In justifying the sheep enterprise, the following points should be enlarged upon:
The level of fixed costs is the average for all the farm.
i.e. If fixed costs were ascribed to specific enterprises, those relating to sheep would be low, whereas enterprises such as dairying carry high fixed costs.
i.e. The sheep flock will 'benefit' subsequent crops in an arable rotation, e.g. a cereal crop grown after a sheep-grazed ley.

8.   For two of the following enterprises, explain why these different results may have been obtained:

Enterprise	Your farm gross margin per hectare (£)	Group of similar average-performance farms
(a) Potatoes	900	1 000
(b) Dairy cows	450	350
(c) Brussels sprouts	1 500	200
(d) Sheep (fat lamb production)	90	160

(*Ref. 1981 City and Guilds Institute Phase IV, Question no. 16*)

Answer (to all four parts):
In answering the above question, candidates should expand upon the following points:
Gross margin is total enterprise output (gross output) less variable costs:

Therefore, the factors which influence levels of gross output and all variable cost items should be considered carefully:

(a) Potatoes

The level of gross output will be influenced by:
1. Yield – this will be influenced by:
   Natural factors, e.g. weather, rainfall, soil type, etc.
   Level of NPK and organic fertilizers
   Incidence of pest and disease
   Variety
   Irrigation
   Damage – mechanical, frost
   Date of planting
   Chitted seed
   Plant population per hectare
   Percentage ware potatoes
2. Price – which is influenced by:
   Time sold
   Merchant or locally
   Variety
   Crisps, chips, canning or for dried consumption
   Washed or dirty

The variable cost items are:

Fertilizer	Herbicide – preplanting or pre-emergence
'Seed'	
Sprays	Fungicide – blight
Contract	?Pesticide – insects
Casual labour	Planting/lifting
Bags	Haulm killer
PMB levy	

(b) Dairy cows

The level of gross output will be influenced by:

	Quantity	Yield
Milk sales		Calving index
	Price	Quality
		Seasonality
Net replacement costs	Cull value, calf value	
	Average herd life of cow	
	Cost of replacements	

The variable costs of dairying will vary according to the use of:
   Concentrates
   Other purchased feeds
   Vet. costs and medicines

Dairy sundries
Forage costs

Note: Answers after 2nd April 1984 will include reference, under "Quantity", to milk quotas.

(c) Brussels Sprouts

The gross output will be influenced by:

Yield – which depends upon: soil fertility
NPK fertilizers applied
Variety grown
Weather and other biotic factors
Incidence of pests and diseases

Price – influenced by: Variety
Size
Time of year sold
Evenness of sample
Volume of Brussels Sprouts in market

The variable costs will depend upon the costs of:
Fertilizers used
Seed price
Sprays used
Casual labour
Contractor (for machinery work)

(d) Sheep (fat lamb production)

The gross output will vary according to:

		Lambing percentage
	Number sold	
		Mortality
Lamb sales		Weight sold
		Quality
	Price per lamb	Seasonality
		Percentage sold fat
		Method of sale
	Weight of fleece	
Wool sales		
	Price per kg	Quality
		Handling
	Price of replacement	
Replacement costs	Rate of replacement	
	Value of cull	

The variable costs will be influenced by the inputs of:

Purchased feed	Vet. and medicines
Sundries	Shearing and services
Forage costs	Consumable equipment
	Haulage

9. The following results were obtained for a mixed arable farm. What further investigations of comparative analysis efficiency measures could be made to identify the reasons for the unsatisfactory levels of performance?

	Mixed arable farm (%)	Group of similar average-performance farms (%)
Return on tenant's capital	12	20
Management and investment income (£/ha)	25	45

(*Ref. 1981 City and Guilds Institute Phase IV, Question no. 17*)

From the information given in the question, it is possible to calculate the levels of tenant's capital per hectare for the farm and the group of similar farms. This is possible since:

$$\text{Percentage return on tenant's capital} = \frac{\text{Management and investment income}}{\text{Tenant's capital}} \times 100$$

Therefore for the farm
$$= 12\% = \frac{25}{X} \times 100$$
$$= £208.3/\text{ha}$$

Therefore for the group of similar farms
$$= 20\% = \frac{45}{X} \times 100$$
$$= £225.0/\text{ha}$$

The farm, compared with the group of similar farms, has a lower percentage return on tenant's capital (12 per cent, cf. 20 per cent), a lower management and investment income (£25/ha, cf. £45/ha) and a lower investment in tenant's capital (£208.3/ha, cf. £225.0/ha). Therefore, the items contributing to the levels of management and investment income and tenant's capital must be investigated.

Candidates' answers should therefore expand upon the following: MII Total enterprise output (gross output) less all variable and fixed costs (including unpaid labour). All the items contributing towards the level of enterprise output and variable and fixed costs should be explained.

Tenant's capital comprises:
Livestock
Crops and cultivations
Stores
Machinery
Car
Tenant's fixtures
The levels of each of these items on the farm and for the group of similar farms should be explained.

10. State in detail the main responsibilities that an employer has towards his staff.

(Ref. 1981 City and Guilds Institute Phase IV, Question no. 23)

Candidates should expand upon the following aspects, in their answers:

safety, job satisfaction, level of remuneration (money and payments), housing (if appropriate), consultation and communications. Also, staff development and career development (within or outside of) the firm and some attention to pension and retirement.

APPENDIX A
BUDGET AND CASH FLOW FOR LITTLEDOWN FARM

A budget and cash flow for Year 3 based on a number of changes to the farm policy has been drawn up on a monthly basis. This has been done to enable monitoring of the business to take place in addition to creating an awareness of the likely financial position for the next year.

Monitoring the budget is vital if the important benefits of early warning are to be taken full advantage of; adjustments and changes if made when and where required can keep the business on target (see Tables A1 and A2).

The appraisal of the existing and budgeted plan should be a continuous process involving partial budgeting techniques as a first step in testing the proposed changes.

THE FORWARD BUDGET AND THE PROJECTED CAPITAL POSITION IN YEAR 3

The data shown in the Appendix A, Tables A1 to A10 is fairly easily followed but a few salient points are worthy of recognition. These are as follows:

Littledown Farm produced a modest profit and return on tenant's capital at the end of Year 2. The level of bank borrowing has increased by £9 560 over the year with the closing bank position standing at (£35 406). At this stage the bank position is not critical to the long-term security of the business as an analysis of the balance sheet (see Table 5.1) would show but an upward trend of the magnitude of 37 per cent is disturbing, since a profit was made and there were no unusual drawings or investments.

In planning the farming operations for Year 3 and developing the cash flow required for monitoring the business and securing the co-operation of the bank, some fundamental changes are to be implemented.

The changes considered necessary for Littledown Farm are made against a background of comparatively low interest rates, which could rise, the implementation of the EEC milk quota system and a farm level of fixed costs £/ha considerably higher than comparative farms.

FUNDS FLOW

In spite of an anticipated decline in the management and investment income relative to Year 2, the business generates a fairly healthy positive cash flow over Year 3. This cash flow has been contributed to by the maintenance of reasonably modest private expenditure and prudent capital investment in machinery, together with a substantial decrease in the valuations of two main assets. This results in a reduction of the end of year bank overdraft. If one refers to the graph on Table A7, then the decline in overdraft would seem to be a trend rather than a temporary aberration.

The farmer having seen the results of a realistic projection may wish to exploit a sound financial base and expand his business in some way. If the scale of the expansion is such that some additional borrowed finance is needed then he may view the prospect of paying interest, at a higher rate than the business can generate (see Table A9), as imprudent. However, a marginal expansion may conceivably yield more than current interest rates (see Table 4.5).

He may consider the repayment of the private loan as important given the reasons stated in Chapter 5, under sources of credit – private mortgages.

Whatever action is taken, it will pay the farmer to explore the possibilities and quantify them, wherever possible in **physical** and **financial** terms before coming to a decision. The quality of the decision will reflect not only the experience and business acumen of the farmer, but also the accuracy of the information supplied.

In this appendix, attention must be drawn to the physical data shown in Tables A1 and A5. No sensible budgeting can be done without the sound development of basic physical data, and it is recommended that a stocks flow should always precede a cash flow.

Table A1 The proposals Year 3
Livestock plans – Year 3

Enterprise	O. No.	Purchases	Transferred in	Deaths	Sales	C. No.	Av. no. yr. 3
Cattle							
Dairy cows	135	—	15	1	40	109	122
0–1 year	35	—	—	—	35 Feb	0	17.0
1–2 years	30	—	—	—	30 March	0	15.0
2–2½ years	26	—	—	—	11 March	0	13.0

Plan to reduce dairy cow numbers to relate to milk quota; discontinue home reared replacements and crop the released land with cereals – spring barley in Year 3, subsequent years with winter wheat. Thirty-five 0–1 year cattle sold in Feb.; thirty 1–2 yr cattle sold in March.

Enterprise	O. No.	Purchases	Transferred in	Deaths	Sales	C. No.	Av. no. yr. 3
Sheep							
Ewes	460	200	—	19	34	607	533.5
Rams	12	8	—	—	3	17	14.5

Budget – stocking rate guide and land released – Year 3

	Av. no.		G.L.U.s		G.L.U.s	
Dairy cows	122	×	1.0	=	122	
Dairy young/stock 0–1	17	×	0.4	=	—	Sold before turnout
1–2	15	×	0.6	=	—	Sold before turnout
2–2½	26	×	0.8	=	—	Transferred into dairy cows
Sheep: Ewes	533.5	×	0.2	=	106.7	
Rams	14.5	×	0.2	=	2.9	
Total					231.6	

Stocking rate Year 2: 1.9 G.L.U.s/Adjusted Forage ha

$\dfrac{231.6}{1.9}$ = requirement of 121.8 adjusted forage ha for grazing and conservation.

Year 2 forage hectares: Leys 130
P. pasture 20 } 150 ha

∴ Approx: 28 ha released for increase in cereal cropping as spring barley in Year 3 and subsequent year into the most appropriate crop – Year 4, winter wheat.

Table A2

Pigs	O. No.	Purchases	Transferred in	Deaths out	Sales/ transfers out	C. No.	Av. No. Yr 3
Sows	88	—	—	—	88 sell	0	44
Boars	6	—	—	—	6 sell	0	3
Sucklers	230	—	—	—	230 sell	0	115

Plan to dispose of the entire pig enterprise in the month of January Year 3. Farm fixed cost structure and poor level of performance suggest that the 'winding up' of this enterprise and the subsequent savings in labour, machinery and power costs is inevitable even though Littledown Farm has a long and in the past moderately successful history of pig keeping. Major capital expenditure on a building programme would be required to sustain the existing unit and this cannot be justified.

Projected cash flow and trading account

Major changes in farm policy are planned for Year 3. An investigation into the repercussions of the changes as shown by the cash flow (see Table A6) and trading account (see Table A8) suggest a significant improvement in the business with a positive annual cash flow of £29 321.

The restructuring and projected improvement in annual cash flow is not reflected in the forecast profit, largely influenced by the predictable drop in valuations of £24 530.

In the following year with valuations stabilizing it would not be unreasonable to forecast an improvement.

Table A3

Cropping	Year 3	To be harvested/utilized Hectares of crops
Winter wheat	50	— Drilled autumn year 2
Winter barley	30	— Drilled autumn year 2
Spring barley	52	— 24 ha originally planned + 28 ha released grassland
M.C. potatoes	8	
Leys	102	— 130 ha originally planned − 28 ha to spring barley
P. pasture	20	
Total	262	

Hay 10 hectares.
Silage 58 hectares.
Reseed 40 hectares.

Table A4   Forward plans
Littledown Farm – Year 4

Livestock plans Year 4

Enterprise	Op. No.	Purchases	Trans. in	Deaths	Sales/Trans out	Clos. No.	Av. No. Yr.4
Cattle							
Dairy cows	109	30	—	Allow 2	30	107	108
Calves 0–1	—	—	—	3	115	—	—
1–2	—	—	—	—	—	—	—
2–2½	—	—	—	—	—	—	—
Sheep							
Ewes	607	125	—	17	150	565	586
Rams	17	7	—	—	5	19	18

Budget – stocking rate

		Av no.		G.L.U.s		G.L.U.s
Dairy Cows:		108	×	1	=	108
Sheep:	Ewes	586	×	0.2	=	117.2
1	Rams	18	×	0.2	=	3.6
	Total					228.8

$\dfrac{228.8}{1.9}$ Yr 2 stocking rate = Approx 120.4 Adj. forage ha.

LIQUIDITY

A glance at the ratios at the bottom of the balance sheet (Table A9) will reveal a marked improvement in liquidity with a current assets to current liabilities ratio of 13.5 : 1. This enhanced liquidity has largely come from the de-stocking of the fixed and current assets which have declined in value by some £34 831 in relation to the Year

Table A5

Cropping	Plans	Year 4 hectares of crops
Winter wheat	75	— Drilled autumn of Year 3
Winter barley	20	— Drilled autumn of Year 3
Spring barley	39	
M.C. potatoes	8	
Leys	100	
P. pasture	20	
	262	

Reseed 30 hectares.

Table A6   Littledown Farm: Cashflow budget – Year 3.

Particulars	Jan B	Jan A	Feb B	Feb A	Mar B	Mar A	Apr B	Apr A	May B	May A	June B	June A
Income:												
Milk	7 397		11 372		10 909		10 354		9 619		8 348	
Calves	584		280									
Cull cows												
Sheep												
Pigs sale of stock	12 000											
Youngstock			3 500		7 800							
Wheat			18 000		18 000		9 000					
Barley (winter)												
Barley (spring)			10 925									
Potatoes	6 000		6 000									
Sundries					500							
Machinery sales			7 000		300							
Sub-total	25 981		57 077		37 509		19 354		9 619		8 348	
Expenditure:												
Feed: Cows	3 416		1 293		4 148		3 660		2 779		1 193	
: Sheep			1 700		852		852					
Vet. and medicines	352		389		439		242		242		439	
Livestock purchases (ewes & rams)												
Sundries (livestock)	338		338		540		342		342		342	
Fertilizers			18 000								18 240	
Seeds			2 080									
Sprays			645		1 478		313		313		1 183	
PMB levy and sundries							2 000					
Wages: Regular	4 192		4 192		4 192		4 645		4 645		4 645	
: Casual												
Repairs and spares, Tax, Ins.	725		725		725		725		725		725	
Power	583		583		583		583		583		583	
Contractor												
Water					370						370	
General ins./Office	350		350		350		350		350		350	
Rates											357	
Rent					10 389							
Machinery							6 500					
Drawings	800		800		800		800		800		800	
Interest					236							
Sub-total	10 756		31 095		25 102		21 012		10 779		10 987	
Opening current account balance	(35 406)		(20 181)		5 801		18 208		16 550		15 390	
Net cash flow for period	15 225		25 982		12 407		(1 658)		(1 160)		(2 639)	
Closing current account balance	(20 181)		5 801		18 208		16 550		15 390		12 751	

Note: Interest charges levied at 14% payable quarterly – March, June, September, December.

B = budget: A = actual

July B	A	Aug B	A	Sept B	A	Oct B	A	Nov B	A	Dec B	A	Totals B	A
7 027		5 362		3 606		3 328		5 917		8 505		91 744	
2 413		2 413		4 064		762		1 524		660		12 700	
3 284		6 455		9 404		3 284		3 284		2 357		28 068	
												12 000	
												11 300	
												45 000	
		23 381										23 381	
				16 675								27 600	
												12 000	
												500	
												7 300	
12 724		37 611		33 749		7 374		10 725		11 522		271 593	
952		729		610		680		1 950		2 952		24 362	
		400		400								4 204	
238		230		352		249		249		365		3 786	
				15 600								15 600	
405		324		351		351		464		371		4 508	
				6 350								42 590	
				4 600		3 700						10 380	
56		1 344		716		672		2 240				8 960	
		2 000										4 000	
5 608		5 608		5 608		4 438		4 438		4 439		56 650	
						2 000						2 000	
725		725		725		725		725		725		8 700	
583		583		583		583		583		587		7 000	
		1 300				500						1 800	
				370						369		1 479	
350		350		350		350		350		350		4 200	
										358		715	
				10 389								20 778	
						4 000						10 500	
800		800		800		800		800		800		9 600	
				28						196		460	
27 957		14 393		47 832		19 048		11 799		11 512		242 272	
12 751		(2 482)		20 736		6 653		(5 021)		(6 095)		—	
(15 233)		23 218		(14 083)		(11 674)		(1 074)		10		—	
(2 482)		20 736		6 653		(5 021)		(6 095)		(6 085)		(6 085)	

: *Supercalc Spreadsheet*: R.A.E. TURNER, K.R.S. WILSON Hampshire College of Agriculture 1984

Table A7   Littledown Farm – Year 3: Monthly cash flow

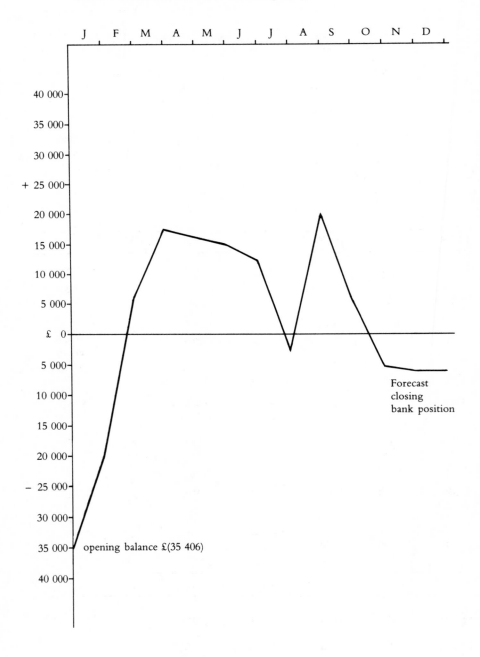

opening balance £(35 406)

Forecast
closing
bank position

Table A8   Littledown Farm: Budgeted trading account – Year 3

Expenditure	(£)	Income	(£)
Opening valuations		From cash flow 271 593	
	231 185	adjusted for: debtors	
		: capital sales	
Purchases			266 216
From cash flow 242 272			
adjusted for: creditors		Private share of farm goods	1 700
: capital purchases			
: private expenditure	219 672	Closing valuations	206 655
Depreciation	15 424		
Budgeted profit	8 290		
	474 571		474 571

Table A9   Littledown Farm – Year 3

	Balance sheet statements	
	At start	End
Fixed assets		
Machinery and Tenant's equipment	110 203	97 979
Breeding livestock	79 270	72 760
Work in progress	10 762	13 182
Total	200 235	183 921
Current assets		
Debtors (receipts due)	13 338	15 261
Non-breeding livestock	23 800	—
Harvested crops on hand	69 675	74 975
Tillages	9 818	12 168
Feed, forage and fertilizer	37 860	33 570
Cash in Hand	350	350
Total	154 841	136 324
Total assets	355 076	320 245
Current liabilities		
Creditors (expenditure owed)	6 500	4 000
Tax owed	—	—
Bank overdraft + interest owed	35 406	6 085
Total	41 906	10 085
Net assets	313 170	310 160
Financed by		
Other loans	12 000	12 000
Farmers share of business	301 170	298 160
Total	355 076	320 245
Current liquidity ratio	3.7 : 1	13.5 : 1
Capital gearing	0.04 : 1	0.04 : 1
Return on owner equity	5.0%	2.8%
Return on total assets	4.3%	2.6%

Table A10   Funds flow for Littledown Farm – Year 3

	£	£
Management and investment income	8 290	
Add:		
Depreciation – tenant's fixtures	—	
– machinery	15 424	
Decrease in valuations	24 530	
Increase in creditors	—	
Decrease in debtors	—	
Capital sales	7 300	
Capital grants	—	
Capital introduced (family labour)	—	
Private income/transfers in	—	
Total		55 544
Less:		
Increase in valuations	—	
Decrease in creditors	2 500	
Increase in debtors	1 923	
Capital expenditure – machinery	10 500	
– other	—	
Loan repayments/interest	—	
Private expenditure	9 600	
Notional benefit	1 700	
Tax	—	
Transfers out		26 223
Surplus/deficit (annual cash flow)		+29 321
Opening bank balance	−35 406	
Less annual cash flow	+29 321	
Closing bank balance	− 6 085	

2 figure. Provided that this de-stocking is not harmful to the business in terms of resource availability, then it could release finance for the expansion of an existing enterprise or the introduction of a new one.

Owner equity and gearing

The farmer and partners' share of the business, as depicted on the projected balance sheet for Year 3 (Table A9) has fallen by one per cent from £301 170 to £298 160 – a decrease of £3 010. This decrease is attributable to the poor profit made in Year 3 (£8 290) and the extent to which private drawings (£9 600 + 1 700 = £11 300) exceeded the profit.

The joint equity of the farmer and his wife is $\frac{298\ 160}{320\ 245} \times 100 = 93.1$

per cent. This is clearly an improvement over the Year 2 figure of 84.8 per cent, having reduced their joint liabilities by some 76 per cent at the expense of selling fixed and current assets by the disposal of the pigs and some young stock (see cash-flow budget, Table A6). This position is reflected in the low capital gearing of 0.04 to 1. Because of low gearing, the relationship between the return on owner equity and total assets is close (see Table A9). Clearly, when it is anticipated that returns will be depressed (the introduction of milk quotas but to name one factor) and there is the likelihood of interest rates rising this is an enviable position to be in.

APPENDIX B
TABLES FOR DISCOUNTED CASH FLOW CALCULATIONS

Table B.1   Discount factors for calculating the present value of future (irregular) cash flows

Year	Percentage										
	5	6	7	8	9	10	12	15	20	25	40
1	0.952	0.943	0.935	0.926	0.917	0.909	0.893	0.870	0.833	0.800	0.714
2	0.907	0.890	0.873	0.857	0.842	0.826	0.797	0.756	0.694	0.640	0.510
3	0.864	0.840	0.816	0.794	0.772	0.751	0.712	0.658	0.579	0.512	0.364
4	0.823	0.792	0.763	0.735	0.708	0.683	0.636	0.572	0.482	0.410	0.260
5	0.784	0.747	0.713	0.681	0.650	0.621	0.567	0.497	0.402	0.328	0.186
6	0.746	0.705	0.666	0.630	0.596	0.564	0.507	0.432	0.335	0.262	0.133
7	0.711	0.665	0.623	0.583	0.547	0.513	0.452	0.376	0.279	0.210	0.095
8	0.677	0.627	0.582	0.540	0.502	0.467	0.404	0.327	0.233	0.168	0.068
9	0.645	0.592	0.544	0.500	0.460	0.424	0.361	0.284	0.194	0.134	0.048
10	0.614	0.558	0.508	0.463	0.422	0.386	0.322	0.247	0.162	0.107	0.035
11	0.585	0.527	0.475	0.429	0.388	0.350	0.287	0.215	0.135	0.086	0.025
12	0.557	0.497	0.444	0.397	0.356	0.319	0.257	0.187	0.112	0.069	0.018
13	0.530	0.469	0.415	0.368	0.326	0.290	0.229	0.163	0.093	0.055	0.013
14	0.505	0.442	0.388	0.340	0.299	0.263	0.205	0.141	0.078	0.044	0.009
15	0.481	0.417	0.362	0.315	0.275	0.239	0.183	0.123	0.065	0.035	0.006
20	0.377	0.312	0.258	0.215	0.178	0.149	0.104	0.061	0.026	0.012	0.001
30	0.231	0.174	0.131	0.099	0.075	0.057	0.033	0.015	0.004	0.001	—
40	0.142	0.097	0.067	0.046	0.032	0.022	0.011	0.004	0.001	—	—

Table B2   Discount factors for calculating the present value of a future annuity (i.e. constant annual cash flow) receivable in Years 1 to n inclusive

Year	Percentage										
	5	6	7	8	9	10	12	15	20	25	40
1	0.95	0.94	0.93	0.93	0.92	0.91	0.89	0.87	0.83	0.80	0.71
2	1.85	1.83	1.80	1.78	1.76	1.74	1.69	1.63	1.53	1.44	1.22
3	2.72	2.67	2.62	2.58	2.53	2.49	2.40	2.28	2.11	1.95	1.59
4	3.54	3.46	3.38	3.31	3.24	3.17	3.04	2.85	2.59	2.36	1.85
5	4.32	4.21	4.10	3.99	3.89	3.79	3.61	3.35	2.99	2.69	2.04
6	5.07	4.91	4.76	4.62	4.49	4.36	4.11	3.78	3.33	2.95	2.17
7	5.78	5.58	5.38	5.21	5.03	4.87	4.56	4.16	3.60	3.16	2.26
8	6.46	6.20	5.97	5.75	5.53	5.33	4.97	4.49	3.84	3.33	2.33
9	7.10	6.80	6.51	6.25	6.00	5.76	5.33	4.77	4.03	3.46	2.38
10	7.72	7.36	7.02	6.71	6.42	6.14	5.65	5.02	4.19	3.57	2.41
12	8.86	8.38	7.94	7.54	7.16	6.81	6.19	5.42	4.43	3.73	2.46
15	10.38	9.71	9.11	8.56	8.06	7.61	6.81	5.85	4.68	3.86	2.48
20	12.46	11.47	10.59	9.82	9.13	8.51	7.47	6.26	4.87	3.95	2.50
30	15.37	13.76	12.41	11.26	10.27	9.43	8.06	6.57	4.98	3.99	2.50
40	17.16	15.05	13.33	11.92	10.76	9.78	8.24	6.64	5.00	4.00	2.50

Table B3   Repayments of capital and interest – Amortization table
Annual charge to write off £1000

Write-off period (years)	Rate of interest (%)									
	5	6	7	8	9	10	12	15	20	25
5	231	238	244	251	258	264	278	299	334	373
6	197	204	210	216	223	230	243	265	301	339
7	173	179	186	192	199	206	219	240	278	316
8	155	161	168	174	181	188	202	223	261	301
10	130	136	142	149	156	163	177	200	239	280
12	113	119	126	133	140	147	162	185	226	269
15	96	103	110	117	124	132	147	171	214	260
20	80	87	94	102	110	117	134	160	205	253
30	65	73	81	89	97	106	124	153	202	251
40	58	66	75	84	93	102	121	150	200	250

APPENDIX C
AGRICULTURAL
INSTITUTIONS

There are a number of agricultural 'institutions' which are important and a number of them are vital for anyone involved in farm management today. The scope of this book does not permit a detailed account of these but a list is given so that students can familiarize themselves with further details of these organizations.

ADVISORY SERVICES

Ministry of Agriculture Experimental Husbandry Farms
Agricultural Development Advisory Service.
Private advisory and consultancy firms

MARKETING BOARDS

The British Wool Marketing Board
The Milk Marketing Board (MMB)
The Potato Marketing Board (PMB)

OTHER 'INSTITUTIONS'

Agricultural Central Trading (ACT)
Agricultural Market Development Executive Committee (AMDEC)
Agricultural Wages Board
British Sugar p.l.c.
Buying groups
Co-operatives

County Council smallholdings
Hops Marketing Board Ltd.
Machinery syndicates
Selling groups
The Agriculture, Horticulture and Forestry Industry Training Board (AHFITB)
The Central Council for Agricultural and Horticultural Co-operation (CCAHC)
The Home Grown Cereals Authority (HGCA)
The Meat and Livestock Commission (MLC)

APPENDIX D
AGRICULTURAL LEGISLATION

Those concerned with farm management should be familiar with the main provisions of legislation relating to farming.

THE MAIN POST-WAR LEGISLATION RELATING TO FARMING IN ENGLAND AND WALES

1947 Agriculture Act

Part I Guaranteed prices and assured markets
To secure *stability* in British farming capable of producing . . . 'such part of the Nation's food and other Agricultural produce as in the National interest it is desirable to produce in the U.K.'

Part II Good estate management and good husbandry
Legislative demand for *efficiency* in management and farming . . . 'That owners of agricultural land will fulfil their responsibilities to manage the land in accordance with the *rules of good estate management* and that occupiers of agricultural land fulfil their responsibilities to farm the land in accordance with the *rules of good husbandry.*'

Part III Agricultural holdings
Deals with the terms of tenancies, rents, tenants' fixtures, notice to quit, compensation for disturbance and improvements, tenant right.

Part IV Small holdings
Provisions of County Council smallholdings.

Part V Administration
(a) ALS (Agricultural Land Service)
(b) CAES (County Agricultural Executive Committees)
(c) ALT (Agricultural Land Tribunal)

1948 Agricultural Holdings Act

This Act consolidated the Agricultural Holdings Act 1923 and Part III of the Agricultural Act, 1947. The main provisions of the Act were:
(a) Provision as to contracts of tenancy.
(b) Provisions affecting relationship of landlord and tenant.
(c) Extenuating circumstances.
(d) Provisions as to Notice to Quit.
(e) Compensation for Disturbance and Improvements.

1957 Agriculture Act

Part I Guaranteed prices and assured markets
Limits set on the total maximum annual decrease of guaranteed prices.

Part II Grants for farm improvements and amalgamations
Grants for long-term improvements of agricultural land (FIS, Farm Improvement Scheme).
Grants towards costs of amalgamation to secure the formation of economic units.

Part III Development of the pig industry
PIDA (Pig Industry Development Authority) was established to develop certain aspects of the pig industry.

1958 Agriculture Act

Covers the following:
(a) Repeal of supervision orders, direction to and dispossession of owners on grounds of bad estate management or bad husbandry (sections 12–20 of 1947 Act, Part II).

(b) Rents determined in arbitration to be at average 'market' levels.
(c) Powers of Agricultural Land Tribunal.
(d) Control of injurious weeds.

1959 Agriculture (Small Farmers) Act

Introduction of a scheme of grants for increasing the efficiency of
the small farm business:
(a) Field husbandry grants.
(b) A farm business grant.

1965 The Small Farm (Business Management) Scheme

The 1959 scheme was modified: grants available only to small
farmers who are prepared to keep farm records. The 'size' of the
business qualifying for these grants was changed.

1967 Agriculture Act

Part I Livestock and meat marketing
Provision for the setting up of the Meat and Livestock Commission.

Part II Farm structure and farm improvements and the promotion of agricultural investment
Includes grants for amalgamations and boundary adjustments and
grants for individuals relinquishing the occupation of uncommercial
units.

Part III Hill land
Grants for benefiting these areas and the provision of Rural Development Boards.

Part IV Co-operative activities
Formation of the Central Council for Agricultural and Horticultural
Co-operation.

Part V Miscellaneous
Various items including financial assistance to bodies making loans, grants for keeping farm business records, etc.

1970 Agriculture Act

Part I Eggs
Arrangements for marketing and subsidy payments for eggs. Provision for the establishment of an Egg Authority, and the revocation of the British Egg Marketing Board.

Part II Capital and other grants
To modernize and simplify capital grants to the industry and to give further encouragement to farm amalgamation.

Part III Smallholdings
Some amendments to Part IV of the 1947 Agriculture Act and a restatement of many of the provisions of that Act.

Part IV Fertilizers and feedingstuffs
This part modernizes the law on fertilizers and feedingstuffs, replacing the fertilizers and feedingstuffs Act 1926.

Part V Flood warning system in England and Wales
(Part VI Scotland)
Provision of grants to river authorities to establish flood warning systems.

Part VII Miscellaneous provisions
Relating to tied cottages, the Agriculture, Horticulture and Forestry Industry Training Board and the payment of its finances through the Annual Price Review.

1972 Agriculture (Miscellaneous Provisions) Act

1972 European Communities Act

1976 Agriculture (Miscellaneous Provisions) Act

1976 Rent (Agriculture) Act

1977 Agricultural Holdings (Notice to Quit) Act

1977 Rent (Agriculture) Amendment Act

1979 Agricultural Statistics Act (Consolidating measure relating to provisions of the 1947 Agriculture Act).

1981 Wildlife and Countryside Act.

1982 The Hops Marketing Act (includes provision for the dissolution of the Hops Marketing Board).

APPENDIX E
METRIC
CONVERSIONS

Quantity	Existing unit	Metric unit	Unit symbol		Conversion factor
Length	mile	kilometre	km	1 mile	= 1.609 km
	yard	metre	m	1 yd	= 0.9144 m
	foot	metre	m	1 ft	= 0.3048 m
	inch	millimetre	mm	1 in	= 25.40 mm
Area	square mile	square kilometre	km^2	1 mile^2	= 2.590 km^2
	acre	hectare	ha	1 acre	= 0.4047 ha (10 000 m^2)
	square yard	square metre	m^2	1 yd^2	= 0.8361 m^2
	square foot	square metre	m^2	1 ft^2	= 0.0929 m^2
	square inch	square millimetre	mm^2	1 in^2	= 645.2 mm^2
Mass (weight)	ton	tonne	t	1 ton	= 1.016 tonne (1 000 kg)
	hundredweight	kilogram	kg	1 cwt	= 50.80 kg
	pound	kilogram	kg	1 lb	= 0.453 kg
	ounce	gram	g	1 oz	= 28.35 g
Volume (capacity)	cubic yard	cubic metre	m^3	1 yd^3	= 0.7646 m^3
	cubic foot	cubic metre	m^3	1 ft^3	= 0.02832 m^3
	cubic foot	litre	1	1 ft^3	= 28.32 litre (1000 litre = 1 m^3)
	cubic inch	cubic millimetre	mm^3	1 in^3	= 16.390 mm^3
	cubic inch	millilitre	ml	1 in^3	= 0.01639 litre
	UK gallon	litre	1	1 gal	= 4.546 litre

APPENDIX F
REFERENCES AND FURTHER READING

Agriculture, Horticulture and Forestry Industry Training Board: *Training grants scheme* (latest edition).

Alfred, A. M. and Evans, J. B. (1971) *Discounted cash flow*. Chapman and Hall.

Aston, P. (1979) *Farm business management and land ownership*. Echo Press Ltd.

Barker, J. W. (1981) *Agricultural Marketing*. Oxford University Press.

Barnard, C. S. and Nix, J. S. (1980) *Farm planning and control* (2nd edn). Cambridge University Press.

Britton, D. K. (1975) *Size and efficiency in farming*. Berkeley Hill.

Butterwick, M. and Neville-Rolfe, E. (1971) *Agricultural marketing and the E.E.C.* Hutchinson.

Butterworth, W. and Nix, J. (1983) *Farm mechanisation for profit*. Granada.

Capstick, M. (1971) *The economics of agriculture*. Allen and Unwin.

Castlè, C. N., Becker, M. H., and Smith, F. J. (1972) *Farm business management* (2nd edn). Collier Macmillan.

Clery, P. *Farming and finance*. Farming Press Ltd.

Currie, R. M. (1977) *Work study*. Pitman.

Dairy Facts and Figures (1980). The Federation of United Kingdom Milk Marketing Boards.

Farm Business Unit (1980)*Farm business statistics for south-east*. England, Suppl. D8.51, pp. 36–7. Wye College, School of Rural Economics and Related Studies.

Fraser, A. K. and Lugg, G. W. *Work study in agriculture*. Land Books.

Giles, A. K. (1980) *The farmer as manager*. Allen and Unwin.

Gordon, F. J. (1979) *Management of the spring calving herd*. Hillsborough, N.I.

Harrison, E. F. (1981) *The managerial decision-making process*. Houghton Mifflin.

Hawkins, S. W. and Rose, P. H. (1979) 'The relationship between the rate of fertilizer nitrogen applied to grassland and milk production: an analysis of recorded farm data', *Grass and Forage Science*, **34**, No. 3, 203–8.

Hosken, M. (1982) *The farm office* (3rd edn). Farming Press.

Lockyer, K. G. (1978) *Critical path analysis.* Pitman.

MAFF (1979) *Farm planning by computer* RB419. Her Majesty's Stationery Office.

MAFF (1980) *An introduction to farm business management* RB 381. Her Majesty's Stationery Office.

MAFF/ADAS (1978) (Booklet 2269) *Definition of terms used in agricultural business management.*

MAFF/ADAS (1982) (Booklet 2420) *Keeping financial records.*

MAFF/ADAS (1983) *The balance sheet* (Leaflet 861)

MAFF/ADAS (1983) *Cash-flow budgeting* (Leaflet 862)

MAFF/ADAS (1983) *Farm Management: computing in the farm office:* 1. *Introduction* (Booklet 2451); 2. *Microcomputer systems and programs* (Booklet 2452); 3. *Dairy management* (Booklet 2453).

Marsh, J. S. (1979) *U.K. agricultural policy within the European Community.* University of Reading.

Meat and Livestock Commission *Meat demand trends.*

Meat and Livestock Commission (1980) *Bull beef production and growth promoters* (Data Sheet 22)

Morley, J. (1975) *British agricultural cooperatives.* Hutchinson.

Nix, J. S. (1983) *Farm management pocketbook* (14th edn). Farm Business Unit, Wye College.

Ridgeon, R. F. (1980) Pig management scheme results for 1980, *Economic Bulletin*, **no. 79**, University of Cambridge.

Slater, K. and Throup, G. (1983) *Dairy farm business management.* Farming Press. (2nd edn).

Warren, M. (1982) *Financial management for farmers.* Hutchinson.

Wilson, B. and Macpherson, G. (1982) *Computers in farm management.* Northwood Books.

Wood, L. S. (1970) *The principles and practice of farm valuations.* The Estates Gazette Ltd.

INDEX

SOCIAL SCIENCE LIBRARY
Oxford University Library Services
Manor Road
Oxford OX1 3UQ
Tel: (2)71093 (enquiries and renewals)
http://www.ssl.ox.ac.uk

This is a NORMAL LOAN item.

We will email you a reminder before this item is due.

Please see http://www.ssl.ox.ac.uk/lending.html
for details on:

- loan policies; these are also displayed on the notice boards and in our library guide.

- how to check when your books are due back.

- how to renew your books, including information on the maximum number of renewals. Items may be renewed if not reserved by another reader. Items must be renewed before the library closes on the due date.

- level of fines; fines are charged on overdue books.

Please note that this item may be recalled during Term.